PUBLIC POLICY EVALUATION

SAGE YEARBOOKS IN POLITICS AND PUBLIC POLICY
Sponsored by the
Policy Studies Organization

Series Editor:

Stuart S. Nagel, *University of Illinois, Urbana*

Other books in this series:

VOLUME II. SAGE YEARBOOKS IN POLITICS AND PUBLIC POLICY

PUBLIC POLICY EVALUATION

KENNETH M. DOLBEARE
Editor

with a section on
Crime Control Evaluation
edited by
John A. Gardiner

 **SAGE Publications**   Beverly Hills / London

For information address:

SAGE PUBLICATIONS, INC.
275 South Beverly Drive
Beverly Hills, California 90212

SAGE PUBLICATIONS LTD
St George's House / 44 Hatton Garden
London EC1N 8ER

Printed in the United States of America

ISBN No. 0-8039-0268-9 (cloth)
ISBN No. 0-8039-0312-X (paper)

Library of Congress Catalog Card No. 75-14631

FIRST PRINTING

CONTENTS

PART III: Applications to Crime Control

PUBLIC POLICY EVALUATION

SERIES EDITOR'S INTRODUCTION

This is the second volume in the series of *Yearbooks in Politics and Public Policy* published by Sage Publications in cooperation with the Policy Studies Organization. The first volume, edited by Matthew Holden, Jr., and Dennis L. Dresang, was devoted to a variety of substantive policy problems from a political science perspective. It seems fitting to follow that volume with one devoted to a variety of methodological problems involved in evaluating public policy, also mainly from a political science perspective. That is what Kenneth Dolbeare and John Gardiner have provided as editors for this volume under the general theme of "Public Policy Evaluation."

In the short time since the last volume in this series and especially since the series was originally conceived in 1972 at the first annual meeting of the Policy Studies Organization, a number of developments have occurred with regard to the methodology of evaluating the effects of alternative public policies. Perhaps the leading development is the greatly increased interest in those methodological problems as manifested in relevant books, articles, convention papers, courses, job openings, foundation grants, and summer institutes which have included material on policy evaluation. This contrasts with the earlier more nearly exclusive emphasis of political science on describing policy decisions (as in the public law field) or on describing how policy is made (as in the legislative process field) rather than on the effects of public policy. When political scientists did hypothesize certain policy effects, they tended in the past to do so without much concern for the methodological problems involved in testing those hypotheses.

Other more specific developments with regard to policy methodology include: (1) a movement away from inductive statistics toward
more building of deductive models whereby one can deduce policy
effects from empirically validated premises; (2) a movement away
from cross-sectional comparison of different cities or states operating
under different policies toward more time-series analysis designed to
determine the effects of policy changes over time in one or more
places; (3) a movement away from just describing what happened
subsequent to the adoption of a policy toward more concern for
determining the causal facilitators and inhibitors responsible for the
post-policy changes; and (4) a movement away from focusing on the
impact of given policies or means toward more of a focus on how
given goals can be maximized or optimized.

The above-mentioned trends have generated new methodological
tools corresponding to those trends such as (1) economic modeling,
(2) quasi-experimental research, (3) causal path analysis, and (4)
operations research. These relatively new methodologies nicely
supplement the more traditional tools used in evaluating alternative
public policies such as case studies, cross-tabulation or correlation
analysis, and input-output or stimulus-response conceptual schemes.
The chapters in this volume reflect or discuss a variety of these
methodological tools. They also provide a variety of concrete
examples.

One unifying feature underlying most public policy evaluation by
political scientists (or others with a political science orientation) is a
concern for political feasibility. This manifests itself in a recognition
of the political constraints that may be present in a partisan sense
with regard to legislative redistricting or in a pressure-group sense
with regard to environmental protection programs. A sophisticated
understanding of those constraints may require substantial awareness
of the knowledge that political science has developed concerning
how and why policy is made.

Another unifying feature in policy evaluation by political scientists is their frequently expressed concern about the effects of
various public policies on the governmental process or on peoples'
attitudes toward the government process. Often this leads political
scientists to emphasize the evaluation of public policies which define

how governmental institutions such as courts, legislatures, and administrative agencies are supposed to operate in dealing with people or each other across substantive fields. Other social and natural sciences tend to concentrate more on specific substantive areas in the realm of their substantive expertise.

The next volume in the Sage-PSO *Yearbooks in Politics and Public Policy* will be devoted to the subject of "Public Policy in a Federal System." It will emphasize the role of national, state, and local conflict and cooperation in the making and implementing of public policy. As with the first two volumes, Volume III will be edited by the political scientist who was responsible for coordinating the previous year's set of public policy panels at the American Political Science Association convention. That coordinating and editing role for Volume III is being performed by Charles O. Jones (University of Pittsburgh) and Robert D. Thomas (Florida Atlantic University). Comments for improving these yearbooks will be welcomed by the volume editors and myself from the members of our international editorial board and especially from our ultimate consumers.

Other policy-relevant publications of Sage Publications include professional papers series like the one in *Administrative and Policy Studies,* book series like the *Sage Criminal Justice System Annuals,* and periodicals like the *Urban Affairs Quarterly.* Other relevant publications of the Policy Studies Organization include the *Policy Studies Journal,* the *Policy Studies Directory,* and the *PSO Policy Studies Series.* It is hoped that this second volume in the Sage-PSO *Yearbooks in Politics and Public Policy* (like those other publications) will also contribute to the application of political and social science to important policy problems.

Stuart S. Nagel
Urbana, Illinois

VOLUME EDITOR'S INTRODUCTION

In most respects, the papers collected in this volume are more than able to speak for themselves; in my view, each is a significant contribution to the literature of policy studies in its own right. In this introduction, therefore, I shall limit myself to a brief review of the way in which the volume developed and a sketch of some of the problems to which the authors have addressed themselves in varying ways.

The crime control section, edited (and separately introduced) by John Gardiner, emerged from a panel which he chaired at the 1973 meetings of the American Political Science Association. The general focus of the public policy panels that year was on evaluative research, its problems and prospects. The papers presented at this particular session proved to be unusually rich in data *and* self-conscious about their usage and implications. Moreover, they were closely related to each other, and thus offered an opportunity for a relatively intensive sort of case-study investigation within the framework of this volume.

The remaining papers were drawn from a wide variety of sources. Some emerged from a set of remarkably good papers submitted in response to the Policy Studies Organization's notice in respect to the nature of this volume; two or more very solid, though perhaps less fully integrated, volumes might have been published from that body of professional work. Other papers were located and included because of their special relevance to the overall theme of this volume. The contribution by James S. Coleman, for example, was first delivered at the SSRC Conference on the Impacts of Public Policy in December 1971. It appears here because it has not been widely available to political scientists, and by the courtesy of the author and the sponsoring SSRC committee chaired by Austin Ranney.

The primary goal of this volume in the Sage Yearbook in Politics and Public Policy series has been to critically assess the state of the art of public policy evaluative (or "consequences") research at this mid-passage point in the social sciences' efforts to develop policy-interpretive capabilities. Political scientists in particular have surged toward "public policy" as a research and theoretical focus in the last few years. Among the wide variety of definitions of "policy," kinds of research undertaken, and purposes involved, one focus that has emerged is that of taking policy as the independent variable and seeking to trace its effects upon people and problems in the larger society. Two purposes have animated this body of research. One is the effort to provide policy-makers with evaluations of the extent to which particular policies have achieved their goals. The other is the longer-range and more scholarly attempt to fill out empirical theories of politics by coming to understand the effects of policies as they diffuse into the social system and process. Both have encountered a number of conceptual and methodological problems, only some of which have as yet been dealt with satisfactorily.

This is not the place to review either the history of this development or the nature of these problems in any detail. My own analysis, expressed elsewhere (Dolbeare, 1974), is that our problems are partly conceptual—in ways that we do not always recognize—and partly inherent in our current empirical social science. The contributors here, most of whom worked without knowledge of each others' efforts, have addressed a number of important aspects of these problems. They have produced a number of new ideas about ways of proceeding in the policy impacts-consequences field, as well as some concrete illustrations and valuable new substantive findings. Their work falls naturally into two general categories, one dealing more or less exclusively with conceptual issues, and the other with the translation of conceptual refinements into actual research activities and findings.

In the conceptual area, James Coleman's important paper raises the question of whether policy research may not require a different foundation, as well as practice, from that familiar to discipline-grounded research. Drawing on his experience in the well-known educational study that bears his name, he develops a set of principles that should govern policy research. Essentially, they involve guidelines for best serving the policy-maker's needs with the tools that we presently have available.

The Best-Connolly paper, on the other hand, addresses those who would do the other kind of policy-consequences research—the wider-ranging and more questioning scholarly kind. The authors point to a set of factors that have, perhaps unconsciously, been taken for granted and built into much extant research. Their preference would be for a much more inclusive approach, but one in which the number of variables involved would be very large.

One of the important issues of policy research is thus joined by these first two papers. Grossly oversimplified, it is whether our desire to be "scientific," to be grounded in demonstrable relationships between measurable variables, does not force us to narrow the focus, concentrate on the measurable, and eliminate uncontrollable factors to such an extent that we may well misinterpret the social reality that we seek to grasp. Coleman frankly acknowledges the need to accept policy-makers' problem definitions, as well as "situational variables" (contextual "givens" not subject to policy controls). Best and Connolly argue that in so doing one necessarily introduces either ideological or other status-quo supporting assumptions. But it is not clear that one could do empirical research on a scale sufficiently broad to include the sorts of variables they consider appropriate.

Ronald Johnson's contribution does not, nor could it, resolve this dilemma. But it does go a considerable distance toward identifying the considerations that should be in researchers' minds as they try to translate purposes and assumptions into manageable research designs. Selection of methods, he makes clear, is in part a reflection of research objectives. His review of these relationships in many ways explains the differences visible in the first two papers, as well as serving as a valuable and conveniently organized overview of much recent policy research.

The implementation category begins with an important paper that extends this analysis to the point of suggesting specific ways to overcome some serious obstacles. Thomas Cook and Frank Scioli, Jr., first present an elegant model, and then show how it can be drawn upon to inform policy-impact research. Their examples come from both their own work and that of others.

The next two papers may serve as illustrations of the increasingly sophisticated use of available data to provide insights into the effects of existing policies and to move beyond this to framing and exploring alternative policy choices. David Caputo and Richard Cole offer some new understanding of the effects of revenue-sharing, as well as an assessment of the uses of the techniques they employ. Stuart Nagel's paper advances a provocative strategy for making necessary choices on sounder evidential bases.

This selection is obviously not exhaustive. Many other examples of good policy studies could have been presented. But, when taken together with the crime control section, this group of papers does appear to have addressed many of the major problems, and to have done so through illustrative solutions. Too often, those who call for new kinds of research or new conceptual formulations never get around to actually doing the research involved, and it remains for others to learn whether or not the latter is really possible. In every case here, ideas are joined to implementation, and the thinkers are also the doers. I am very glad of the opportunity to thank the contributors for their good work.

Kenneth M. Dolbeare
Amherst, Massachusetts

REFERENCE

DOLBEARE, K. M. (1974) "The impacts of public policies," in C. P. Cotter (ed.) Political Science Annual 5. Indianapolis and New York: Bobbs-Merrill.

PART I

CONCEPTUALIZATION

PROBLEMS OF CONCEPTUALIZATION AND
MEASUREMENT IN STUDYING POLICY IMPACTS

JAMES S. COLEMAN

University of Chicago

I will begin from the beginning. That is to say there is no body of
methods, no comprehensive methodology, for the study of the
impact of public policy. When we ask why there is not, two points
rise above the rest: First, it is a very recent development in the
practice of governments to seriously ask questions about the impact
of policy, and to expect or even hope to get a scientific answer. It is
only very recently, for example, that social legislation began to
contain provision and budget for evaluation of the effects of that
legislation. Second, the policy sciences have not really regarded
themselves as policy sciences, with the exception of some parts of
economics and a few of the older areas of political science. In
general, as the social sciences have come to be self-conscious as
disciplines, they have busied themselves with internal or immanent

AUTHOR'S NOTE: *Further development of the ideas in this paper is carried out in* Policy
Research in the Social Sciences *(Morristown, N.J.: General Learning Press, 1972).*

development of the discipline. The systematic methods they have developed are methods for aiding this disciplinary development, not for such externally imposed irritants as the evaluation of public policies. The philosophical bases of the methods are all oriented in this direction—toward the development of "theory," toward the generation and testing of hypotheses to confirm, refine, and enlarge the theory.

The first and most important order of business, then, is to recognize that these disciplines which comprise the policy sciences *are* policy sciences, and to follow that recognition with attention to some of its implications. A central implication is that a coherent and self-conscious methodology for studying impacts of public policy must be developed.

Some steps toward that development have already taken place. There has been, during the past several years, attention to research methods to evaluate specific policies, and attention to the design of these policies in such a way that they *can* be evaluated. The most interesting and most comprehensive of these is a paper by Donald Campbell (1971), as yet unpublished, titled "Methods for the Experimenting Society." Campbell takes seriously a conception of Haworth (1960) about a society of the future: a society which attempts innovations as solutions to problems, which has explicit mechanisms for evaluating these innovations, which goes on to attempt further innovations, engages in further evaluations, and through such processes attempts to resolve those problems that arise. The conception is of a society that has an explicit evolutionary mechanism built in, an evolutionary mechanism that employs scientific methods. In this conception of a future society, it will be a scientific society, not in Marx's sense of a state of society based on a scientific theory, but in the sense of a society that uses scientific methods for changing itself. The relation of the policy sciences to such a society is a relation in which social science theory plays a small and secondary part, but methods of the social sciences play a central part. It is these methods, together with the institutional structure that insures their employment, that constitutes the feedback mechanism which such a society needs.

THE PROPERTIES OF METHODS FOR POLICY ANALYSIS

It is important at the very outset to sharply distinguish a methodology that has as its philosophic base the testing and development of theories from a methodology that has as its philosophic base a guide to action. This is not to say that the methods developed as an aid in theory construction cannot be used as components of a methodology that constitutes guides to action. It is rather to say that, at the most fundamental philosophical level, a difference exists: the goal is not to further develop theory about an area of activity, but to provide an information basis for social action. Cronbach and Suppes (1969) have expressed the difference in a pair of terms that they use to describe research in education: The first is "conclusion-oriented research," in which the aim is to arrive at certain conclusions about what is, descriptively, the state of affairs. This research is designed to contribute to knowledge in a substantive area, and directly or indirectly to contribute to theory. The second is "decision-oriented research," in which the aim is to provide information that is important for policy decisions that must be made. Here I will not use these terms, but will call that research which is designed to advance knowledge in a scientific discipline "discipline research," and will call that research designed as a guide to social action "policy research."

When we adjust our ideas in this way, and explore the implications of a change in the philosophical base from research for the discipline to research for social policy, a number of differences emerge. I will not present an exhaustive catalog here, because no such exhaustive catalog exists. What I will do is to urge that serious attention be devoted to discovering and examining these differences, and to examine a few of the differences that are apparent to me now.

First, and probably more important, is the recognition that in research for social policy, a decision will be made at a certain time, action will be taken at that time, and it cannot be based on information that is available later. (It may not be based on information available at that time, but that, for the moment, is not the question. The institutional structure that can make the most appropriate use of social science information is an important problem, but not one that I will examine at this point.) In contrast, theory development, or more generally the advancement of knowledge in a discipline, proceeds at a pace dependent on research results. As a general principle, then, we can say this: *For policy research, partial information available at the time an action must be taken is better than complete information after that time.*

The implications of this principle for research design are not trivial. It means the design of research fitted to the time sequencing of social actions. It means the design of research which provides partial results at various time points, in the anticipation that the final results may be delayed for one of the many reasons that impedes social research. It means a steady *cumulation* of research results that can aid policy decisions, rather than a single complete research result at the end.

There is a second principle that leads to the same pattern in research design. This is the recognition that the user or consumer of the research will not himself be a social scientist, but will be involved in social policy and will likely be a social science layman. The general principle can be stated as follows: *For policy research, the ultimate product is not a "contribution to existing knowledge" in the literature, but a social policy modified by the research results.*

A major implication of this principle is that policy research is a first stage in a social learning process: if they are to affect action, research results must be assimilated by those upon whom the action depends. One of the most feasible ways to insure this is to make partial research results available at various points during the research activity. I have seen many cases—in market research, in political polling, and in research for government agencies—in which a client responsible for policy was presented with a single grand research report, which he was unable to digest. Such indigestion, largely the fault of the researcher, means that the research is a failure, whatever the substantive quality of the material that lay between the covers of the report. Ruefully, I must admit that I have been guilty of such failures. Perhaps the most important was research for the *New York Times,* carried out at the time of the 1962 elections, designed to provide election projections and analysis in the New York elections and the national congressional elections. On election night, our system was perfected, and we gave excellent projections and analyses: projections of election outcomes and sizes of majorities that were superior to any on television or radio, and analyses of the voting behavior of various population groups that subsequently proved to be accurate. After the election, we produced a paper describing both the sophisticated projection and analytical techniques and some of the results (Coleman, Heau, Peabody, and Rigsby, 1964). But on election night almost none of the *Times'* political reporters were willing to use the results, because in trial runs the elaborate system had not worked, we had no simple system to give partial or approximate results, and the reporters had not had the experience in use of *any* of the material with which they were confronted on election night.

Another principle that is closely related to the timing principle is that the value of research results lies in a high probability of giving approximately the right guides to action rather than in their derivation from, or correspondence to, a good theory. The general principle can be stated thus: *For policy research, results that are with high certainty approximately correct are more valuable than results which are more elegantly derived but possibly grossly incorrect.* I will give two examples from the physical world to illustrate the principle. First, consider estimation of the trajectory of a cannonball after the development of Newtonian theory of motion. There are two ways to estimate the trajectory. One is to use Newtonian theory and calculate the expected trajectory based on the known exit velocity of the cannonball, a calculation of the distance to the target, and the known gravitational constant. The second is to shoot the cannon, see where the ball lands, and adjust the aim to compensate for the deviation. The first is an elegant method, but likely to be very wrong. Only when the theory was made far more sophisticated through knowledge of the effect of air resistance, wind effects, effects of the shape of the projectile, and other factors, and only when calculations came to be instantly achievable, did the elegant method come to be better than the inelegant method.

A second example is similar in some respects. I had a colleague at one time who had flown light airplanes in Burma during World War II. He then came back to instruct pilots in training on navigational methods to use there. His methods, however, outraged the stateside instructors who were teaching the methods they had learned from books. Their methods involved calculation of full details of the flight plan from the point of departure designed to achieve an arrival exactly at the designated landing point. His methods, in contrast, paid much less attention to the precise flight plan in its early stages, but concentrated intensely on the use of landmarks in the general but very broad vicinity of the designated landing point. His procedures were designed to get the pilot roughly in the correct area, and then when he was there, to find his way from the *incorrect* place at which he found himself to the correct place of landing. Obviously, in the context of my general principle, my point here is that his method was the better one. Why? It was better because it got the pilot roughly to where he wanted to be by the use of very ad hoc, inelegant, and approximate methods, but providing means by which he would end up where he wanted to be even if he had made early mistakes. The other methods provided him with a greater chance of being exactly where he wanted to be, but also a greater chance of missing his goal by a wide mark and being unable to recover.

The application of this general principle in social science implies the use of research design and research procedures that give good results with high probability rather than more sophisticated techniques that give excellent results if they are correct, but have a high probability of being far off if some of their assumptions are not met: if there is measurement error, if there is sampling bias, if some variables have been overlooked and left out, or if the other of the frequent sources of defective data exist.

A fourth principle of a methodology for policy research is that the variables involved in an analysis are in three classes, while they are in only two classes for discipline research. In discipline research there are ordinarily "independent variables" and "dependent variables." In policy research, however, there are certain results or *outcomes of policy*—some of them intended, others not intended, but all equally candidates for investigation; there are *policy variables,* that is, those variables which can be or have been amenable to policy control; and there are *situational variables*—variables that play a part in the causal structure which leads to the outcome variables, and thus must be controlled in the analysis or the design, but are not subject to policy control. In discipline research the latter two classes are indistinguishable, both being merely "independent variables." The principle stated generally can be put as follows: *For policy research, it is necessary to treat differently policy variables which are subject to policy manipulation, and situational variables which are not.*

The implications of this principle include both differences in statistical and design roles of policy and situational variables, and differences in the kinds of problems posed in the research. While it is important to measure or take account of control variables, their effect on the outcome variables are not of interest. The questions posed should involve the policy variables and the outcome variables, but not the control variables except in their capacity to confound or distort the effect of policy variables on outcome variables.

This general principle might appear to be straightforward and self-evident; but many researchers engaged in policy research fail to make such a distinction in their work, and give to their client answers that he cannot use because they give him no handles for action.

There are technical implications as well of this difference between policy variables and situational variables in policy research. When a policy is implemented in a pilot program with some aspects of experimental design, the set of control variables is the set of variables to be protected against in some fashion—through randomization, through the use of samples for the pilot program stratified by the important control variables, through use of an individual or a city or another unit to which policy variables are applied as a control for himself by before-after measurements, and through other design strategies. When an ongoing policy is to be evaluated, and no experimental application of policy variables is possible, then the control variables play a different role in the statistical analysis. For example, in the U.S. Office of Education research that resulted in the report (Coleman et al., 1966) on equality of educational opportunity, a child's family background characteristics were control variables. In regression analysis, which was extensively used in that report, these variables were always used as statistical controls. The strategy we used there was to include as many as possible of those variables, to attempt to correct as fully as possible for individual differences in children that were *not* due to school factors before examining the relation of school factors to educational outcomes. School factors, in contrast, were introduced into the analysis both individually and in concert, with the aim of getting a variety of estimates of their effects. An estimate when such a variable is introduced alone is likely to be too *great,* due to its correlation with some other effective school factor that is not included in the equation. An estimate when such a school factor is introduced with all others is likely to be too *small,* due to its correlation with some other ineffective variable in the equation which, given the presence of measurement error, reduces its apparent effect.

A fifth principle in a methodology for policy research involves the very initiation of the research. In the initiation of discipline research, the primary starting point is an intellectual problem posed by previous research or theory. The solution of that intellectual problem will bring about the advancement of knowledge in the discipline. In contrast, policy research begins with a problem as formulated outside the discipline. The general principle can be stated in this way: *For policy research, the research problem enters from outside any academic discipline, and must be carefully translated from the real world of policy or the conceptual world of a client without loss of meaning.* In some cases, there is little difficulty. The problem is clear by the very nature of the policy intervention itself. But in other cases it is not. As an example of the first, it is clear that the study of the impact of Head Start had as its central problem the effects of Head Start—effects in several dimensions, and effects over the long run as well as the short run—on the children who participated in the program. Details remained problematic, such as just what types of changes (health, reading readiness, attitudes, preparedness for a school regime) should be examined. But in this case, and in many others like it, the nature of the policy intervention dictates in a straightforward way the problem.

An example of the other set of cases, in which the policy intervention does not point directly to the research problem, is a voucher experiment in several cities that OEO planned to initiate. In that case, the policy intervention is one that changes radically the whole structure of an educational system. Consequently, to take as the primary policy outcome the effect of participation in the voucher plan on a child's academic achievement would be quite inappropriate. This is only one of many effects that vouchers might have: effects on the existing public school system, effects in generating new schools in the private sector, effects on the supply of teachers, effects on the degree of racial, religious, or other segregation in the system, effects on the range of curriculum content among different schools. The intervention itself does not in any simple and straightforward way dictate which of these effects should be studied. What must be known in addition is what questions are problematic from the policy-maker's point of view, and what questions are capable of being answered with the given pilot program. For example, in a three-year pilot program with educational vouchers, it is likely that little can be learned about the ability of vouchers to generate new schools, since opeing a school to operate during a three-year period is a very different enterprise from opening a school to operate indefinitely. Consequently, although a policy-maker would like answers to this question, he cannot expect to get good ones from such a pilot program.

This fifth principle of translation without loss of meaning from the world of reality to the research design is illustrated in an especially complex way by the study which led to *Equality of Educational Opportunity* (Coleman et al., 1966). The research was initiated as a result of a short provision in the Civil Rights Act of 1964, section 402, which went as follows:

> SEC. 402. The Commissioner shall conduct a survey and make a report to the President and the Congress, within two years of the enactment of this title, concerning the lack of availability of equal educational opportunities for individuals by reason of race, color, religion, or national origin in public educational institutions at all levels in the United States, its territories and possessions, and the District of Columbia.

This directive to the Commissioner of Education gave only a starting point in formulation of the problem. The words could be interpreted to mean any of several things, and the first research task was an investigation of what they meant to those who imposed the directive—congressmen—and to those who could have an interest in the research results. For the staff of the survey, this meant that two things were necessary at the outset: discovering the "intent of Congress," and discovering the interests of various groups which could be experiencing inequality of educational opportunity. The first and surprising result was that there had been a shift in the intent of Congress from the initial inclusion of Section 402 to the final passage of the bill. Initially, the section, in different form, was of principal interest to the Justice Department, which probably was responsible for its initiation, and was not a matter of policy research at all. It was instead designed to discover intentional acts of discrimination on the part of school systems, to allow for prosecution by the Justice Department. Then, as the civil rights bill proceeded through Congress, the Justice Department lost all interest in the section. It would have been dropped had it not been picked up by some senators and transformed into a policy research question. It was clear from our investigations that the intent of Congress was to discover inequalities in educational opportunity, and sources of inequalities, as the basis for future policy designed to reduce them.[1]

This left, however, a thorny conceptual problem: what was meant by "inequality of educational opportunity?" A review of the statements of members of Congress indicated that different congressmen meant very different things by it. Consultation with members of interest groups (Black civil rights groups, religious groups, ethnic interest groups, as for Puerto Ricans) gave no narrowing of the range of things that were meant by the term, no convergence on a single generally accepted meaning of "equality of educational opportunity." Finally, an historical examination of the meaning of the concept showed an evolution involving several distinct meanings, and generally involving an increasing responsibility of the community beyond a relatively passive provision of services.[2] But the historical examination did not show a discarding of the earlier concepts as modifications emerged. Rather, there came to be multiple meanings of "equality of educational opportunity," different ones held by different segments of the population. What became clear was that if this survey was to be responsible to the society and its representatives who directed that it be done, it must necessarily examine a number of *different* conceptions of equality of educational opportunity. In the design stage of the research, an internal staff memorandum was written which describes the conceptual diversity and indicates how the survey would proceed. A portion of that memorandum is reproduced below:

> The point of second importance in design [second to the point of discovering the intent of Congress, which was taken to be that the survey was not for the purpose of locating willful discrimination, but to determine educational inequality without regard to intention of those in authority] follows from the first and concerns the definition of inequality. One type of inequality may be defined in terms of differences of the community's input to the school, such as per-pupil expenditure, school plants, libraries, quality of teachers, and other similar quantities.
>
> A second type of inequality may be defined in terms of the racial composition of the school, following the Supreme Court's decision that segregated schooling is inherently unequal. By the former definition, the question of inequality through segregation is excluded, while by the latter, there is inequality of education within a school system so long as the schools within the system have different racial composition.
>
> A third type of inequality would include various intangible characteristics of the school as well as the factors directly traceable to the community inputs to the school. These intangibles are such things as teacher morale, teachers' expectations of students, level of interest of the student body in learning, or others. Any of these factors may affect the impact of the school upon a given student within it. Yet such a definition gives no suggestion of where to stop, or just how relevant these factors might be for school quality.
>
> Consequently, a fourth type of inequality may be defined in terms of consequences of the school for individuals with equal backgrounds and abilities. In this definition, equality of educational opportunity is equality of results, given the same individual input. With such a definition, inequality might come about from differences in the school inputs and/or racial composition and/or from more intangible things as described above.
>
> Such a definition obviously would require that two steps be taken in the determination of inequality. First, it is necessary to determine the effect of these various factors upon educational results (conceiving of results quite broadly, including not only achievement but attitudes toward learning, self-image, and perhaps other variables). This provides various measures of the school's quality in terms of its effect upon its students. Second, it is necessary to take these measures of quality, once determined,

and determine the differential exposure of Negroes (or other groups) and whites to schools of high and low quality.

A fifth type of inequality may be defined in terms of consequences of the school for individuals of unequal backgrounds and abilities. In this definition, equality of educational opportunity is equality of results given *different* individual inputs. The most striking examples of inequality here would be children from households in which a language other than English, such as Spanish or Navaho, is spoken. Other examples would be low-achieving children from homes in which there is a poverty of verbal expression or an absence of experiences which lead to conceptual facility.

Such a definition taken in the extreme would imply that educational equality is reached only when the results of schooling (achievement and attitudes) are the same for racial and religious minorities as for the dominant group [Coleman, 1968: 16-17].

The problem as defined by the survey staff from this array of meanings is described at another point in the memorandum:

Thus, the study will focus its principal effort on the fourth definition, but will also provide information relevant to all possible definitions. This insures the pluralism which is obviously necessary with respect to a definition of inequality. The major justification for this focus is that the results of this approach can best be translated into policy which will improve education's effects. The results of the first two approaches (tangible inputs to the school, and segregation) can certainly be translated into policy, but there is no good evidence that these policies will improve education's effects; and while policies to implement the fifth would certainly improve education's effects, it seems hardly possible that the study could provide information that would direct such policies.

Altogether, it has become evident that it is not our role to define what constitutes equality for policy-making purposes. Such a definition will be an outcome of the interplay of a variety of interests, and will certainly differ from time to time as these interests differ. It should be our role to cast light on the state of inequality defined in the variety of ways which appear reasonable at this time [Coleman, 1968: 17].

The last paragraph in this quotation expresses well the appropriate task of the policy researcher in formulating his research problem. His task is to carry out a sensitive and accurate translation of societal interests—potential or expressed—so that the very framing of the research problem will not myopically or intentionally favor interests of certain segments of society or further his own ideology. The research results might very well strengthen the hand of certain societal interests, as was certainly the case for *Equality of Educational Opportunity;* but the design must be such as to allow the possibility of results that benefit any interested parties—whether or not their interests coincide with those of his immediate client or his own values.

Altogether, this fifth principle in a methodology for policy research, concerning translation of the research problem, can be seen as analogous to principles 1 and 2, involving the reporting of research results. The essential point here is that policy research involves two acts of translation: translation of the problem from the world of reality and policy into the world of scientific method, and then a translation of the research results back into the world of reality and policy. If either translation is faulty, then even the best research activity that intervenes between problem and results cannot compensate. A methodology for discipline research need not address itself to these translation problems, for that research operates within the realm of disciplinary discourse. There are not two worlds to shift back and forth between, but only one. In contrast, a methodology for policy research must explicitly recognize these two worlds, and develop techniques to cope with the translation problems in each direction.

Disagreements in the translation from policy problems to research design are well illustrated by a criticism of *Equality of Educational Opportunity* by two economists, Eric Hanushek and John Kain (1972), in which they argue that the study made a serious mistake in attempting to study all five of the above definitions of equality of educational opportunity. They argue that the study should have carried out a careful study of inputs, as the necessary minimum, before it could consider more esoteric questions, such as the effect of school inputs on achievements.

As the survey was defined and carried out, it was intended to serve three purposes: to provide an accurate description of resouce inputs for six different racial and ethnic groups at elementary and secondary school; to provide an acfurate description of levels of achievement of each of these groups at three points in elementary school, grades 1, 3, and 6, and two in secondary school, grades 9 and 12; and to provide the basis for an analysis of the effects of various inputs on achievement. In terms of the five definitions of educational opportunity described above, such measures of effects were necessary for the fourth and the fifth, to provide weights for various inputs, so that the "effective" inequality of opportunity could be assessed, and attention could be focused on those input resources that are effective in bringing about educational opportunity, or by their unequal distribution, effective in maintaining inequality of opportunity.

As Hanushek and Kain point out, the sample design requirements and the kinds of measurement are different for each of these three purposes. In the first, the sampling variability is at the level of the *school,* even if reporting is ultimately to be done in terms of exposure of the average student to school resources, as the report did. The second and third aims, on the other hand, require measurements on students, in effect reducing the number of schools that can be included within the scope of such a study. The third, analysis of the relation between input and output, imposes different design requirements than the second, in the way that analysis of relationships generally imposes a different sample design than does description of population characteristics, with less attention to sampling error, and more attention to the range of variability in the independent variables. Kain and Hanushek argue that the survey attempted too much; by attempting all three of these things, it failed to do well the first, minimum requirement.

The alternative, as proposed by Kain and Hanushek, was to do well the minimum necessary task: to measure carefully the input resources to schools attended by Blacks and those attended by whites, to show what is in fact the kind and degree of discrimination in schooling experienced by Blacks.

I believe, however, that the defect of the apparently simple and straightforward approach they suggest is the most serious possible: by selective attention to one of the definitions of equality of educational opportunity, that is, equality of inputs, it implicitly accepts and reinforces that definition. In contrast, I believe that the major virtue of the study as conceived and executed lay in the fact that it did not *accept* that definition, and by refusing to do so, has had its major impact in *shifting* policy attention from its traditional focus on comparison of inputs (the traditional measures of school quality used by school administrators: per-pupil expenditure, class size, teacher salaries, age of building and equipment, and so on) to a focus on output, and the effectiveness of inputs for bringing about changes in output.

This effect of the study in shifting the focus of attention did not come about because the study gave selective emphasis to that definition of educational opportunity which entailed examination of effects; only one section of one chapter of the report was devoted to it. The study presented evidence relevant to all five of the definitions that had been initially laid out. It was the audience who, with evidence on all of these before it rather than only the comparisons of inputs that have traditionally served as the basis for comparisons of school "quality," focused its attention on the more relevant questions of output, and effect of inputs upon output. As I indicated above, I regard this shift of attention as the most important impact on policy of the study. It raised questions where none had been before, questions which had been prematurely answered in the absence of facts. If the study had taken the apparently straightforward careful approach that Kain and Hanushek propose, they would have continued to be answered prematurely, in the absence of facts. The study would have been celebrated for its careful accuracy, its measurement of inequality, and its irrelevance would have gone unnoticed as policy-makers busily worked to eradicate those irrelevant inequalities.

I will introduce here a sixth principle for the development of policy research methodology, though I do so much more tentatively than was true for the others. I regard it perhaps more as an important question to be seriously examined rather than as a principle to be dogmatically observed. The principle is this: *For policy research, the existence of competing or conflicting interests should be reflected in the commissioning of more than one research group, under the auspices of different interested parties where possible. Even in the absence of explicitly conflicting interests, two or more research projects should be commissioned to study a given policy problem.*

The basis for this principle is the recognition that the different time frame of policy research does not allow the self-correcting procedures that exist in discipline research. In discipline research, one researcher's results are subject to the careful scrutiny of the discipline, and others in the discipline find it in their interest to try to show him wrong, For example, researchers attempt to carry out *replications* of the research of other researchers; and they gain attention in the discipline if they show the results are not replicable. This constitutes a built-in adversary or competitive structure which is the primary self-correcting device for science. But such a sequence of steps, such a dialectic, does not exist in policy research. Any competitive structure or adversary procedure or self-correcting devices must be simultaneous, because the world of research is connected to the world of policy in real time. Given this connection, the only way of mirroring the competitive, self-corrective structure of discipline research that takes place sequentially is to commission policy research in parallel to study the same question. Without that, one of the most important elements in the refinement of knowledge that occurs in scientific disciplines is gone.

The principles listed above give some indication of the kinds of points that a methodology for policy research sould include. Their principal aim here is to show that important differences between policy research and discipline research do exist, and that it is possible to develop a methodological foundation for policy research.

Apart from these principles, there are some points, both technical and nontechnical, which are especially important in one or another kind of policy research. Campbell, in the paper (1971) cited earlier, has begun to develop a number of these. I will mention below a few others, without any suggestion of being exhaustive, comprehensive, or even systematic. These points are those which have arisen in my experience, which appear to have general relevance. I suspect that in the development of a policy research methodology it will for some time be necessary merely to collect such points before putting them in any systematic and coherent order.

METHODOLOGICAL POINTS FOR POLICY RESEARCH

ANALYSIS OF POLICIES AS AN AID TO
METHODS FOR POLICY RESEARCH

Although, as I have indicated, theory must play a distinctly secondary role in policy research, this does not imply that certain theoretical efforts may not be extremely useful. Certainly the existence of confirmed theory about an area of activity is quite valuable in the design and analysis of policies and research when the policy implementation is accompanied by research. That should be trivially evident. There is another matter, however, that may not be so evident. This is the importance of developing a theory about policies, in the sense of an understanding of important differences between types of policies. For example, there are policies that involve resource distribution (such as a Head Start program) versus policies that do not (such as the Supreme Court decision in 1954 outlawing a racially dual school system). Those policies that involve resource distribution allow, for example, research designs that trace the resources as they flow through a system (say a school system, or a housing program) and reach their final destination (or are diverted on the way). I will discuss such research designs later in the paper and will not go into further examination here. The point here is that nonresource distribution policies do not allow such a research design. Thus to make such a distinction immediately gives an indication of the kind of research that can be carried out.

As another distinction, policies can be distinguished according to the relation between the direct receptor of policy and the locus of its ultimate intended impact. If the ultimate impact desired is upon children in school, and there are funds allocated to (or directives given to) a school system, then there is a long organizational path which mediates impact of the policy on its ultimate intended recipients. The research design can, and probably should, include some examination of this path. In contrast, if the ultimate desired impact is on children, and resources are given directly to them or their families, such as in educational voucher systems mentioned earlier, the types of research designs that may be fruitfully used are different.

It is not my intention to develop systematically the relation between types of policies and types of research designs, but only to indicate that this can be done, and that it should be done as part of the development of a methodology for policy research. As that task is done, then knowledge of the type of policy to be investigated immediately brings into play a certain set of possible research designs, and excludes others. It is this kind of linkage that is important in the movement of policy research from an art to a science.

TWO TYPES OF RESEARCH:
INPUTS AND OUTPUTS VERSUS SOCIAL AUDITS

I want to describe here two types of research that may be used to study the same problem, to draw sharply the contrast between them, and then to come out strongly in favor of one of them. The type of policies to which these designs are relevant are policies involving resource distribution. In studies of resource distribution where the aim is to examine the effectiveness of these resources, the usual kind of research design has involved measurement of resource inputs, measurement of policy-relevant outcomes, and establishment of a relation between them (either through research design, as in experimental design, or in ex-post statistical controls, as in analysis of the impact of an ongoing program. The study I have referred to before, *Equality of Educational Opportunity,* is one such example in which the effectiveness of various school resources was studied by measuring the resource inputs and by measuring achievement outcomes of schooling. Or the Westinghouse evaluation of the impact of Head Start (Cicarelli et al., 1969) studied the effectiveness of the resource inputs of Head Start by examining the cognitive and affective skills of children exposed to these resources.

The essential characteristic of this research design is that the policy inputs are measured, policy outcomes are measured, and the two are related (with, of course, the use of experimental or statistical controls to neutralize the effect of control variables). Whatever institutional structure intervenes is taken in effect as a black box into which the input resources go, and out of which the desired outcomes and side effects come. In the first research mentioned above, the school was the black box. Inputs to it were teacher salaries, pupil-teacher ratio, age of textbooks, size of library, and a variety of other traditional measures of school resources. Outputs studied were achievement of students in verbal and mathematical skills. In the second study, the resource inputs were the additional resources provided by Head Start; the outputs were cognitive and affective measures on the children.

I want to contrast this general research design with another that might be called a social audit. In a social audit, resource inputs initiated by policy are traced from the point at which they are disbursed to the point at which they are experienced by the ultimate intended recipient of those resources. It is, then, those resources as experienced that are related to the outcomes in the research, rather than the resources as disbursed. For there are two possible causes of the ineffectiveness of resources: the resources as experienced may be ineffective in bringing about any change; or the resources as disbursed never reach the ultimate intended recipient and are instead lost somewhere on the path between point of initial disbursement and point of experience by the ultimate recipient. In research that does not trace the resources along this path, it is impossible to distinguish these two causes of ineffectiveness, and the assumption is ordinarily made that resources as experienced are the same as resources as disbursed. But this may not be true at all. Consider a few examples in schools: a school board can spend identical amounts on textbooks in two different schools (or two school boards can spend identical amounts in two different systems), so that the inputs as disbursed by school boards are identical. But if texts depreciate more rapidly, through loss and lack of care, in one school or one system than the other, then the text as received by a given child (say the second year after a new text is issued) constitutes a lesser input of educational resources to him than if he were in the other school or the other system. Or if teacher salaries in a city and the surrounding suburban area are equal, then the city is not competitive in salary and loses the best teachers to the suburbs. Again, the inputs as disbursed by the school boards are equal, but the inputs as received by the children are not. As another example, if the expenditures on window glass in a city school in a lower-class neighborhood and a suburban school were equal, the child in the city school would spend much of his time in classrooms with broken windows, while the child in the suburban school would not. Furthermore, many of the examples in which this "loss of input" occurs between disbursement and reception go in the same direction, that is, to reduce the resources received by the average lower-class child.

The above examples of resource loss between disbursement and experience all involved loss imposed on a student by other students. There is another general source of resource loss, the administrative system through which resources flow. For example, a major cause of the ineffectiveness of funds from Title I in the Elementary and Secondary Education Act lay in loss through the administrative system of schools. Funds were used in a variety of ways, but a relatively small fraction of them ever led to a change in the experience of a child in school.

Whatever the place in the path from government to child that resources get drained off or lost, the end result is the same: the resources never reach the child. There is a loss of input between disbursement and experience.

Research which is designed to trace such resource loss might be described as a "social audit." Just as with a financial audit, the flows of resources are examined to discover the paths that resources take and the possible loss of these resources through diversion. As in a financial audit, proper use of resources does not insure the ultimate effectiveness of the resources; but it does tell whether the resources are available at point of use, and if they are not, where and how they got lost. A social audit is not a substitute for a study of the effectiveness of resources which have reached their destination. It should be accompanied by such an examination. But the crucial value of the social audit as compared to research which relates inputs to outputs is that it simply gives much more information for policy. Research that relates input resources stemming from social policy to various possible outcomes of policy can tell only the levels of effectiveness and kinds of effectiveness. If it shows little or no effectiveness of certain resources, as much recent policy research in education has shown, there is little more that can be learned. It is not possible to learn from this research design whether ineffectiveness was due to intermediate resource loss or due to ineffectiveness of resources, and if the former, to see just where and how resources got diverted.

The methods for social audits have not been developed, and obviously they would differ according to the kind of institutional structure through which resources flow. The development of such methods would, however, constitute an important development in methods for policy research. Social audits would be appropriate only to certain kinds of policies, those involving resource allocation; but for those policies, they would constitute, I believe, a far superior research method than those which concentrate on relating inputs as disbursed to final outputs.

This kind of design would constitute an important change for policy research generally. For it applies to a very wide range of "evaluation research" such as that called for in much current social legislation in the United States. Most evaluation research is now carried out largely according to some "inputs versus outputs" design, without any kind of tracing of resource flow. Change to a social audit design would give much greater insight into what kind of modifications are needed for effective policies.

CONCLUDING NOTE

In this paper, I have attempted to do two things: first, to show how a fundamentally different methodological foundation is needed for policy research than exists for discipline research; and second, to show some of the elements that such a methodology should have. It is clear that the ideas for such a methodology are still in the formative stage; but what is important, even at this early stage, is to recognize that policy research requires methodological development of its own, beginning at the most fundamental philosophical or conceptual level.

NOTES

1. It is curious that, by an ironic twist, the results of the report (Coleman et al., 1966) have probably been used more by the courts in the prosecution of cases on school desegregation than by either the Congress, the executive branch of government, or local school boards.

2. Some of this historical development of the concept is traced in Coleman (1968).

REFERENCES

CAMPBELL, D. T. (1971) "Methods for the experimenting society." Northwestern University, Department of Psychology. (mimeo)

CICARELLI, V. et al. (1969) The Impact of Head Start: An Evaluation of the Effects of Head Start on Children's Cognitive and Affective Development. Washington, D.C.: Government Printing Office. Distributed by Clearinghouse for Federal Scientific and Technical Information.

COLEMAN, J. S. (1968) "The concept of equality of educational opportunity." Harvard Educational Review 38, 1 (Winter): 7-22.

———, E. HEAU, R. PEABODY and L. RIGSBY (1964) "Computers and election analysis: The New York Times project." Public Opinion Quarterly 28 (Fall): 418-446.

COLEMAN, J. S., E. Q. CAMPBELL, C. J. HOBSON, J. McPARTLAND, A. M. MOOD, F. D. WEINFELD and R. L. YORK (1966) Equality of Educational Opportunity. Washington, D.C.: Government Printing Office.

CRONBACH, L. J. and P. SUPPES [eds.] (1969) Research for Tomorrow's Schools. New York: Macmillan.

HANUSHEK, E. A. and J. F. KAIN (1972) "On the value of equality of educational opportunity as a guide to public policy," in F. Mosteller and D. P. Moynihan (eds.) On Equality of Educational Opportunity. New York: Random House.

HAWORTH, L. (1960) "The experimenting society: Dewey and Jordan." Ethics 71, 1 (October): 27-40.

MARKET IMAGES AND CORPORATE POWER: BEYOND THE "ECONOMICS OF ENVIRONMENTAL MANAGEMENT"

MICHAEL H. BEST
WILLIAM E. CONNOLLY

University of Massachusetts, Amherst

The policy sciences, one might reasonably suggest, meet their social responsibilities effectively when they articulate public problems understood only vaguely by those affected and when they formulate strategies to attack the structural sources of those problems before they reach crisis proportions. On these criteria political scientists and economists of the last generation have performed dismally in at least one area: the social costs of environmental degradation became a national disgrace before they became a serious subject of policy analysis.

A perusal of respected textbooks in each discipline written before 1965 does reveal a singular lack of attention to environmental issues.[1] But maybe this omission looks like a deficiency of inquiry only in retrospect. Perhaps, until quite recently, the adverse environmental effects of the American political economy were too unobtrusive to be captured within the frame of *any* theoretical system. Unfortunately, the work of two maverick social scientists, K. William Kapp (1950), and economist, and Grant McConnell (1954, 1966), a political scientists), defeats that hypothesis before it can be entertained seriously.

Kapp's documentation of the "social costs" of economic transactions cover the

> destructive effects of air and water pollution . . . . [and] occupational diseases . . . , the competitive exploitation of both self-renewable and exhaustible natural wealth such as wildlife, petroleum and coal reserves, soil fertility and forest resources . . . ; the diseconomies of the present transport system [Kapp, 1950: 229].[2]

These social costs have gone unnoted and untended in the economic system, according to Kapp, because they "do not enter into the cost calculations of private firms." And economists have failed to detect them, too, not because they indulged in "wilful apologetics" for the private enterprise system, but because "the phenomena of social costs" seemed to "have no room in the conceptual system of traditional value and price analysis" (1950: 229, 230).[3] Particularly important, he thought, was the faulty attempt by his professional colleagues to separate economic from political analysis, as if each could be treated as a distinct system. The ironic outcome of such an effort was a set of assumptions and concepts which maintained an unacknowledged and thus undefended "union between economic analysis and political liberalism" (Kapp, 1950: 236).

McConnell's early analysis of the political obstacles facing any conservation movement was built upon assumptions and concepts quite similar to those adopted by Kapp. He castigated pluralist political scientists for their refusal to see that the aggregation of organized private interests often produced results opposed to the "public interest" (his corollary to Kapp's idea of the social costs of private transactions), for their failure to identify the corporation as "the most important form of private government in America today," and particularly for their continued acceptance of the "historic liberal" image of "an autonomous economy and its corollary, an autonomous politics" (McConnell, 1966: 129, 247).

Michael H. Best and William E. Connolly [43]

The prescience of Kapp and McConnell would be merely of historical interest (and academic embarrassment) amidst the universal attention to environmental issues today except for one further development. Contemporary policy scientists, adopting assumptions and concepts very much like those which Kapp and McConnell thought had blinded their predecessors to the environmental impact of the American political economy, today purport to have a program to restore environmental integrity while it retains the autonomy of the market economy.

In contemporary America, policy scientists who perceive the economy as a competitive market system invariably see pluralism as its mirror image in politics. Indeed, since pluralist theory is basically market theory transposed to politics, we can say that each market image is a mirror to the other: if either is blurred, the other will shift out of focus, too. We shall argue, first, that the assumptions, concepts, and policy priorities of those policy scientists gripped by the market image of the economy are disconnected today from the environmental problems their predecessors failed to detect yesterday. Our critique of the market model of environmental management will require massive revisions in the pluralist theory of politics as well. While Kapp and McConnell may have failed to convert their critique of market imagery into a theory of political economy, they did expose two decades ago theoretical defects in the policy sciences that remain unrepaired today.

THE MARKET MODEL OF ENVIRONMENTAL MANAGEMENT

"Perfect efficiency is generally defined in terms of a Pareto optimum, a situation such that no one can be made better off without making someone else worse off" (Koplin, 1971: xiii-xiv). And the virtue of competitive markets, according to neoclassical theory, is their ability to provide price signals which lead to Pareto optimality.

The market provides an environment conducive to Pareto optimality if individuals are utility maximizers, if neither producers nor consumers have any influence on prices, if markets are universal, and if transactions do not affect the utility of nonparticipants. If the market worked perfectly (no one claims that it does) there would be perfect information, no transaction costs, and absence of uncertainty. Under such conditions the social prices (the aggregate costs and benefits to society) of any transaction are exactly equal to the private prices (the specific costs and benefits to market participants).

When actual arrangements roughly approximate these conditions the market model predicts that transactions will continue until the necessary conditions for Pareto optimality are satisfied. Any divergence of social from private prices will result in economic inefficiency and a violation of the conditions for Pareto optimality.[4]

One form of divergence is caused by the existence of externalities.[5] Externalities occur when transactions generate unpriced side effects diffused to parties who typically are not directly involved in the transactions.[6] In such circumstances the social cost/benefits are uncompensated because the market provides neither a measure of the cost/benefits nor a mechanism for enforcing a compensation claim. If Pareto optimality is to be attained (or restored), a means must be found to account for these unpriced social costs and benefits.

Pollution, a reduction in environmental services, is an example of an externality. Unfortunately, the environmental effects of market transactions are dispersed over time and across persons within a particular time frame so that it becomes irrational for any producer or consumer to incorporate these costs into market transactions. Thus a company which purifies its water before disposing it into streams adds to its own costs, contributes only marginally to the purification of the nation's water, fails to benefit itself from the purified water which flows downstream, and weakens its competitive market position with respect to those companies which refuse to institute purification procedures. Since it is reasonable to assume that other companies in a market system will not voluntarily weaken their position in this way, it is irrational for any single company to choose to do so. The same logic applies to the consumer who assesses the rationality of, say, placing an emission control device on his automobile exhaust system.

Thus a range of activities which are desirable from the vantage of the collectivity are irrational from the vantage point of any particular consumer or producer. And a range of policies which are rational from the vantage point of individual consumers and producers are destructive of the collective interest in preserving nonrenewable productive resources and in maintaining the environment's capacity to assimilate wastes. This is the "tragedy of the commons" (Hardin, 1968; also Arrow, 1970; Musgrave, 1959).

Environmental "externalities" can be priced in several ways. All individuals and firms affected by a transaction could be merged into one collectivity so that third-party victims or beneficiaries become participants in any transaction. If externalities were pervasive, the achievement of Pareto optimality could require cumulative merger activity until finally all externalities were "internalized" by the establishment of one collectivity, or socialist unit (see Lange and Taylor, 1938). Alternatively, a complex system of private property relations could be created and extended so that individuals or firms suffering from air or water pollution could press legal claims against those responsible for these effects.[7]

Other proposals have also been advanced.[8] But the method most economists clearly favor is to adjust market prices through a system of charges and subsidies processed through the political system. Environmentally degrading transactions will then either become prohibitive or will reflect the costs of repurification processes and the development of new resources. "Internalizing the externalities" in this way will force a decline in the rate of throughput (about five pounds of solid wastes per person per day is "disposed" in the U.S.). a change in the composition of products, and an expansion of recycling. These reforms will also have the secondary effect of stimulating private businesses to specialize in treating and disposing wastes in ecologically rational ways.

Even when the assumptions which underlie this analysis are granted, certain problems emerge. First, it is not at all clear that the intrusion of politics into the market place on the massive scale required would not create severe dislocations in the delicate, self-adjustive market mechanisms. Certainly, a huge bureaucracy would be required to identify the extensive environmental costs of a vast array of production processes and waste disposal systems and to administer a tax and subsidy program which reflected these assessments.

Moreover, the problems of measuring and assessing environmental costs are magnified when issues of *intergenerational* equity are introduced. The environmental effects of current transactions are often deflected to future generations. But how are current populations to incorporate the needs and claims of future generations into current market transactions? What makes proponents of this model, with their assumption that individuals are utility maximizers, think that current generations will be willing to build the interests of future generations into the pricing system?[9]

Finally, a market system which retains private control of the investment and pricing functions seems to require continued economic growth as a spur to investment. But a point may well be reached when growth itself is incompatible with environmental imperatives. It is known that a steady rate of growth will eventually (within several generations) generate atmospheric heat levels incompatible with human life (see Heilbroner, 1974; Ayres and Kneese, 1972). Many suspect that other factors such as the depletion of key resources before adequate substitutes are found will force an end to, or a profound slowdown of, economic growth. The ecological effects of economic processes are often delayed, but when they emerge they can be overwhelming and pervasive. If it is true that market capitalism flourishes on growth and dies on stagnation, then the market response to the environmental crisis so long ignored by its theorists may be woefully inadequate to the magnitude of the problem.[10]

A number of revisionist market economists, reacting in part to problems internal to the neo-classical model and in part to a growing perception that the model does not correspond to the actual economic system at crucial points, have introduced a series of adjustments into this framework. The recent study by Freeman, Haveman, and Kneese (1973) applies such a revisionist view to an understanding of environmental issues. They seek to show how the "economics of environmental management" can enable us to curb the worst effects of pollution within the parameters of the market economy. Their basic acceptance of the market model is expressed when they assert that "unlike most other kinds of resources, choices involving the allocation of environmental resources cannot be left to individuals acting separately in unregulated and decentralized markets" (Freeman et al., 1973: 33).

But then a series of adjustments is introduced. The authors concede that manipulative advertising affects consumer choices in important ways; they acknowledge that a highly unequal distribution of income allows privileged minorities to impose the heaviest burdens of pollution and the largest costs of pollution control on low-income groups; they agree that their proposals to incorporate ecological costs into the pricing system are inadequate to cope with considerations of intergenerational equity; and they agree that biases in the pluralist political system make it an exceedingly intractable vehicle for incorporating environmental costs into the market system. Indeed, they conclude, "the most formidable barrier to controlling pollution is probably not technology, population or public attitudes, but the politics of power" (Freeman et al., 1973: 170).

These adjustments and concessions could provide the catalyst for a quite different analysis of environmental issues. But none of these leads is in fact pursued. Inequality is noted as a problem, but its systematic causes and environmental effects are not explored;[11] the problem of future generations is mentioned, but institutional reforms which might enable citizens to forego immediate consumption benefits in the interests of preserving future environmental supports are never considered; biases in the pluralist political system are described as the most "formidable barrier" to ecological integrity, but only a brief (and rather quaint) reference is made to "institutional arrangements such as the Congressional seniority system and loose campaign financial regulations that encourage economic power to be readily transformed into political power" (Freeman et al., 1973: 168). In effect, these modifications function as ad hoc adjustments which protect the theory from disconfirmation while its basic form remains untouched: the newly identified factors, though acknowledged to be important, are neither explained within the model nor reflected in policy proposals drawn from it.

Such an analysis moves too hesitantly beyond those very assumptions and categories which led social scientists to ignore the environmental effects of prevailing arrangements until they reached crisis proportions. The analysis is abstracted from the basic structure of corporate capitalism; the technical proposals for reform are disconnected from any grasp of the political constituencies and structural reforms required to implement them. In fact, proposals which incorporate environmental costs into the market system while retaining the structural arrangements which have generated these effects promise to divide the very constituencies which must be united if environmental deterioration is to be forestalled.

These are the charges we seek to sustain. To do so we must move beyond the artificial division between the economic and political systems postulated in the market model to a perspective which probes the connections between the dangerous deterioration of the natural environment and the political economy of corporate capitalism.

TOWARD AN ALTERNATIVE THEORY

CORPORATE POWER

Market theorists systematically underplay the role of the modern, oligopolistic, multinational corporation in the economy. And this omission is particularly pertinent to an understanding of the environmental crisis.[12]

According to neo-classical economic theory a corporate monopoly impedes market forces by enabling the corporate unit to raise prices above market levels. But a related and more serious matter is the ability of such a corporation to exercise control over the range of products available to the public. It is necessary to probe this form of corporate power, for the product priorities of corporate elites often diverge significantly from the range of products compatible with environmental integrity.

Consider an example of such product control. In America of the 1920s the automobile and truck industries were rather competitive and the entire industry faced stiff competition from railroads, streetcars, trolleys and buses. But as Snell (1974) has documented in a report to the Senate Judiciary Subcommittee on Antitrust and Monopoly, that competitive situation was short-lived. During the middle twenties General Motors, often in conjunction with Standard Oil of California and Firestone Tire, launched an investment program enabling it first to control and then to dismantle the electric trolley and transit systems of 44 urban areas in 16 states. Often operating through a holding company, National City Line, the three corporations acquired electric rail systems, uprooted the tracks, and substituted diesel-powered bus systems. After acquisition and conversion, the systems were sold back to local groups, but only with a contractual clause which precluded the purchase of new equipment "using any fuel or means of propulsion other than gas" (Snell, 1974: 31).

The life of a diesel bus is 28% shorter than that of its electric counterpart; its operating costs are 40% higher. Thus the typical result of the substitution of one system for the other was "higher operating costs, loss of patronage, and eventual bankruptcy" (Snell, 1974: 37). General Motors pursued a similar program of acquisition and conversion with rail lines.[13]

General Motors and its satellite companies benefited in two ways from this policy. First, its profits from the sale of buses and diesel-powered locomotives are higher than if trolleys and electric trains were retained. Second, the financial difficulties faced by these converted transportation systems has encouraged consumers to buy more cars. General Motors' *incentive* to make cars and trucks the basic vehicles of American ground transportation is clear enough: its gross revenues are 10 times greater if it sells cars rather than buses and 25 to 35 times greater if it sells trucks rather than locomotives (Snell, 1974: 38). Its expansion into mass transportation systems thereby enhanced its *ability* to make cars and trucks more attractive to consumers than alternative modes of ground transportation.

Its policy of acquiring, converting, selling, and strangling mass transportation systems, in combination with the escalating pressure from the American Road Builders Association, American Trucking Association, and American Petroleum Association to launch massive state and federal highway construction programs (see Mowbray, 1969, and Kohlmeier, 1969) helped to make the truck and the automobile dominant vehicles for shipping and transportation in the country.[14] Sandwiched between a private corporation with impressive market power over ground transportation and a governmental pressure system biased in favor of those organized corporate interests that pressed successfully for $156 billion in highway construction between 1945 and 1970, it was inevitable that mass transportation systems would eventually lose out to the "competition."

But as profitable as the operation was to the corporations involved, it was disastrous for the country. It has created cities crisscrossed with highways, straddled by distorted housing patterns, smothered in toxic emissions of carbon monoxide, lead, and other deadly chemical combinations from gasoline-powered vehicles. It is the primary source as well of the serious strains on our fuel resources. For it takes six times as much fuel to haul a ton of freight from Los Angeles to New York by truck as it does by rail (Commoner, 1971: 169) and the automobile uses many times more fuel per passenger mile than mass transit systems do.

It is absurd to argue that consumers have *chosen* cars and trucks over transit and rail systems after having considered each option in the light of its comparative costs and benefits, including the costs of highway construction and the effects on the environment. But rather a few corporations with effective market power helped to eliminate one mode of transportation as a viable consumer option and thereby stimulated consumer demand for the only option available.[15] Thereafter, market control in this area was further solidified as national patterns of employment (for example, automobile factories, oil production, highway construction) and satellite entrepreneurial activities (e.g., motels, tourist businesses) developed around this system and established a vast constituency whose immediate interests are tied to the maintenance and expansion of an ecologically irrational transportation system.

Corporate control over product options is matched by similar control over the technologies of production with similar consequences for the environment. As Barry Commoner (1971) has shown, neither affluence nor population growth has contributed as much as systematic changes in the materials and technologies of corporate production to the rapid increase in air and water pollution in the United States since 1946. The trend of recent history is that technologies with marginal environmental impact are displaced by those with massive environmental impact. Thus, as corporate forms of agricultural production have grown, there has been a steady decline in land acreage used in farming matched by multiple increase in the use of fertilizers to reach high production levels; the self-purifying aquatic cycle has been unable to assimilate the material received. The substitution of nylon and other synthetic fibers for cotton and wool, of plastic for wood, of aluminum for steel, have combined to accelerate the accumulation of nondegradable, heat increasing, air- and water-polluting wastes.

The effects of ecologically unsound technologies are felt most directly and severely in the workplace. Market economists, whose assumptions and concepts encourage them to focus on the exchange side of the economic system as opposed to the organization of productive processes, have generally ignored the unhealthy "side effects" of work conditions in which legally established pollution standards are more permissive and pollution levels are higher than they are outside the workplace. What price are we to calculate for the 400 deaths annually from pneumoconiosis (black lung)? What is the appropriate trade-off when 34 out of every 100 asbestos workers die prematurely from asbestiosis or cancer? What about the one in six uranium miners expected to die of cancer? (See Wallick, 1972; Stellman and Daum, 1973; Special Task Force Report to the Department of HEW, 1973; Sexton and Sexton, 1973.)

Each year 3,000 new chemicals are introduced into the productive system with little or no prior analysis of their vapor, dust, or toxic effects on workers. It is estimated that 17 million workers suffer from noise levels above reasonable safety and health levels. Over 2 million suffer serious disabilities from occupational diseases, including brain damage. And these figures must be expected to grow as our information about the connections between job conditions and mental illness, heart disease, ulcers, arthritis, and deafness becomes more complete. To confront these effects of environmentally irrational technologies political intervention in the exchange system must be matched by political intervention in the corporate system of production.

Unfortunately, the failure to confront the realities of corporate power in explaining environmental degradation also contributes to a profound misreading of that political process which is to provide the vehicle for market reform. Market economists consistently adopt a pluralist image of politics; they assume that the balancing processes in the political system are quite analogous to those at work in the market economy.[16] But the growth of the large corporation undermines both sets of assumptions: the erosion of the market system is a manifestation of the same forces which have eroded the pluralist balancing process in politics. Corporate control over productive technologies and product forms has generated a work force and a system of subsidiary corporations dependent on the continuation of these forms. Political efforts to convert to new forms of energy use, production systems, and products more in line with environmental imperatives tend to mobilize these workers and satellite businesses in support of the corporate structures which provide them with employment and markets. The dependency of the blue- and white-collar worker and the subsidiary businesses in this way tends to neutralize the very constituencies needed to place the appropriate price tag on environmentally irrational corporate prac- tices through the political process.[17] Put another way, corporate capitalism introduces "imperfections" into the pluralist system which reflect those it has introduced into the market system; it seems implausible in such circumstances to look to the political system as a means to remedy those imperfections while the private corporations itself is to remain intact.

Even if short-run pressures to introduce the needed pricing and enforcement systems were successful, the retention by the private, multinational corporation of investment and pricing prerogatives would give it powerful leverage to force a relaxation or rollback of these policies over the longer term. Both the pluralist theory of politics and the market theory of the economy assume that economic units are basically national in scope and that they are thereby subject to effective control by the nation-state within which they are located. But the progressive internationalization of capital or, described another way, the rise of the multinational corporation, increasingly undermines the viability of that premise (see Hymer,

1972). If a multinational corporation finds environmental controls in the United States to be too stringent, it can divert a portion of its capital to other countries where profit margins are greater and environmental controls less corrosive of its prerogatives. Such a diversion contributes to unemployment and recession in the United States, and as "business confidence" is undermined here, those domestic labor constituencies most immediately affected (for example, truckers affected by pollution charges and by efforts to modernize railroads, auto workers displaced by mass transit systems) will press militantly for a relaxation of those policies and controls. The multinational corporation can thus use its international investment capability to protect its domestic economic autonomy.

We agree with market economists in concluding that the political process must play the crucial role in incorporating environmental imperatives into the productive system, but such an approach cannot work unless it succeeds in taming unilateral corporate power, unless, in particular, it converts the privately owned multinational corporation into a publicly owned corporation which is subject to the effective control of a national constituency.

If we lived in the age of the small economic unit operating in a decentralized market economy, the mere incorporation of environmental costs into the system which remains intact in other respects might produce some positive results. But that era, if it ever did exist, is over now: reforms proposed within the frame of market assumptions are anachronistic at best. Only public control over the investment and pricing functions of the modern corporations can render that unit reasonably accountable to the population which must live in the environment it produces.

WORK LIFE AND INCENTIVE SYSTEMS

Workers are victimized not only by the workplace as a collection point for pollution, safety, and health hazards. The structure of work itself is deadening for vast numbers of blue- and white-collar workers: the incentive system that structure sustains and the motivational system it accentuates produce exactly the set of consumer pressures which must be displaced if environmental degradation is to be forestalled.

Routinized, repetitive, mindless work which is only very imperfectly productive of goods and services in the general welfare cannot be *intrinsically* satisfying to the workers. In such circumstances work must be organized almost completely around *external* incentives. Since, moreover, continuous inter-class and intergenerational movement in a highly stratified society officially committed to class mobility ("equality of opportunity") erodes extended kinship ties and breaks up stable neighborhood communities, the external incentives to work must be restricted within a narrow range. Incentives tied to the general welfare of internally unified collectivities (community recreation centers, health programs, transit systems) tend to be displaced by incentives tied to private consumer goods (stylish clothes, exotic foods) or to goods which can be enjoyed by the individual in conjunction with the nuclear family (cars, television sets, private houses).

We do not contend, of course, that all consumer satisfactions geared to private individuals and to nuclear families are evil; nor do we think that a work incentive system tied strictly to collective goals would be feasible or desirable. But it is clear that private incentives are unnecessarily accentuated by the structure of work and social life which prevails in our society, while the potential connections between inherently fulfilling work and the attainment of more durable collective interests are systematically depressed. Deprived of the opportunity for communal satisfactions inside and outside of work, the satisfactions available must become increasingly privatized; this limited range of private satisfactions available *must* then provide the central incentives to work and the central forms of consumption.

The organization of work, the restriction of opportunities for improvement to *individual* mobility, and the resulting breakdown of persisting communal ties combine to sustain (or to require) a privatized mode of life which is intrinsically unfulfilling and in opposition to the imperatives of ecology. Public policies which seek to divert patterns of *consumption* to ecologically rational forms, while leaving this historically specific set of *productive* and *social* arrangements untouched, are doomed to magnify the discontent and resentment of those caught in the bind. Ecological imperatives must then be discounted or met by the coercion of some by others.

Should I voluntarily support a transit system in this area when I can best improve my life chances by moving elsewhere in a few years? Are the costs of recycling and of moderning waste disposal systems worth it to *us* when there is no internalized *we* that any of us naturally identifies with? Is the future condition of this stream, this park, this local atmosphere, this soil, of deep concern to me when my relatives live elsewhere and my progeny are also likely to move? When I am likely to be a transitory resident myself? Will I then tolerate high tax levels and the curtailment of consumer purchases to protect the environment for others when the promise of consumer pleasures and the dangers of personal insecurity provide my basic incentives to work?

Economists and other social scientists gripped by the theory of abstract individualism, by the view of atomic individuals as private utility maximizers, are unable to explore the ecological import of these structural arrangements. They simply assume that the incentives to work must always and everywhere match those dominant in our society; they suppose the private consumer satisfactions predominant here to be the paradigm satisfaction available to the human species as such. In effect, they take as given what needs to be explained. When confronting the basic dimensions of work, sociality, and patterns of motivation in our society one must not lose sight of the simple insight enunciated in another context by Schattschneider (1960: 57):

> Anyone watching the crowds move about Grand Central Station might learn something. . . . The crowds seem to be completely unorganized. What the spectator observes is not chaos, however, because the multitude is controlled by the timetables and the gates. *Each member of the crowd finds his place in the system (is organized by the system) because his alternatives are limited* [our emphasis].

Those who, analogously, comprehend that the prevailing patterns of work and opportunity within our stratified social order provide a set of "timetables" and "gates" which shape and limit the modes of life open to citizens will understand as well that efforts to channel consumption habits into ecologically sound forms will be resisted bitterly by those confined within these structures. In the absence of new possibilities for fulfillment within work itself, in the absence of new possibilities for stable community relationships which stretch beyond the space and time frame of the nuclear family, apprehensive blue- and white-collar workers will militantly oppose environmental management programs which threaten the private forms of satis- faction that are available. The organizations to which they belong can be expected to coalesce with corporate interests to oppose environmental controls.

There is nothing about the environmental crisis itself which ensures that the political will and muscle to respond to it will surface. Only an environmental movement which connects prevailing structures of work and opportunity to persisting patterns of environmental destruction can hope to build a progressive coalition which responds affirmatively to the one form of exploitation while it copes with the other.

INEQUALITY AND SOCIAL SERVICES

In a highly stratified individualist society, those with the highest incomes tend to seek private solutions to collective problems while those in the lowest brackets lack the power to implement collective solutions and the means to secure private remedies. In an egalitarian society, by contrast, it is rational for citizens to seek collective solutions to those collective problems which no one is in a position to escape privately. This simple fact, enunciated and explored by Rousseau, is of critical importance to a viable analysis of the environmental crisis.[18]

We must initially clarify the meaning and import of inequality in income and security in an affluent stratified society such as ours. It is not correct to assume that today those members who receive the lowest incomes, have the least job security, and face the heavy burdens of regressive state and local taxes are to be described merely as *relatively* deprived by comparison to their affluent contempo- raries; nor is it quite accurate to conclude, after citing statistics of economic growth, that a family of four earning, say, $6,000 in constant dollars today is better off than a similarly placed family of four earing $3,000 in 1924. Such a judgment falters because of the tendency to abstract income levels from the historically specific support systems within which each family strives to meet its needs for food, shelter, work, health, education, transportation, and recreation. If, for instance, it costs the contemporary family $6,500 to plug into the basic institutions and services around which the life of its society is organized because the nature of these services has changed radically since 1924, it is hardly clear that its real standard of living is better than that of its 1924 equivalent. If $2,500 was sufficient in 1924 and $6,500 is required today, we must conclude that the contemporary family's income has increased while its comparative standard of living has probably declined.

In 1924 one could store food in an icebox because the iceman delivered ice to the house: the production and delivery of ice was one of the established social services of the day. Today one must buy a refrigerator to keep perishable food; electricity has replaced ice as the established social support for storing food. The fact that middle- and upper-income groups can easily afford refrigerators and, until recently, charges for electricity has rendered it economically infeasible for the iceman to serve the needs of those who cannot. The refrigerator has thus become a household necessity.

The shift from the icebox to the refrigerator only symbolizes, of course, a much broader shift in institutions and services which have together contributed to the plight of the underclass and generated serious ecological consequences. When transit, bus, and railroad systems are increasingly displaced by automobiles, airplanes, trucks, and interstate highways, those in the middle- and upper-income levels can afford to purchase the vehicles needed to plug into the transportation system supported by government programs (for example, highway construction programs, tax subsidies for oil companies, public air terminals). Those at the bottom of the society are then forced to buy and maintain cars or else they find themselves unable to travel from residences in the inner city to jobs on the urban fringe, to buy clothing and food at bargain prices (for example, cut-rate shopping centers located on urban fringes) or to take advantage of the least expensive recreation and vacation opportunities available (state parks, public beaches, tourist motels located near interstate highways).

When one adds to the refrigerator and the car other requirements of contemporary life such as television (displacing the neighborhood and the local newspaper as the central vehicle for news, culture, and entertainment in the society), day care for the children of working mothers (required by the eclipse of the extended family), the need to travel longer distances for fresh air, recreation, and vacations (occasioned by urban blight), the necessity to spend a portion of one's income on old-age insurance (again forced by the breakdown of extensive kinship ties), and the cost of modern waste disposal and energy creation systems, it seems not unlikely that the relatively low-income family of four in 1924 was better able to afford the essential support services of its day than its similarly placed equivalent can in our contemporary system. An affluent, stratified, capitalist system imposes severe burdens on its underclass by maintaining a system of support services geared to its affluent members, and it is also quite apparent that those support systems typically impose a heavy load on the ecological system.

When these same systems of support are viewed from the top we can see how they encourage the affluent to evade the most direct effects of environmental degradation by private expenditures that at once accelerate the destructive processes and undermine the political will of privileged minorities to cope with these consequences. The affluent can secure work that is environmentally safe; they can move to suburbs where the air and water are cleaner, escape summer heat through air conditioning, take vacations by jet to undefiled areas, locate their residences away from nuclear power plants, and replace shoddy products which break or perish. But since they must then commute to work in the inner city by automobile their private escape worsens the pollution problem in the city they have left behind. Their dependence on air conditioning, air travel, and shoddy products similarly increases the load imposed on the environment. Most importantly, since they have invested heavily in the private escapes available and since their affluence often flows from eco-logically unsound business enterprises, they are often inclined to oppose public policies and regulations which would make energy production ecologically safe, establish mass transit systems, institute building construction regulations which reduce the need for air conditioning, restore parks and waterways in urban centers, improve garbage and disposal systems, ensure the production of durable goods. The availability of an expensive *private* escape renders the affluent unwilling to accept the tax assessments, changes in productive processes, and alterations in privileged life styles implied by the application of collective solutions to these *public* problems.

In these interconnected ways, inequality combines with the system of corporate power and the weakness of communal ties to encourage the growth of ecologically devastating support systems; it imposes the most direct and oppressive effects of these unsound systems on a politically weak underclass which often remains imprisoned in the inner city; and it encourages the affluent to seek private escape routes which deepen the system's debt to nature and dampen political support for effective public responses. These are the reasons that income redistribution, a worthy objective in its own right, will also form an essential part of any political movement which seriously seeks to cope with the environmental crisis. These considerations also reinforce the case for bringing the private corporation under greater public control, for inequality cannot be materially reduced until corporate pricing, investment, salary, and location decisions are subjected to public debate and accountability.

A more egalitarian society would not necessarily maintain rational ecological policies, but it would be more likely to do so. For, to paraphrase Rousseau, when life chances are distributed so that all can feel the effects of collective achievements and collective failures, so that all are in a position to benefit from a public resolution of common problems, and so that none can afford to escape the problems through the use of private resources unavailable to others, then the political system is very likely to generate collective responses to the common dangers and burdens imposed by the depletion of nonrenewable resources and the destruction of environmental supports essential to human life.

HUMAN NATURE, NORMATIVE PRIORITIES AND
POLITICAL STRATEGIES

The neo-market theory of environmental management first postulates a theory of individuals motivated by self-interest narrowly
defined. It then projects a model of entrepreneurial activity guided
by the profit motive, workers motivated by the fear of unemployment and the promise of enhanced commodity pleasures, and an
impersonal market mechanism which regulates prices and wages to
promote total welfare. Belatedly, proponents of this model have
come to acknowledge the market's failure to regulate pollutants and
environmental supports in the public interest. The imperfection is to
be remedied by incorporating environmental costs into the pricing
system via the political process. There are problems acknowledged by
proponents of this model: politically established trade-offs between
consumption and environmental protection are likely to be skewed
against the environment, the political tampering with delicate market
mechanisms is likely to magnify dislocations and to distribute the
costs of environmental control unevenly. But, given the basic
assumptions underlying this model, these tensions are unavoidable;
the policy prescriptions advanced provide the only viable way to fuel
the economy while protecting the environment within which it
operates. Those who try to slide around these tensions simply engage
in self-deception: there is no such thing as a free lunch.

According to assumptions informing the alternative program of
environmental control, the individual as private utility maximizer
emerges out of a particular set of conditions in which market
relationships have penetrated the fabric of social life itself. Within
more favorable contexts, where work provides more intrinsic
gratifications, where opportunities for rich and persistent social
relationships are available, where extreme inequalities in income and
security are eliminated, members of the productive community can
be motivated in part by a self-interest which includes but transcends
private material welfare and in part by a shared concern for the
welfare of the larger communities with which they identify. A
rational response to the environmental crisis, within the frame of
these premises, is tied to a reconstitution of the institutions and

attached attitudes which have generated it and which now pose obstacles to its resolution. These structural changes will make the needed trade-offs between economic productivity and environmental imperatives more acceptable to members of the community. Moreover, by identifying a community of concerns between environmentalists and blue-collar workers, this model encourages the very political coalition it sees as required to apply effective pressure within a political economy biased in favor of corporate elites. Only such a movement for structural reform can create the space within which environmental imperatives become political priorities.

Two points emerge from this comparative summary: (1) each explanatory model *generates* a distinctive set of normative priorities in the form of policy prescriptions and political strategies; (2) the normative priorities supported by each model rest in large part upon a distinctive theory of human nature which sets the frame within which the crisis is comprehended and in terms of which alternative policy-strategic options are appraised.

EXPLANATORY THEORY AND ENVIRONMENTAL PRIORITIES

The intelligent layman, unencumbered by the philosophical presuppositions of mainstream social science, would perceive a natural congruence between the market economists' explanation of environmental destruction and the policy prescriptions he supports. That perception, in our view, is superior to the one sanctioned by those social scientists caught in the grip of the positivist disjuncture between scientific explanation as a rational, objective enterprise and normative judgment as a nonrational, subjective process.

An explanatory theory specifies the phenomena to be described, postulates the range within the phenomena are expected to vary, and identifies a set of factors which tell us why the phenomena vary in these ways and not others. The rules of moral, or more broadly, normative, discourse specify the *sorts of considerations* which warrant norms, which justify judgments of good and bad. If one adopts these rules of normative discourse (and this includes everyone who adopts our shared moral language without explicitly tacking special provisos onto it), then *to accept a particular explanatory theory is to advance a set of reasons for ratifying a range of policy prescriptions and strategic orientations.*

The evaluative disagreements among radical and liberal social scientists are thus not coincidental facts which happen to accompany the divergent assumptions, categories, and test procedures within their respective explanatory theories. The disagreements in normative priorities flow out of and reflect these differences in explanatory theory. The reason this is so becomes clear when one examines more closely the grammar of normative concepts.

Normative judgments are more than mere expressions of emotion detached from understanding. To conclude that some project is "good" or "desirable" *may* be to express a favorable attitude toward it (though this is not always so), but it is definitely to conclude that it will, by comparison to other known alternatives, fulfill an array of human interests, wants, and purposes effectively. Moreover, if the claim is not explicitly restricted to a narrow group within the relevant social unit (good for me, desirable for the managers), use of the normative vocabulary conveys the idea that the claim ranges over all the members: the good or desirable policy is, on balance, good for all of us.

It is not that the concept of good, for example, is reducible or equivalent to statements such as "y is in A's interests" or "y makes A content," but that given the grammar of "good" and that of other normative concepts, evidence that project y makes collective A more content than other alternatives is always a prima facie reason for accepting y as more desirable. Charles Taylor, who has presented the best, brief account of this view, makes the point in the following way:

> "good" does not *mean* conducive to the fulfillment of human wants, needs or purposes, but its use is unintelligible outside of any relationship to wants, needs and purposes. . . . For if we abstract from this relation, then we cannot tell whether a man is using "good" to make a judgment, or simply to express some feeling; and it is an essential part of the meaning of the term that such a distinction can be made (Taylor, 1967: 55).[19]

Taylor's thesis can be given a weak or a strong interpretation. The weak thesis is that most of us just happen to use normative concepts in this way, we accept and employ the conventions of our society in this respect. Just as we conventionally distinguish saying "I am *glad* the sky is blue" from "I am *proud* the sky is blue" by tacitly understanding the person who utters the second statement to be claiming not only that he *likes* a blue sky but that he in fact has *contributed* to its blueness, we also distinguish "I like capitalism" from "capitalism is the ideal economic system" by understanding the second assertion to include the claim that capitalism promotes the desires and interests of its members more fully than other possible economic systems. In each case the conventions of our language lead the listener to build more into the second claim than the first, and a person using our normative language sincerely will honor that expectation: if one wishes to make the lesser claim one can simply use the language of "liking," "being glad," and the like for that purpose.

The weak version of the thesis affirms that normative concepts, as used by members of our linguistic community, embody ingredients which differentiate them from the mere expression of feelings or emotive states. Because the normative language has these ingredients, normative conclusions can only be warranted by revealing how in fact arrangements x or y promote the interests, and so on, of the requisite community. Since the explanatory theory one accepts performs exactly this function of identifying interests and showing under what conditions they are promoted or frustrated, the theory thereby warrants or justifies a set of policy prescriptions.

The strong version of this thesis is that social life itself could not be sustained unless some such distinction between normative judgment and the expression of feelings were sustained in the conventions of language. We think the stronger thesis is indeed correct, but it is sufficient for our purposes here to note that even if only the weaker thesis were correct, the sharp disjuncture between explanatory theory and normative judgment presupposed by mainstream social science is false. Social scientists who say, with Paul Samuelson for instance, that "judgments of better or worse involve *subjective* evaluations" and that such judgments in "the realm of ethics" are disconnected from subjective, scientific explanation, misread the nature and import of their own work (Samuelson, 1973: 7-8).[20]

Given these connections the social scientist who purports to explain the environmental crisis has not fulfilled his intellectual responsibilities until he clarifies the normative import of that theory, until he compares the theory to competing interpretations with variable normative import to ascertain the extent to which the available empirical evidence is compatible with more than one set of normative priorities, and until he self-consciously probes the possibility that his acceptance of a particular explanatory theory reflects as much the pull of his *previous* attachment to the normative priorities it sustains as it does the constraints of evidence. The connection between explanatory theory and normative judgment provides methodological support for the proliferation of competing explanatory-normative theories within social science and makes the conscious juxtaposition of opposing theories a precondition of good empiricism (see Connolly, 1973; Feyerabend, 1968).

The tacit rules governing a practice are generally richer than the explicit formulations offered by those engaged in that practice. Such a discrepancy persists in the practice of social science: the practitioners tacitly understand the close connection between accepting an explanatory theory and sanctioning a set of political commitments, even though the explicit methodological formulations of mainstream social science discount that connection. This fact helps to explain the suspicion and anxiety with which proponents of the market model view challenges to their interpretation of environmental degradation. For to accept the mainstream theory is to legitimize a set of policy ideals and political strategies well within the range of tolerance of corporate and governmental elites, while to accept (or even to explore sympathetically) the alternative model is to place oneself and one's profession in direct opposition to those same elites.

These considerations do not, certainly, undermine the validity of the neo-market theory, but they do help to explain why the vast preponderance of environmental research in America has remained comfortably within the frame of that model. And we are now better able to understand as well why those who challenge the assumptive substructure of neo-classical theory tend to be defined by their professional colleagues less as intellectual protagonists to be answered and more as political adversaries to be isolated and controlled (see Lifshultz, 1974).

HUMAN NATURE AND ENVIRONMENTAL MANAGEMENT

The normative priorities ratified by neo-classical theory find their most basic underpinning in a postulate which proponents of the theory have subjected to minimal examination: the profile of the individual as "homo-economicus" who prudently calculates private advantage narrowly defined and rationally selects the policy or strategy which will optimize that advantage (see Dallmayr, 1974; also Lukes, 1973; Bottomore, 1963).

To explain and to justify contemporary economic practices it is imperative that "homo-economicus" be represented not as a particular manifestation of contemporary capitalist society but as the manifestation of invariant characteristics of human nature which are allowed to flourish in market society. For to acknowledge significant historical variations in patterns of individual motivation and social interaction would be to call into question contemporary forms of production organized around private profit, work as simply a means to security and consumption, the stratified labor force as instrumental to productivity, and equality of opportunity as a vehicle for placing individuals efficiently within the stratified system. Affirmation of a more flexible and social theory of human nature would extend the parameters within which alternative responses to the environmental crisis and to other symptoms of social malaise could be seriously explored. It would thus tend to undermine the policy priorities of the environmental managers.

When Frank Knight contended that "the strongest argument in favor of such a system as ours is the contention that this direct selfish motive is the only dependable method for guaranteeing that productive forces will be organized and worked efficiently" (Knight, 1951: 11-12), it must be emphasized that only a very narrow reading of the phrase "direct selfish motive" will suffice to discredit efforts to create alternative modes of production and consumption more congruent with environmental imperatives. If the assembly-line worker who works only for pay and the scientist who works partly for pay, partly because of the intrinsic interest of the work itself, partly because of a desire to create socially useful results, and partly because of the hope that his social contribution will enhance his social status, are to be lumped together as guided *equally* by "direct selfish motives," then the image of "homo-economicus" is preserved by making its content vacuous. For the mix of reasons and incentives which enter into the worklife of the latter are quite congruent with our proposals to restructure the worklife of the former and to reorient social relationships so as to diminish environmental pressures. Moreover, the fact that the economic behavior of many individuals in our system more or less fits the model of "homo-economicus" tells us very little about the comparative validity of the two models. For that fit is quite compatible with the contention that the system of corporate power, work incentives, and individual mobility requires individuals to internalize such a style in order to get along within it. The fact that inmates in a concentration camp eat garbage tells us less about the culinary propensities of human beings as such and more about the conditions of life in the camp.

The tragic flaw in the image of "homo-economicus" is this: a vast array of historical and anthropological evidence undermines any reading of the image sufficient to sustain the normative priorities of the environmental managers, while any reading flexible enough to assimilate the range of historical variations is quite congruent with a distinctly different set of priorities (see Berger and Luckmann, 1966; Durkheim, 1947; Gurley, 1970; Piaget, 1965; Turnbull, 1962).

The image which underpins our own normative system is influenced strongly by the Marxian theory of alienation and by Rousseau's theory of personal development through participation in community life. But our orientation does not require a *perfectionist* interpretation of such theories. A perfectionist version would hold that if the specified conditions were established, all members of the community would consistently and voluntarily strive to promote the general welfare. In such an order (even if conceived only as a limiting case), the need for coercion and for any private incentives for productive effort would disappear. Citizens would consent to policies and workers would maximize their productive efforts simply because these policies and efforts were seen to contribute to the collective welfare.

Our view diverges from perfectionism in certain essential respects. We hold that structural reforms in work life, especially those which reestablish the connection between mental and physical work and build social interaction into the work process, will make work itself gratifying, thereby decreasing dependence on incentives and threats external to the work setting itself. And we also hold that a reduction in income inequality joined to an expansion of opportunities to enter into fulfilling social relationships will further dampen the consumptive and self-aggrandizing tendencies endemic to market society. Even under ideal conditions, though, the need for democratically established legal rules backed by coercive sanctions and for a range of material incentives in the work process would persist, but they would play a subordinate role within a much richer social and productive setting. In the absence of *any* such sanctions and incentives a Gresham's law would operate to bring the system back where it is today: a few would manipulate the system for private advantage and then build upon that advantage to further improve their relative standing; others, responding defensively to these pressures, would strive to protect themselves from such incursions; and the life of the relatively integrated society would gradually erode into that of the competitive market society marked by extreme inequality.

Even though private incentives and coercive sanctions would find a place within each of the two models outlined, the practices permitted and those proscribed would vary quite significantly in the two systems. Corporate capitalism applies coercive pressures primarily to those at the bottom of the pyramid and positive incentives to those at the top, while the alternative model broadens the meaning of "incentive" beyond its paradigm use in capitalist society and distributes the positive incentives and supportive social arrangements more equally among members of the system.[21]

ENVIRONMENTAL IMPERATIVES AND POLITICAL REALISM

When the market model of environmental management is stripped of the image of human nature which props it up, its advocates still retain a fall-back position. The alternative model, they say, is unrealistic politically (it is naive, utopian, impractical). At least the program of internalizing the externalities within existing market mechanisms has a chance of gaining political acceptance. We agree. But a few additional points are required to fill this picture out.

(1) If the market program is now to be justified not because it copes effectively with imperfections in an otherwise healthy system, but because theoretically viable alternatives are unacceptable to corporate and governmental elites, the argument for political realism becomes more an indictment of the power structure than a justification of the market system.

(2) Neo-classical economists and pluralist political scientists who have helped to legitimize the market images of the economy and the polity by claiming these systems reflect invariant features of human nature bear a measure of responsibility for the political unrealism of efforts to institute structural reforms today. Scholars who now see defects in assumptions underlying these models, and who define themselves as defenders of the truth, are today obligated to explore the theoretical viability of alternative responses to environmental control, even if these alternatives presently face intractable political barriers.

(3) The policies of the environmental managers may gain limited short-run support, especially from constituencies which can easily assimilate the costs involved and/or displace the costs to the underclasses. But initial successes, as the war on poverty demonstrated, can contribute to defeat over the long run. The program of the environmental managers, as we have argued, promises to drive that segment of labor employed in the corporate sector into an alliance with corporate elites against environmental reform. The immediate difficulties in our strategy are outstripped only by the long-run political unrealism of the economics of environmental management. Moreover, the labor-corporate backlash it encourages threatens to heighten the repressive tendencies in American politics.

(4) When one construes the problem as more political than technical, it is clear that the most important strategic objective is to mobilize a progressive labor-environmentalist coalition around issues immediately compelling to each party and to generate thereby momentum for more basic reforms at a later date. Such a strategy is not easy to develop. But the most promising focal point is the workplace itself; workers and environmentalists can find common ground in an effort to eliminate the hazards of pollution within the workplace. And as environmentalists come to see that worklife

reform is an essential precondition of sound environmental control, that alliance could develop into a movement for broader structural reform.

Clearly, the direction the environmental movement takes in the next few years will help to determine whether a labor-environmental or labor-corporate coalition gains ascendancy. If economic growth is curtailed (as we expect) and the labor movement coalesces with corporate elites, we can expect a suppression of environmental issues while labor in the corporate sector solidifies its advantages over labor in the market sector of the economy. If, alternatively, an early alliance between environmentalists and organized labor forestalls these developments, there is a chance that the economics of environmental management can be displaced by the political economy of work life reform, income redistribution, and environmental integrity.

No one group can alone shape forces as large as those discussed here, but an environmental movement which is strategically alert has some capacity to encourage that labor-environmentalist coalition which is necessary to attack the institutional sources of environmental decay.

NOTES

1. In Paul Samuelson's classic text, *Economics* (1948, 1951, 1955, 1958, 1961, 1964, 1967, 1970, 1973), there is no discussion of pollution until the 1961 edition where a very brief mention of smoke is made. By 1964 there were a couple of paragraphs on "external diseconomies" in general; by 1967 a brief justification of governmental intervention to compensate for market externalities such as air and water pollution. There is no comparable classic text in political science. But the Frederic Ogg and R. Orman Ray, *Essentials of American Government* (1932, 1936, 1940, 1943, 1947, 1950, 1952, 1961, 1963; Young, 1969), covers a long span and has been widely used. The 1950 edition contains only a brief, optimistic discussion of recent government protection of land, soil, water, forest, and mineral resources. But by 1969, William and Sara Young, who revised that edition, were moved to warn that "our forests are still being slashed and depleted; soil is being washed and blown away. . . . Bays and estuaries, rivers and lakes are brown with silt and rank with wastes. Our cities are choked with traffic, smog and blight" (p. 400). A more contemporary, behavioral text, Marian D. Irish and James W. Prothro, *The Politics of American Democracy* (1959, 1962, 1965, 1968), has four chapters dealing with the "outputs of the political system," but none touches the politics of ecology.

2. Some of the chapter headings indicate the range of social costs probed in this study:

"The Social Costs of Air Pollution;" "The Social Costs of Water Pollution;" "The Premature Depletion of Energy Resources;" "Soil Erosion, Soil Depletion and Reforestation;" and "Social Costs in Transportation." We are indebted to Barry Commoner for calling this study to our attention and for many other helpful suggestions as well.

3. Kapp notes that Pigou (1932) discussed such externalities in general, but more often they were treated as a "minor disturbance" which "need not be assimilated into the main body of economic analysis."

4. For a discussion of the optimum conditions sufficient for Pareto optimality, see Koplin (1971: 305-308) and Mishan (1960). Mishan examines various criteria for comparing economic situations. The compensation test for economic efficiency, that a change should be made if the gainers *could* compensate the losers, is also commonly used in economic studies and forms the basis of the benefit-cost method for public policy decision-making. It sidesteps the question of distributive justice. Although broader than the Paretian test for an increase in welfare, the compensation test also requires an assessment of unpriced social costs.

5. Divergence can also be caused by imperfect competition, declining cost industries, public goods, and transaction costs. The ecological implications of corporate power, which extend well beyond price divergencies, will be explored later. For an analysis of market failure and of conditions under which nonmarket allocating mechanisms seems superior to the price system, see Arrow (1970).

6. Some would replace our term "unpriced side effects," preferring the vocabulary of excessive transactions costs that impede or block the formation of markets (see Arrow, 1970: 60). In either case, social costs/benefits escape market evaluation.

7. Two substantial barriers to relying on property rights are generally mentioned. First, the size of environmental units is often large and indivisible, which would necessitate highly concentrated ownership. Second, given the public good nature of environmental resources, nonpayers could not be excluded from the benefits. Therefore, the allocation of costs would require cumbersome and costly legal procedures. In one of the most far-reaching proposals, Mishan argues for placing the burden of proof on polluters rather than victims. However, the compatibility of such a policy with the maintenance of a favorable private investment climate is not explored. See Mishan (1972) and Calabresi (1972).

8. For example, direct regulation. But market economists stress the inefficiencies inherent in such a policy. Market charges, by comparison, are thought to maintain the elements of market discrimination, marginal variation, and price incentive—all components of an efficient allocative mechanism.

9. This latter problem could be remedied by assuming, as we do, that the individual as utility maximizer is more a product of, and less the cause of, the market system of economic competition. But that shift in assumptions erodes support for the private-enterprise market system, since it is now seen as developing a motivational system which unnecessarily depletes resources and erodes environmental supports. More about this later.

10. There are other difficulties more or less internal to this theory which we cannot discuss here: the assumption of a smooth exchange function between any two items (how many ice cream cones will you exchange for your left arm?), the assumption that the environment (including animals) is merely to be viewed and valued as a human resource; and (a view we will oppose in our alternative model) the tendency to reduce complex social relationships to exchange relationships between private utility maximizers. For impressive elaboration and criticism of these tendencies among utilitarians in general and market economists in particular, see Hampshire (1973); Tribe (1972); Wolff (1968: ch. 5).

11. As the authors put it, "We must assume that there is some political mechanism through which collective choices are made and that through this political mechanism the society has determined the rules that govern the distribution of income and wealth in the society" (Freeman et al., 1973: 70).

12. For a liberal version of the thesis that the political economy of contemporary America is divided into two systems, the market system in which multiple units are regulated by impersonal market forces and the industrial system in which the oligopolistic corporation exercises significant power over markets, see Galbraith (1973). A radical version of this thesis is presented in O'Connor (1973). Our analysis draws upon this distinction, but we, like O'Connor, would emphasize internal connections among the investing class in both systems and we would also call attention to the impact of the "industrial system" on the forms of production and the range of product options as well as its impact on exchange markets. These differences in emphasis are quite necessary for an understanding of resource depletion and pressures on the environment as a receptacle for waste. For a critique of Galbraith which develops such points, see Best (1974-1975).

13. Today General Motors produces 50% of all U.S. cars. General Motors, Ford, and Chrysler produce 84% of all trucks; G.M. builds 75% of all city buses, 100% of passenger train locomotives, and 80% of freight locomotives (Snell, 1974: 26-27).

14. The dominant role of the automobile is clear enough. There are today over 15 million trucks on our roads which carry 22% of intercity freight, 90% of livestock shipped, and 63% of market produce. Approximately 10 million persons work in the manufacture, maintenance, and commercial use of trucks, creating a massive political constituency in support of a shipping system that is ecologically irrational (Mowbray, 1969). Notable in the history of this development was the Presidential Commission in 1944 that proposed the Highway Trust Fund in which gasoline taxes are received for highway construction. The Commission "failed to give any consideration to the relative efficiency or need of rail, water, and air, as well as highway transportation" (Kohlmeier, 1969: 154).

15. General Motors did, according to findings by the Interstate Commerce Commission, make cost claims for its diesel locomotives to potential buyers that were "erroneous," "inflated," and "manifestly absurd" (Snell, 1974: 41). And corporate elites knew about the dangerous levels of pollution from cars and trucks as early as 1953. Nevertheless, our argument leans less on an assessment of corporate *intent* formed in the twenties to dismantle trolley and train systems, more on the identification of policy tendencies that emerge when a small group of corporations dominate all forms of ground transportation, some of which are more profitable than others. Moreover, as this brief review indicates, the acknowledgement by Freeman et al. (1973) that consumer "tastes and preferences are not strictly given, but are subject to the influence of *advertising*" (underlining added, p. 71) barely scratches the surface of the forces at work in corporate capitalism that shape consumer demand by controlling product options.

16. Indeed neo-classical economists have made important contributions to contemporary pluralist theory. Schumpeter (1947) helped to lay the foundations for contemporary pluralist theory. Lindblom (1965) continues in that tradition. In these cases and many others the assumptions and categories of market economists are transposed to political processes.

17. The basic problem is the tendency of political scientists and economists to assume the autonomy of political and economic *spheres,* when in fact political and economic transactions are not confined to particular spatial spheres but are dimensions of activities with variable spatial locations. The modern corporation has a political dimension both in its

application of pressure to government and in its unilateral policy decisions which affect the well being of broader segments of the population. When "politics" is understood in this way it becomes clear that the disciplines of political science and economics must give way to the study of political economy. For arguments which move in this direction, see Bachrach (1967) and Connolly (1969).

18. As Rousseau was careful to point out, a society can be egalitarian enough to encourage collective solutions to collective problems if the range of inequalities in property and power do not force some to bear alone the burdens of policies initiated by others: "As for equality, this word must not be understood to mean that all individuals must have exactly the same amount of power and property, but rather that power must be exercised only in accordance with rank and the laws, so that no one should have so much as to be able to use violence upon another, and as regards property, that no one is rich enough to buy another or poor enough to be forced to sell himself" (Rousseau, 1954: 119).

19. There are, clearly, many other ingredients in normative judgment which require specification as well. Perhaps the best start is provided by Frankena (1970).

20. A. J. Ayer's classic defense of this disjuncture rests on such a mistake about the actual conventions of our moral language: "What we are denying is that the suggested reduction of ethical to non-ethical statements is consistent with the *conventions of our language*" (Ayer, 1936: 105; our emphasis). Many have noted the primitive view of definition represented here (naturalists seldom *reduce* ethical terms to nonethical terms), but it is equally important to see that Ayer rests his case on a (faulty) reading of the *conventions* of our language.

21. A serious issue remains which cannot be explored here. Tyranny is *possible* in any society, but some systems generate internal resources for limiting or expunging tyrants more effectively than others. Thus the difference between Stalinism and Nixonism turns largely on the presence of a relatively independent judiciary and press in the latter system (even though those institutions are clearly biased) while Stalin faced no such resistance. We assume that the requisite degree of institutional autonomy can be established in a humane socialist system, but we have not argued in support of that assumption here. For thoughtful, comparative statements of the issues involved, see Parkin (1971) and Ricoeur (1972: 337-367).

REFERENCES

ARROW, K. J. (1970) "The organization of economic activity: issues pertinent to the choice of market versus nonmarket allocation," in R. H. Haveman and J. Margolis (eds.) Public Expenditure and Public Analysis. Chicago: Markham.
AYER, A. J. (1936) Language, Truth and Logic. New York: Dover.
AYERS, R. V. and A. V. KNEESE (1972) Economic and Ecological Effects of a Stationary Economy. Resources for the Future, reprint No. 99.
BACHRACH, P. (1967) "Corporate authority and democratic theory," in D. Spitz (ed.) Political Theory and Social Change. New York: Atherton.
BERGER, P. and T. LUCKMANN (1966) The Social Construction of Reality. New York: Doubleday.
BEST, M. (1974-1975) "Galbraith on the transition to corporate capitalism." Maxwell Review 11: 58-69.

BOTTOMORE, T. B. [ed.] (1963) Karl Marx: Early Writings. New York: McGraw-Hill.

CALABRESI, G. (1972) "Transaction costs, resource allocation and liability rules," In R. and N. Dorfman (eds.) Economics of the Environment. New York: W. W. Norton.

COMMONER, B. (1971) The Closing Circle. New York: Alfred A. Knopf.

CONNOLLY, W. E. (1973) "Theoretical self consciousness." Polity 6: 5-35.

——— [ed.] (1969) The Bias of Pluralism. New York: Atherton Press.

CRENSON, M. (1971) The Unpolitics of Air Pollution. Baltimore: Johns Hopkins University Press.

DALLMAYR, F. (1974) "Empirical theory and the images of man," in W. E. Connolly and G. Gordon (eds.) Social Structure and Political Theory. Lexington, Mass.: D. C. Heath.

DALY, H. E. [ed.] (1973) Toward a Steady State Economy. San Francisco: W. H. Freeman.

DOWD, D. (1974) The Twisted Dream. Cambridge, Mass.: Winthrop.

DURKHEIM, E. (1947) The Division of Labor in Society. Glencoe, Ill.: Free Press.

EDWARDS, R. C. (1972) "The logic of capitalist expansion," in R. C. Edwards, M. Reich, and T. E. Weisskopf (eds.) The Capitalist System. Englewood Cliffs, N.J.: Prentice-Hall.

FEYERABAND, P. K. (1968) "How to be a good empiricist," in P. H. Nidditch (ed.) The Philosophy of Science. New York: Oxford University Press.

FRANKENA, W. (1970) "The concept of morality," in G. Wallace and A.D.M. Walker (eds.) The Definition of Morality. London: Methuen.

FREEMAN, M., R. H. HAVEMAN and A. V. KNEESE (1973) The Economics of Environmental Policy. New York: John Wiley.

GALBRAITH, J. K. (1973) The Economics of Public Purpose. Boston: Houghton Mifflin.

GURLEY, J. (1970) "The new man in the new China," The Center Magazine 3: 25-33.

HAMPSHIRE, S. (1973) Morality and Pessimism. London: Cambridge University Press.

HARDIN, G. (1968) "The tragedy of the Commons." Science 162: 1243-1248.

HEILBRONER, R. (1974) "The human prospect." New York Review of Books (January 24): 21-34.

HYMER, S. (1972) "The internationalization of capital." Journal of Economic Issues 6: 91-110.

IRISH, M. and J. PROTHRO (1968) The Politics of American Democracy. 4 editions. Englewood Cliffs, N.J.: Prentice-Hall.

KAPP, K. W. (1950) The Social Costs of Private Enterprise. Cambridge: Harvard University Press.

KNIGHT, F. H. (1951) The Economic Organization. New York: A. M. Kelley.

KOHLMEIER, L. M., Jr. (1969) The Regulators. New York: Harper & Row.

KOPLIN, H. J. (1971) Micro-economic Analysis and Efficiency in Private and Public Sectors. New York: Harper & Row.

LANGE, O. and F. TAYLOR (1938) On the Economic Theory of Socialism. Minneapolis: University of Minnesota Press.

LIFSHULTZ, L. S. (1974) "Could Karl Marx teach economics in America?" Ramparts 12: 27-59.

LINDBLOM, C. (1965) The Intelligence of Democracy. New York: Free Press.

LUKES, S. (1973) Individualism. New York: Harper Torchbooks.

McCONNELL, G. (1966) Private Power and American Democracy. New York: Alfred A. Knopf.

——— (1954) "The conservation movement, past and present." Western Political Quarterly 7: 463-478.

MISHAN, E. J. (1972) "Property rights and amenity rights," in R. and N. Dorfman (eds.) Economics of the Environment. New York: W. W. Norton.

––– (1960) "A survey of welfare economics, 1939-1959." Economic Journal 70: 197-256.
MOWBRAY, A. Q. (1969) Road to Ruin. Philadelphia: Lippincott.
MUSGRAVE, R. A. (1959) The Theory of Public Finance. New York: McGraw-Hill.
O'CONNOR, J. (1973) The Fiscal Crisis of the State. New York: St. Martin's.
PARKIN, F. (1971) Class Inequality and Political Order: Social Stratification in Capitalist and Communist Societies. New York: Praeger.
PIAGET, J. (1965) The Moral Judgment of the Child. New York: Free Press.
PIGOU, A. C. (1932) The Economics of Welfare, 4th ed. London: Macmillan.
RICOEUR, P. (1972) "The political paradox," in Hwa Yol Jung (ed.) Existential Phenomonology and Political Theory. Chicago: Henry Regnery.
ROUSSEAU, J. J. (1954) The Social Contract. Chicago: Henry Regnery.
SAMUELSON, P. (1973) Economics, 9th ed. New York: McGraw-Hill.
SCHATTSCHNEIDER, E. E. (1960) The Semi-Sovereign People. New York: Holt, Rinehart & Winston.
SCHUMPETER, J. (1947) Capitalism, Socialism and Democracy. New York: Harper.
SEXTON, P. and B. SEXTON (1971) Blue Collars and Hardhats. New York: Random House.
SNELL, B. C. (1974) American Ground Transport: A Proposal for Reconstructuring the Automobile, Truck, Bus and Rail Industries, presented to the Subcommittee on Antitrust and Monopoly of the Committee on the Judiciary, U.S. Senate. Washington, D.C.: Government Printing Office.
Special Task Force Report to the Department of Health, Education and Welfare (1973) Work in America. Cambridge: M.I.T. Press.
STELLMAN, J. M. and S. M. DAUM (1973) Work Is Dangerous to Your Health. New York: Vintage.
TAYLOR, C. (1967) "Neutrality in political science," in P. Laslett and W. G. Runciman (eds.) Philosophy, Politics and Society, 3rd ser. New York: Barnes & Noble.
TRIBE, L. (1972) "The policy sciences: science or ideology." Philosophy and Public Affairs 2: 66-110.
TURNBULL, C. (1962) The Forest People. New York: Simon & Schuster.
WALLICK, F. (1972) The American Worker: An Endangered Species. New York: Ballantine.
WOLFF, R. P. (1968) The Poverty of Liberalism. Boston: Beacon.
YOUNG, W. H. (1969) Ogg and Ray's Essentials of American Government, 10th ed. New York: Appleton Crofts.

3

RESEARCH OBJECTIVES FOR
POLICY ANALYSIS

RONALD W. JOHNSON

Pennsylvania State University

Policy research can occupy a unique and possibly critical position in
the development of the social sciences. Few social science research
enterprises do not involve extensive public funding, and few public
agencies are still willing to fund research for the sake of "pure"
knowledge. What we are discovering in the social sciences, however,
is that we are woefully unprepared to understand what is meant by
the requirement to justify our research in terms of public policy
implications. If we look at the research in the last twenty years in
political science that has a policy label, we should be badly
disappointed. The most important policy implication that seems
derivable from much of the state and local policy input/output

AUTHOR'S NOTE: *The capable assistance of Terry M. Thomas in background work for this
essay is gratefully acknowledged. My friends and colleagues who will all agree that I should
have listened to their comments more than is reflected here are Gene Meehan, Bob
O'Connor, and Jack Wikse.*

correlational analysis is that if more expenditures for human services are desirable we should alter per-capita income. In some cases it might also help if we would alter the degree of party competition.

Analyses which "explain" expenditure levels by demonstrating correlations with social, economic, or political characteristics could only pass for knowledge in an environment isolated from the rest of the world and the needs of human beings. If we ask for the relationship of this "knowledge" of correlations to the problems to which public policies are presumably directed, I think the answers are short. The defect is not a lack of interest in policy, but is rather a defective epistemological position. There seems to be no self-conscious attempt in policy research to address the question of how we know what we know. Instead, we rely on finding new variables to add to the regression equations and assume that each variable added, or each reduction in unexplained variance, is an accumulation of knowledge. The way out of what would otherwise be an endless "filling in the gaps" in the policy literature is to address directly the question of public policy criticism and policy recommendation.

In this essay I work with three concerns:

(1) the implications of a self-conscious reflection on the purposes of policy research;

(2) a framework for evaluating policy research as an activity directed toward human purposes; and

(3) an application of the framework to measurement problems in policy research.

In the first section of the essay I examine policy research as an active engagement of the researcher with human purposes. This orientation requires self-conscious choice of substantive policy area, range of conditions to be examined, and the nature of policy recommendations to be made. My argument is that these choices must stem from an explicit understanding of the policy choices that have been made and a critical stance that permits evaluation of those choices. Each research choice we make as social scientists is thus a value judgment.

In section two, I provide a framework for evaluating policy

research in terms of its adequacy for solving human problems. The criterion implicit in this framework is that policy research which is not oriented toward human purposes is inadequate. The internal standards of a discipline are inadequate guidelines for making research choices and encourage perpetuation of fraudulent academic claims on scarce societal resources. In this position, I am supporting the Meehan (1974) critique of most social science, but I am specifically charging policy researchers with the greatest responsibility for connecting our research to standards of purpose outside the discipline.

I conclude the essay by looking at measurement problems in policy research. Specifically, I show how the position argued in the first two sections helps answer two measurement problems—what to measure, which implicitly means what not to measure, and how to establish the claim that our indicators are adequate representations of our concepts.

I.

The policy research of the last decade and a half can be classified initially in two categories—analysis of policy-making as a process and evaluation research. The first is not new to political science, a good example of the genre being Wildavsky's (1964) *Politics of the Budgetary Process.* Numerous syntheses of the public policy process have also been produced in the last five years.[1] The more recent emphasis on the policy process includes a variety of data analytic pieces usually operationalizing policy as the amount of a jurisdiction's budget spent on various public functions.[2] From the initial important work of Dye on state policy outputs, we have in some ways regressed to a search for new and better aggregate data correlates of state or local government budget expenditures (see Hofferbert, 1968; Sharkansky, 1970; Gray and Wanat, 1974).

Policy research of the evaluation type is more hopeful in the sense that its focus is not on an intermediate aspect of the policy process such as a budget decision or a piece of legislation but on the consequences of policy decisions. Cook and Scioli (1972), for example, have argued that the researcher must become involved in analyzing the impacts of policy decisions on target populations. While an important advance over the more traditional focus of policy research, however, evaluation research is only the first step in developing a systematic approach to explanation and criticism of public policy.

The argument for a critical approach to policy research can be posed in two ways. From a social utility perspective, policy research which does not have any implications for improving the choices of policy-makers cannot justify a claim on public resources. While there is merit in having policy research carried out in a variety of academic and nonacademic settings, that useful variety does not justify avoiding the connection between research findings and policy recommendations on the grounds of pursuit of knowledge for its own sake. Meehan's description of this position states the problem plainly:

> By asserting that the search for knowledge is the search for truth, that the purposes of inquiry need be nothing more than the satisfaction of human curiosity, and that there is no need for the academic to justify his privileged position in society by his contribution to that society, knowledge has been made an end in itself, related to no human need or purpose, and subject to criticism on conventional rather than pragmatic grounds. Social science remains "art for art's sake" [Meehan, 1971: 25].

Policy research which has no policy implications is simply a drain on public resources which the academic community can ill afford.

Aside from the utilitarian argument for providing useful research to those who fund us, there is the more important epistemological question of whether research results which do not imply recommendations for testing in use have any status as knowledge. The usual claim to knowledge in the social sciences involves a comparison for consistency with other social scientists' claims to know. Even the most sophisticated testing situations involving complex patterns remain internal to a discipline or a slightly larger academic community unless the theories imply interventions in an environment where change can either be observed or not. Relying on the judgment of our fellow academicians is perhaps the safest way to academic success, but ignorance of whether our research can be put to use is a form of complete ignorance.

In the natural sciences the epistemological problem is better understood. Generations of scientists may cling dogmatically to a view of the world which fits their theories, but as engineers attempt to build physical structures that do not work or collapse, either the scientists abandon or modify their theories or the engineer recognizes their irrelevance and invents his own theoretical understanding which he tests in use. A suspension bridge built with an inadequate theory of stress forces has a dramatic way of revealing to us that our theories are suspect. Theories about human beings, however, have a double way of hanging around. Either we fail to test them by putting them to use, or they are advocated so strenuously that humans begin to act as if they were true and provide confirmations which may last for generations (Vickers, 1965).

A way out of the circularity of relying on internal disciplinary tests is to recommend intervention in the environment to test in use, and it is to this capacity that policy research should be most adaptable. What it means in practice is that the foremost question for the researcher is what are the implicit policy recommendations embedded in a given piece of research. The guidance that this basic question provides is considered explicitly in the next section.

II.

Meehan's (1971) analysis of the structure of human inquiry suggests a taxonomy of policy research objectives which provides the basis for evaluating policy research and solving some of its problems. Among the methodological tools necessary for systematic inquiry, Meehan includes description, forecast, explanation, and value judgments.[3] Considering policy-oriented research in Meehan's methodological terms, my taxonomy distinguishes four objectives:

(1) *Description.* Description involves reporting the observed behavior of participants in policy-making and noting the values of various operational indicators of the researcher's concepts. The

research objective is limited to describing a sequence of events over time or the static associations among pairs or larger sets of variables.

(2) *Forecast.* One obvious step beyond description is to predict an observed pattern of events or a statistical relationship to continue into a future time period. Such a forecast may be a raw empirical extrapolation of data or may be an extrapolation accompanied by an argument that most human behavior follows predictable, usually linear, patterns.

(3) *Explanation.* Most of the evaluation research has as its purpose relating variable program impacts to variable program conditions. The experimental and quasi-experimental program evaluations advocated by Cook and Scioli (1971) are of this type and have as a basic purpose the experimental determination of optimum program level.

(4) *Criticism.* A critical piece of policy research would extend beyond the explanation involved in evaluation research to include criticism of policy choices in terms of alternative choices that could have been made. This involves the researcher not only in describing and explaining policy-makers' value judgments but also in making our own value judgments about the range of choices that could have been but were not considered by policy-makers.

Each of the classifications in the taxonomy describes a different basic purpose behind a given piece of research. Orienting the taxonomy to research purposes is my understanding of the research process as a choice-making activity. As a choice-making activity, research involves making value judgments about the questions to be pursued, the method of study, and the policy choices which are the object of study.

Present policy research is heavily descriptive. Most of the quantitative studies of public policy in political science have taken level of expenditure as the operational conception of policy and have gone on to describe the extent to which various social, economic, and political indicators are or are not correlated with expenditure amounts.[4] Most of these studies are static comparisons of states or local governments at one point in time; they either assume that the observed correlations would extend over time, or they make no reference to future projections. Thorough critiques from both conceptual and methodological points of view have already been offered of this type of literature (Rakoff and Schaefer, 1970). My point here is to put it in the light of a classification of research purposes. As descriptive studies, analyses of spending levels and their correlates lead to no expectations about the future behavior of citizens or policy-makers and suggest no policy recommendations. In fact, only if one is willing to assume that there is something interesting in the fact in and of itself that Mississippi spends less per capita for welfare than New York does it make any sense simply to examine expenditures in the first place. A description is only a rudimentary step in understanding policy. And it would make more sense to use as a description of policy something beyond dollars spent as a first step.

Few policy studies involve the second purpose described in the taxonomy. The Davis, Dempster, and Wildavsky (1966) study of budget requests and appropriations is an example of a longitudinal study, again of budget dollars, which implicitly projects that budget expenditures for most federal agencies will vary only slightly from year to year in a predictable linear pattern. A glance at several years of federal budgets confirms this projection without plugging in the statistical models, although the significance of the fact that federal agencies usually spend a little more each year is uncertain.[5]

To date, the most important policy research has involved evaluation of actual programs in action. Although very little evaluation research has been conducted by political scientists, there is good evidence that its stature is increasing in the discipline.[6] Policy evaluations range from those which take the measures of program success as those given by program administrators and attempt to assess the extent of impact to long-term major research efforts such as the Westinghouse evaluation of the Head Start program. Generally, these studies would fall into the category of explanation in the taxonomy of purposes. In the more comprehensive studies, changes over time in measures of program success are associated with changes in program operation or level or with varying program conditions. Natural or field experiments and deliberately designed experiments provide means of control over nonprogram variables.[7]

The last type of objective that policy research might entertain is what I have called policy criticism. Criticism involves taking a stance that policy choices are not simply matters of fact, that policy outcomes cannot only be explained, but that they can also be criticized in terms of other possible outcomes. Criticism is a function happily endorsed in literary and rhetorical analyses as well as other arts but not one normally accepted by the social sciences as part of our professional domain. Political scientists who engage in empirical research suspend judgment about whether policy choices are correct or not, and ethical theorists who examine questions of right or wrong carefully avoid confronting the world of real policy choices.

The policy critic's function is twofold. First, we must explain the outcomes, intended and unintended, of policy choices. That is, we must be able to show the connection between actual choices human beings have made and the consequences that we observe. In this I follow Meehan's argument that consequences which follow from environmental events or even unavoidable human actions cannot be criticized meaningfully since the criticism could not lead anyone to alter their behavior. The second task of the critic is to enlarge the conceptual framework within which policy choices are made. An unintended consequence of a policy choice is just as much a critical concern as an intended one. Unintended is a meaningful designation only within a conceptual framework which does not include those unintended consequences as possible outcomes of policy choices.

Expanding the policy-maker's frame of reference means more, however, than just attempting to incorporate all consequences of choice. It also means being prepared to judge an intended or unintended consequence unacceptable. While it may be appropriate to stay within an impressionist's framework to evaluate the artistic worth of an impressionist and not use a cubist's perspective, policy choices have consequences that must be considered from outside the particular frame of reference of the policy-maker. As critics we may, for example, criticize policy outcomes which are a fully intended extension of state socialism as undesirable interventions in the private economy. Since every critic is in some sense trapped within his own conceptual framework, there is no single critical stance. It is important, however, to view this argument not from a "one person's ethics are as good as another's" position. By examining alternative policy choices as producers of different outcomes for human beings and recommending different choices based on those outcomes, we accept the responsible role of examining over time those outcomes for their adaptability to human survival capacities. If we refuse that job, we remain both irresponsible and obscure. In the following section my understanding of the responsibilities of the policy analyst are applied to two basic measurement problems.

III.

Two measurement problems seem most critical for the policy researcher. The first is conceptualizing and then finding indicators for policy outcomes. The second is assessing the validity of those indicators. Both are classical problems familiar to any empirically oriented social scientist, but the purposive framework argued in the first two sections adds some resolution to these problems.

There are two basic positions on the relation of an indicator (or set of indicators) to the concept measured. Operationalists define a concept strictly in terms of the operations performed to measure it. The indicators are then assumed to exhaust the meaning of a concept. Operationalists thus assume that the language of theory and the language of empirical observation are identical. This assumed identity severely limits the prospects for theory development by limiting the meaning of complex human behavior to only that which is observable. Since my interest in this essay is to enhance the role of the social scientist in dealing with real human problems, I assume the less restricted argument that no set of operations which identify sets of indicators completely exhausts the meaning of a concept. Thus, every set of measures is a partial representation—is in fact a kind of mini-theory which hypothesizes the relation between concepts and indicators.

If we take as hypothetical the relation between concept and indicators, the researcher's measurement choices amount to a selection of indicators which are at best a partial representation of the complex problems investigated. Although there is usually no explicit discussion in present policy literature of the selection problem, the amount of space devoted to budget expenditures as the indicator of policy suggests that we now pay little attention to the selection process. Starting with the notion of measurement as choosing a partial set of indicators suggests first that any set chosen must be justified in two respects:

(1) the indicators selected must be shown to be a meaningful description of policy choices; and

(2) the indicators selected must be useful for explicating the consequences, intended or not, of policy choices.

As an indicator of policy, budget expenditures, number of agency personnel employed in a given program, or other such intermediate indicators of agency effort are difficult to justify in either respect. These output measures may be a good indication of the political standing of different bureaus, but they are inadequate descriptions of the bureaus' policies or of legislative policy intentions. Further, indicators of governmental activity have no assumable connection with either desirable or undesirable consequences for the human subjects of public efforts.

To do a piece of policy research which we can legitimately claim to have some connection with real policy choices, therefore, the set of concepts which have to be considered are the following.

(1) *Program characteristics.* Characteristics of governmental programs would include those aspects of agencies and activities which might be reasonably expected to be related causally to change in the target population. Expenditure and personnel levels are meaningful indicators only if variations in level are expected to produce different consequences among the target population. Types of intervention strategies such as income-maintenance strategies versus service provision for welfare clients are relevant program characteristics.

While these are often treated as indicators of dependent behavior in political research, their status in policy research is as causes of policy outcomes.

(2) *Population condition.* In order to analyze and criticize public policy, some assessment of the condition of both a specific target population and the general population in a beginning state is necessary. Without some indication of change from time one to time two, there is no meaningful understanding of policy consequences. Public relations survey research which gathers the public's likes and dislikes for public servants may tell us about the popularity of officials and of particular programs, but it tells us nothing about whether public policies are effecting change in life conditions.

(3) *Program consequences.* Although a set of indicators describing the condition of the population at successive points in time is closely related to indicators of program consequences, I classify them separately to stress that policy consequences are often more far-reaching than any given inventory of population conditions may describe. It is our responsibility within our own understanding of relevant consequences to try to find indicators of policy outcomes whether intended or not. This might include, for example, indicators of program personnel's attitudes and behavior as one set of consequences.

Obviously, the set of three concepts does not provide a ready-made formula to determine relevant indicators. I am arguing only that any policy research must begin not with an assessment of census data, budget documents, and other available data sources as a grocery store of variables. Policy research begins with the understanding that selection of observable indicators is a choice-making activity which has to clarify the condition of the target population, the operating characteristics of programs intended to reach that population, and the consequences of human policy choices.

If we pair the three concepts for which indicators must be selected with the classification of research purposes from section two, the selection problem in measurement is further clarified, as shown in Table 1.

Table 1

	Program Characteristics		Population Conditions		Program Consequences	
	t_1	t_2	t_1	t_2	t_1	t_2
Description						
Policy input/output studies	X					
Politics of policy-making	X					
Forecast						
Policy output studies	X	X				
Politics of policy-making	X	X				
Explanation						
Program evaluations	X	X			X[a]	X
Criticism[b]	X	X	X	X	X	X

a. Evaluation research is usually limited to relating program characteristics to indicators of intended impacts. Although there is a lot of research seeking to establish sets of social indicators, this as yet is not connected to policy research which attempts to assess changes in population conditions as consequences of specific policy choices. See note 8.

b. I have here indicated that critical research would have to involve all three basic concepts, but the classification does not elaborate sufficiently what criticism involves in considering population conditions and program consequences. An obvious example first. From a classical liberal-democratic perspective, the distribution of income across individuals is not a condition to be manipulated by public policy other than by preventing special privileges by class and by guaranteeing some form of equal opportunity. From a socialist perspective, the distribution of income across individuals is an important indicator of the condition of the population and is a variable to be affected by public policy. Less obvious is a critical stance which takes as an important indicator of population conditions the distribution of occupations by sex. Choice of indicators, in other words, is not according to rule of logic or any fixed standard but is itself subject to criticism.

Although I have loosely classified major types of current policy research within Table 1, my purpose is not so much to castigate current research as to argue what research has to involve if it is to be relevant to policy choices. Most of our current research is restricted to describing the behavior of political actors—bureaucrats, legislators, lobbyists, and so forth. Even that which we call policy research generally ignores the effects of political actors on the population, and presumably that is what policy is all about. Evaluation research is an important progressive move because it focuses on program consequences for target populations—sometimes unintended consequences as well—and it usually involves beginning condition comparisons with after-program conditions. Even evaluation research, however, is too limited. The policy choice implications from evaluation studies are limited to modifications in program characteristics to maximize desired program impacts. Wider policy implications are evident only if we include in our concerns the condition of the population beyond selected indicators of specific program impacts and subject our understanding of relevant indicators of population condition to criticism from a variety of social perspectives.

The act of choosing relevant indicators of the three basic policy concepts, therefore, is inseparable from the choice of research purpose. From this perspective, the problem of assessing the validity of the indicators chosen seems less a technical or statistical one and more one of awareness of the perspective within which we make our claim that a set of indicators is a valid measurement of a concept. Every statement about validity is an argument that a given indicator as a measure of a concept serves the research purpose. We commonly phrase these arguments in one or more of three ways. We make the claim that an indicator is subjectively understood by the population, political actors, and the research community alike to be related to the underlying concept. The shared intersubjectivity of common language and common culture is the evidence base for what we usually term *face* validity. Personal income is understood by most people as an indicator, although incomplete, of economic well-being. A second argument that an indicator is a valid measure of a concept uses a more restricted reference group, making essentially the same claim. This appeal to *convention* argues that a given subgroup—the scientific community, policy-makers, and so forth—agrees that an indicator is a valid measure of a concept. A third argument depends on showing that an indicator fits with other indicators in a manner predictable by the researcher's theory. Thus, if an indicator correlates well with some indicators as predicted (converges) and correlates less well with other indicators as predicted (diverges), it is a valid measure of a concept (Campbell and Fiske, 1959). I call this the *fit-to-theory* argument.

Each of these arguments based on face, convention, and *fit-to-theory* depends upon the researcher's purpose as the final deter-minant of validity, whether the researcher is conscious of this or not. In the descriptive policy research, and the forecasting as well, the indicators of behavior of political actors are so well accepted that rarely does anyone mention a validity problem. A budget decision to spend $43 million in one agency is generally accepted on its face as a decision. I doubt if the general population is ever consulted, but I imagine most people would agree that here we have a decision. The independent correlates of budget decisions are more obscure because, except in a very complex way, things such as per-capita income, degree of party competition, region of the country, and so forth are not exactly related to any political actors' decisions. And there is a problem as far as policy implications are concerned. If the indicators selected have no connection with the choice behavior of people, then we can draw no implications for policy choices. More attention to what sorts of policy choices and what policy-makers we are describing or forecasting might prevent any more of this research.

Evaluation research presents more of a validity problem. At least research which has no policy implications is probably not dangerous. But evaluation research has policy implications, and claims for the validity of indicators must be taken seriously. A validity argument based on convention is common to most evaluation research. Program personnel determine the indicators of program characteristics. Established by legislation and interpreted by program managers, the indicators of program consequences are given to the researcher performing an evaluation. Fairweather (1967: 123) states this argument most strongly: "The validity of a measure in the field of social innovation is simply an empirical matter because it can be defined as the magnitude of its correlation with the social change outcome criterion." The social change outcome criterion is defined as "the consensus of a society's representatives about an acceptable solution to a given social problem" (Fairweather, 1967: 123), presumably a policy's official objectives.

While an empirical test of the relationship of the researcher's chosen measures to the official policy objective(s) may be made, the *claim* to validity of the measures is based on the assumed validity of the "social change outcome criterion." The claim is thus based on convention among political and program actors. Fairweather would have the researcher suspend judgment and ignore the whole question of whether the policy-making group's framework is an adequate perspective on the problem. Using my purposive framework, we can see the limitations of this argument.

Ronald W. Johnson

If we take as a research purpose the criticism of policy choices, we cannot stay within the policy-makers' framework in establishing the validity of our indicators. We have to specify our own normative framework and select indicators which enable us to compare alternative policy choices, both those that were and those that were not made, in terms of their consequences and in terms of general population conditions. While a fit-to-theory argument for the validity of a set of indicators is useful for any of the research purposes described here, it is unavoidable in criticism. And the most important point is that any given research framework, no matter how much more encompassing it is than the policy-maker's perspective, is always subject to judgment from still another critical stance. The ultimate test of the validity of indicators as well as the value of our research therefore must be external to our research community. At least as far as policy research is concerned, the relevant external community is the human population on whom policy consequences are perpetrated. Our research is useful, our indicators are well selected and valid if we discover alternative policy choices and those policy choices over time enhance the survival capacity of the human population.

SUMMARY AND IMPLICATIONS

The implicit rationale for a good part of current policy research seems to be an assumed need to continue an established line of descriptive research which is best characterized by inattention to the basic concept of policy. While I have not argued, as others have, that all empirical social science research must be concerned with policy, I have argued that to claim a connection with policy we must conduct our research with deliberate attention to policy implications. Policy refers to human choices, and policy research must have something to say which potentially can improve human choices or we must abandon both our claims on public resources and the status of our claims to knowledge.

If we take our job of improving human choices seriously, we have to consider our research not as pursuit of knowledge for its own sake. Our research and our writing will be demonstrably different than much of what is presently considered policy research. The four research objectives described in part two provide a classification against which we can compare both current and prospective policy research. Whether the purpose is description, forecast, explanation, or criticism, policy research has to argue for the relevance of the indicators selected to represent policy. Beyond that, however, understanding different research objectives forces us to consider the value of research limited to any one of the first three objectives. If we do not adopt criticism as one of our objectives, our ability to evaluate a claim to know is in question. Specifically, criticism involves both the examination and advocacy of alternative policies, based upon alternative outcomes. Thus, it is the only one of the four research objectives which includes testing in the environment alternatives outside the policy-makers' frames of reference. Meehan (1973: 164) best summarizes this epistemological argument: "The quality of scientific knowledge ... depends on the content of the knowledge claim, compatibility with other accepted knowledge claims, correspondence with observation, and successful use in the environment to achieve human purposes."

Although current evaluation research involves examination of policy consequences as a testing in use, we still shy away from going beyond the policy-maker's frame of reference and advocating alternatives. While Campbell (1973) is correct to warn against over-advocacy, he misunderstands the problem. From his position that our social science theories are too inadequate to allow policy recommendations, we are forced to sharpen our methodological tools for the service of policy-makers. But the tools involved in Campbell's conception of research design at best stop with explanation. We are then trapped within a circle of fellow professionals for determining what we should measure and the validity of our indicators. It is only by observing the consequences of changing policy in light of our research implications that we can determine whether we have adequately conceptualized policy and whether our measured indicators adequately represent our concepts.

Thus, as I understand the epistemological problem, we cannot choose to restrict our inquiry and ignore the necessity of policy criticism except at the price of irrelevance. Doing policy analysis means doing criticism. Doing criticism means exposing the implicit values that guide our research and recognizing that research which precludes implications for alternative policy choices is not worth doing.

NOTES

1. Good examples of the recent emphasis on the policy-making process are Dye (1972), Jones (1970), Wade (1972), and Woll (1974). Wade (1972) and Wade and Curry (1970) focus less on the policy-making process and more on the analytics of policy in an economic (or political economy) framework.

2. Dye (1966) is the best lengthy treatment of policy outputs and their correlates. Dawson and Robinson (1963) may be fairly said to have started the correlative aggregate data research.

3. Meehan (1971) also includes language as one of the tools necessary.

4. Gray and Wanat (1974) include a nonexpenditure measure of policy—the number of personnel employed. While it is not an expenditure measure, it says very little about policy choices. For example, day-care programs jointly funded by state and federal sources may contract with local governments (hence there would be employees to count) or with private organizations (hence no governmental employees to count).

5. Gist (1974) has an effective critique of both the theoretical and methodological significance (lack of) of Davis, Dempster, and Wildavsky (1966) and other statistical studies purporting to demonstrate the incremental nature of budgetary decision-making.

6. The *Policy Studies Journal* reflects this development and is a good source of short pieces of policy research.

7. Several large-scale program experiments have been conducted or are underway. Among them are the negative income tax experiments (OEO), performance contracting in education (OEO), and HEW's income maintenance experiments.

8. Meehan (1974) has a destructive critique of the value of much of the current work on social indicators, along with a description of what would be necessary for a useful inventory of population conditions.

REFERENCES

CAMPBELL, D. T. (1973) "The social scientist as a methodological servant of the experimenting society." Policy Studies Journal (Autumn).

——— and D. W. FISKE (1959) "Convergent and discriminant validation by the multitrait-multimethod matrix." Psychological Bulletin (March).

COOK, T. J. and F. P. SCIOLI, Jr. (1972) "Policy analysis in political science: trends and issues in empirical research." Policy Studies Journal (Autumn).

DAVIS, O. A., M.A.H. DEMPSTER, and A. WILDAVSKY (1966) "A theory of the budgetary process." American Political Science Review (September).

DAWSON, R. E. and J. A. ROBINSON (1963) "Interparty competition, economic variables and welfare policies in the American states." Journal of Politics (May).

DYE, T. R. (1972) Understanding Public Policy. Englewood Cliffs, N.J.: Prentice-Hall.

——— (1966) Politics, Economics, and the Public Interest. Chicago: Rand McNally.

FAIRWEATHER, G. W. (1967) Methods for Experimental Social Innovation. New York: John Wiley.

GIST, J. (1974) "The effect of budget controllability on the theory of incrementalism." Presented at the annual meeting of the Midwest Political Science Association (April 26).

GRAY, V. and J. WANAT (1974) "Public policies in the American states: new formulations of old problems." Presented at the annual meeting of the Midwest Political Science Association (April 26).

HOFFERBERT, R. (1968) "Socio-economic dimensions of the American states, 1890-1960." Midwest Journal of Politics (August).

JONES, C. O. (1970) An Introduction to the Study of Public Policy. Boston: Duxbury.

MEEHAN, E. J. (1974) "Social indicators, policies and inventories." Prepared for the annual meeting of the Public Choice Society (March), New Haven, Conn.

——— (1973) "Science, values, and policies." American Behavioral Scientist (September/ October).

——— (1971) The Foundations of Political Analysis: Empirical and Normative. Homewood, Ill.: Dorsey.

RAKOFF, S. H. and G. F. SCHAEFER (1970) "Politics, policy, and political science: theoretical alternatives." Politics and Society (November).

SHARKANSKY, I. (1970) Policy Analysis in Political Science. Chicago: Markham.

VICKERS, G. (1965) The Art of Judgment: A Study of Policy Making. New York: Basic Books.

WADE, L. L. (1972) The Elements of Public Policy. Columbus: Merrill.

——— and R. L. CURRY, Jr. (1970) A Logic of Public Policy: Aspects of Political Economy. Belmont, Calif.: Wadsworth.

WILDAVSKY, A. (1964) Politics of the Budgetary Process. Boston: Little, Brown.

WOLL, P. (1974) Public Policy. Cambridge, Mass.: Winthrop.

PART II

IMPLEMENTATION

4

IMPACT ANALYSIS IN
PUBLIC POLICY RESEARCH

THOMAS J. COOK
FRANK P. SCIOLI, Jr.

University of Illinois,
Chicago Circle

Public policy analysis has long been a province of inquiry for political scientists. Since the early 1960s numerous political scientists have applied multivariate research methodologies to questions focusing on factors affecting policy formulation by state and local governmental jurisdictions.[1] The expression "policy output analysis" has generally been employed to characterize this area of research. Briefly stated, a central concern of scholars working in this area has been a determination of the relative explanatory power of selected variables (for example, governmental structure versus socio-economic characteristics) in accounting for differences in policy outputs (for example, dollar expenditures).

Policy impact analysis entails an extension of this research area while, at the same time, shifting attention toward the measurement of the consequences of public policy (see Cook and Scioli, 1972). In other words, as opposed to the study of *what causes policy,* impact analysis centers on the question of *what policy causes.* For example, what is the impact of revenue sharing? What will be the consequences of passing the Equal Rights Amendment to the United States Constitution? How effective is the Head Start program in achieving its stated objectives? These are all examples of the type of questions addressed in a policy impact study. Although the substantive areas may differ, the research question is basically the same: assessing those consequences which may reasonably be attributed to a given policy action.

While the necessity for scholarly debate on the desirability of governmental objectives, or goals, that may underlie governmental action is readily acknowledged, this debate is most often cast within a philosophical mode of discourse (Cook and Scioli, 1974). Policy impact analysis, on the other hand, is directed at questions having empirical content. Once the policy objectives, however controversial, have been established and action to achieve the objectives has been initiated, the researchers' task entails determination of the form and strength of the empirical relationship between policy action and policy consequences.

In this paper we will discuss two distinct research approaches toward analyzing policy impacts—experimental and quasi-experimental design—and the methodological linkage between them. These approaches are discussed in terms of their general utility for policy impact analysis conducted within diverse research settings and across varying substantive policy areas. As will be pointed out, the choice between the alternative approaches is contingent upon the unique contextual features of each particular research situation.

A POLICY IMPACT MODEL

The main reference point for the discussion to follow is contained in the "Policy Impact Model" displayed in Figure 1. In Figure 1, $P_1 \ldots P_n$ refers to any set of specific programs which have been established in order to carry out a given public policy decision. The model analyzes a specific public policy in terms of its implementation through a variety of social programs.

An example is the Economic Opportunity Act of 1964 (Kershaw, 1970). The Act, at least in principle, was heralded as the cornerstone of the Johnson Administration policy to wage an all-out "war on poverty." In its implementation, the policy was an umbrella for a heterogeneous mix of social programs: community action programs, youth programs, anti-poverty programs for rural areas, work experience programs, small business loan programs, and so on. Each of these programs may be further broken down in more specific terms. For example, the Community Action Program (CAP) was implemented through various "special emphasis" programs such as the Head Start program, the Legal Services program, and the Family Planning program. As the model of Figure 1 emphasizes, the overall success of a given social policy is a function of the success of its component programs. Thus, the *program* is the basic unit of analysis for assessing policy impacts.

The model serves to explicate a given program in terms of three main components: program objectives, program activities, and program effectiveness criteria. Program objectives may be distinguished in terms of *procedural* and *outcome* objectives. In the case of procedural objectives, the emphasis is upon the performance of the administrative functions by the agency personnel responsible for implementing the overall program. Questions of cost-efficiency and administrative performance are relevant here. Thus, for example, a procedural objective of a police response-time program may be to reduce the response time between the receipt of a call for assistance and the arrival of a patrol car to the complaint site. Similarly, a Volunteers In Probation program may have a procedural objective to recruit more male volunteers to serve as one-to-one counselors in a juvenile court. Essentially, then, procedural objectives refer to objectives relevant to the *internal* administration of the program (that is, program implementation and service delivery). Outcome objectives, on the other hand, set targets *external* to the program operation whereby program performance/effectiveness may be evaluated. To take the response-time example, the question here concerns the effectiveness of reducing response time relative to increasing the probability of apprehending a criminal offender, where "offender apprehension" represents an important overall outcome

[98]

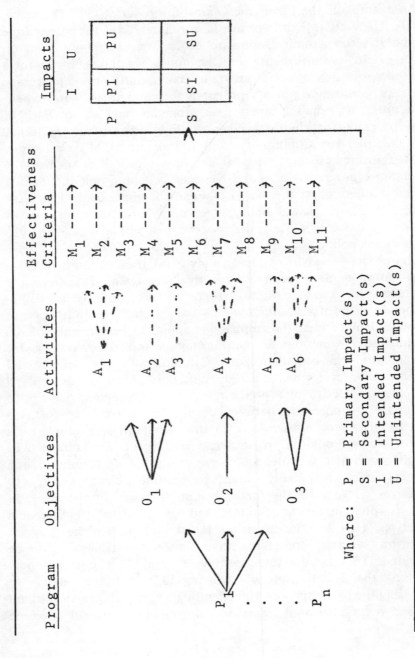

Figure 1: POLICY IMPACT MODEL

objective. In the case of a Head Start program, the outcome objective would refer to the expected gains in pre-school cognitive abilities (however measured) as a function of participation in the program. In both examples, the research focus centers upon the impact of the program on a specific socio-physical target within the environment of the program; thus, the shift from what causes policy (for example, Head Start program activities) to what policy causes (for example, changes in preschool cognitive abilities).

In a sense, the central question of a policy impact analysis may be restated as follows: is the attainment of procedural objectives (i.e., cost-efficient program implementation) a necessary and sufficient condition for the attainment of the outcome goals or objectives?

In line with the above, program activities refers to the specific *content* of program implementation. Terms such as "workload measures" and "task performance" are relevant to the activity component of the model. It is important that the specific procedures, or operations, associated with each activity be carefully detailed so it can be determined "what it is" in the program implementation that is, or is not, successful in achieving outcome objectives. A careful specification of the program activity would entail a consideration of several factors, such as the source of the program activity, the characteristics of the implementing personnel, location characteristics of the program implementation, and the administrative/organizational characteristics of the program delivery system. Also, the temporal aspects of program implementation, such as the timing and duration of service delivery, should be delineated. In a human service program (e.g., health care program), for example, the timing, frequency, and duration of treatment exposure would be important factors to consider in estimating program effectiveness.

An important related point concerns the assumption of "program continuity" which posits a constancy of program operation over the time period covered in the evaluation of program impact. This assumption becomes especially important when a time-series or trend analysis-type design is used. Several events could, for example, occur during the life of the program and might serve to vitiate the program continuity assumption, such as changes in the operating characteristics of the program and changes in composition (that is, characteristics) of the administrative and operational personnel responsible for implementing the program. Also, the goals or objectives of the program may have been modified following the initial implementation period. Thus, the researcher should seek direct evidence for the equivalence of program operation across the time periods covered in the assessment of program impact.

The argument for careful specification of program activity is justified not only in terms of evaluating a program in a particular location, but also in order to assess the potential utility of the program vis-à-vis implementation at some other location or point in time (i.e., the generality of program impact). Without "operationally" defining the set of program activities in terms of the factors discussed above, we could not be confident that a program implemented at Site A was similar to the program implemented at Site B. The importance of this point is underscored in the controversy over evaluations of the Head Start program. A recent study by Richard Light and Paul Smith (1970), for example, questions the overall evaluation conclusions stated in the Westinghouse report. Light and Smith, in a secondary analysis of the Head Start data, found that the impact of Head Start participation was not constant across all program sites. Factors such as the characteristics of the administrative personnel of the various centers and characteristics of the children in the centers were found to be related to the performance of the children on the impact criteria. The authors concluded that the failure to control for these factors masked a significant amount of variation in several important aspects of the program's operation.

Program effectiveness criteria refer to the specific performance measures associated with each outcome objective. Several measurement criteria are associated with the selection of effectiveness criteria: in particular, the extent to which the effectiveness measures are standardized, objective, reliable, and valid.

Standardization refers to the extent to which the measurement procedure provides safeguards against interpretive errors. In other words, do the effectiveness criteria provide a clear-cut set of norms against which changes in the value of the criteria may be evaluated? Without some type of comparative baseline, changes in criteria measure values are generally uninterpretable. The requirement of objectivity serves to minimize the possibility that the personal bias of the investigator(s) enters into the measurement procedure. The key point is that the results obtained from the measurement procedure should be independent of the particular individual performing the measurement operation. The third criteria, reliability, refers to the amount of random error present in the measurement procedure. It is evidenced by the degree of inconsistency of results obtained from repeated applications of a measuring instrument to similar phenomena at different points in time. The greater the inconsistency, the lower the reliability of the measurement, and, therefore, the greater the amount of measurement error present. Closely related to reliability (in a statistical sense) is the question of measurement validity.[2] Whereas the above criteria are important to a full assessment of a given measurement procedure, the concept of validity is what might be called the "acid test" for any measurement operation. A measurement procedure may entail standardized norms for comparison, be fully objective in providing guidelines for reproduction of the measures, highly consistent in repeated application (i.e., reliable); but if the resultant measures are not validated indicators of the decision-relevant concepts contained in the study, they are suspect—suspect in the sense that they may be irrelevant to the analytical question(s) posed in the study. The attitudes of prison inmates toward different brands of cigarettes may be of interest to a tobacco industry official but on "face validity" alone seem to be of dubious value as a predictor of post-release job stability. Furthermore, the measurement procedure should be particularly sensitive to the various procedural safeguards against the various "threats to validity" of measurement as discussed in social science literature (see Webb, 1966)—in particular, threats resulting from the person performing the measurement, the reactivity of the phenomena being measured, and the measurement context.

The effectiveness criteria in the model refer to the specific impact indicators selected (for example, decrease in the absolute probability of recidivism, increase in job attainment, and work stability) as measures of program impact. The difference between *primary* and *secondary* impacts refers to the immediate changes resulting from program activity as opposed to the long-term consequences of program action. These two contingencies require that the analyst specify both the immediate and secondary consequences of program action. The dichotomization of *intended* versus *unintended* consequences recognizes the necessity of estimating both the main as well as the external, or spill-over, effects of the program. The unintended consequences, of course, may be either positive or negative. Thus, a program to retrain prison inmates for a particular occupation (intended impact) may result in the exertion of downward pressure on the wages of existing employees in the occupation category (unintended impact). Likewise, a 55-mile-per-hour highway speed limit may reduce the number of highway traffic fatalities (unintended effect) as well as serve to reduce the consumption of gasoline (intended effect).

DESIGN CONSIDERATIONS

In general terms, the design of a research project serves as a "blueprint" for the overall research effort. As such, it spells out how the researcher organized the various aspects of the research problem for purposes of data collection and analysis. Relative to impact analysis, the design delineates the organization of objectives, program activities, and effectiveness criteria. In addition, it provides a means of integrating relevant contextual variables into the analysis for purposes of evaluating both the main and the interactive components of the overall program impact. If, for example, the researcher is attempting to measure the effect of Program X upon effectiveness criteria M_1, M_2 under conditions C_1, C_2, C_3, his design would consist of the set of rules governing the way the X, M, and C are combined for analysis. The design, in other words, would specify the exact nature of the analysis which underlies the claim that Program X did (or did not) have an impact and under what conditions (C_1, C_2, C_3) the impact was the greatest.

The major consideration in developing a research design for an impact study is the extent to which the design of the study overcomes what Donald Campbell (1969) calls "threats to validity."

These various threats are of two kinds—internal and external. Internal threats constitute "plausible rival explanations" for the effects observed and serve to cast doubt on the argument that a specific program action produced the specified changes in the effectiveness criteria. They are labeled "internal" because they raise questions about whether or not a "true" impact was observed and the extent to which this impact can reasonably be attributed to a given program action. "External validity" refers to the generalizability of the research findings from a particular study to other locations, time periods, program variations, or effectiveness criteria. Thus, external validity is most important in terms of policy utility. A primary concern of public policy analysis is the development of general-purpose solutions to social problems. While the effectiveness of a program action in a specific location is an important concern, the realities of public decision-making under the ever-present budgetary constraints necessitates the search for problem solutions (i.e., social programs) whose utility is not limited to a particular point in time or space: thus, the importance of external validity (i.e., the general utility of research findings for decision-making in other settings).

Because of their importance to a discussion of research design, we are including the various threats to validity below, with a brief explanation of each one. As Campbell has pointed out, these threats apply equally to true experimental and quasi-experimental designs. They are particularly relevant in the area of applied experimentation.

INTERNAL VALIDITY THREATS

(1) *History:* events other than the experimental treatment,[3] occurring between pre-test and post-test and thus providing alternate explanations of effects (for example, changes in the actual administration of the program).

(2) *Maturation:* process within the respondents or observed social units producing changes as a function of the passage of time and not from the particular experimental treatment.

(3) *Instability:* unreliability of measures, fluctuations in sampling persons or components, autonomous instability of repeated or "equivalent" meas-

ures in the presence of these kinds of problems; can be detected with statistical tests of significance.

(4) *Testing:* the impact that taking a test has on repeated testing (that is, test sensitivity or greater experience with testing may cause differences in scores).

(5) *Instrumentation:* changes in the calibration of a measuring instrument, changes in the observers, or scores used may produce changes in the obtained measurements.

(6) *Regression artifacts:* pseudo-shifts occurring when subjects or treatment units have been selected because of their extreme scores. A "gain" in the performance of the experimental group (originally lower on the particular measure) versus the control group may be due to natural tendency of movement toward the mean.

(7) *Selection:* biases resulting from differential recruitment of comparison groups, producing different mean levels on the effectiveness criteria prior to treatment.

(8) *Experimental mortality:* the differential loss of respondents from comparison groups (that is, due to mobility, dropping out of project, and the like).

(9) *Selection-maturation interaction:* selection biases resulting in differential rates of "maturation" or autonomous change within comparison groups.

EXTERNAL VALIDITY THREATS

(1) *Interaction effects of testing:* the effect of a pre-test in increasing or decreasing the respondent's sensitivity or responsiveness to the experimental variable, thus making the results obtained for a pre-tested population unrepresentative of the effects of the experimental variable for the unpre-tested universe from which the experimental respondents were selected.

(2) *Interaction of selection and experimental treatment:* unrepresentative responsiveness of the treated population.

(3) *Reactive effects of experimental arrangements:* "artificiality" of conditions making the experimental setting atypical of conditions of regular application of the treatment (for example, "Hawthorne effects").

(4) *Multiple-treatment interference:* where multiple treatments are jointly applied, effects atypical of the separate application of the treatments may result.

(5) *Irrelevant responsiveness of measures:* all measures are complex and all include irrelevant components that may produce pseudo-effects.

(6) *Irrelevant replicability of treatments:* treatments are complex, and replications of them may fail to include those components actually responsible for the effects.

In terms of the relative importance of the two categories of validity threats, internal validity stands as the most important concern for the policy analyst. Without internal validity, the question of external validity is a moot point. The analyst must have confidence that his research design has produced valid evidence of a cause-and-effect relationship between a policy action and changes in the behavior of his/her effectiveness criteria before there is a concern for the generality of the results to other settings. Given the limited space of this paper, we will concentrate on the question of internal validity and refer the reader to discussions elsewhere of the external validity issue (Bracht and Glass, 1968).

OVERCOMING THREATS TO INTERNAL VALIDITY

Threats to internal validity may be handled within two distinct design frameworks. The first approach is discussed under the heading of true experimental design. The sine qua non of true experimental design is found in the principle of randomization—in particular, the random assignment of experimental units (that is, individuals, groups, research sites, and so on) to treatment conditions.

Based on a sophisticated mathematical rationale, random assignment serves to eliminate most threats to internal validity by a nonsystematic (i.e., random) distribution of subject or group bias across all treatment conditions. Random assignment thus assures that the given characteristics of either the individual or the group will not be systematically associated with the presence or absence of the treatment condition.

This latter point introduces a second feature of the experimental procedure: control groups. Control groups provide a baseline from which to measure the effect of the treatment upon the criterion measures. Control groups are equated with the experimental units through random assignment and yet do not receive the experimental treatment. This point is displayed in Figure 2.

In Figure 2, the O refers to the observation of effectiveness criteria. The X refers to the exposure of a group to an experimental variable or event the effects of which are to be measured. R indicates random assignment to separate treatment and control groups. Random assignment, in effect, provides the basis for measuring the effects of the treatment variable. If random assignment does in fact equate the two groups, then the only systematic difference lies in the exposure of one of the groups to the experimental treatment. The difference between the O_2 and O_4 measurements indicates the effect of the experimental treatment. This follows from the fact that, given the randomization argument, the two groups differ primarily with respect to the presence (or absence) of the experimental treatment, and any O_2-O_4 difference should be attributable to treatment effect.

In like fashion, an expanded treatment control group design may include several alternative approaches toward attaining an outcome objective. In addition to the nontreatment group, the design may include several other groups which receive variations of the program activity service/treatment. Again, the comparison is initially between the nontreatment control groups and the alternative treatment groups. In addition, the design allows a comparison between the various treatment groups to determine which type of program activity achieves the best results within the given cost-utility parameters of the particular program(s). The underlying justification for the expanded comparison lies, as in the single treatment-control group case, in the random assignment procedure. An example of an expanded control group design is displayed in Figure 3.

The reader may recognize the design in Figure 3 as a variant of the "randomized block design" common to research in experimental psychology (Kirk, 1968). The blocks represent sets of experimental

$$R \quad O_1 \quad X \quad O_2$$
$$R \quad O_3 \qquad O_4$$

Figure 2: PRE-TEST/POST-TEST CONTROL GROUP DESIGN

Blocks	A_1	A_2	A_3	A_4	C_1	C_2
B_1	B_1A_1				B_1C_1	
B_2		B_2A_2				
B_3						
B_4						

Program Activity

Figure 3.

units (people, locations, and the like) that are grouped on the basis of hypothesized important variables (sex, age, SES, geography, and so on) so as to maximize the within-group homogeneity of each block relative to the overall variability of the total study population. This type of design is especially recommended when it is suspected that there may be wide differences in the measured responses on the dependent variables (i.e., effectiveness criteria), and the treatment effects observed may not be especially pronounced (as in the case in most human service programs). Thus, the purpose of the design is to remove these initial differences (that is, pre-program participation differences) on the dependent variable and hence increase the possibility of detecting significant treatment effects, relative to the randomized groups design displayed in Figure 2. In analysis of variance terms, the attempt is to decrease the error mean square concomitant with an increase in the treatment mean square.

The procedure for allocating experimental units to treatment and control conditions is straightforward: once the units are grouped into blocks of similar units ($B_1 \ldots B_N$) the units within each block are randomly assigned to a treatment ($A_1 \ldots A_N$) or a control ($C_1 \ldots C_2$) conditions. The random assignment assures that each unit within each block has an equal chance of being assigned to one of the treatment or control conditions, thus removing the selection threat.

An illustration of this design approach can be found in the series of income-maintenance experiments being conducted throughout the United States (see Kelly, 1968). Each of the four experiments employed a variant of the randomized block design. In the

Seattle-Denver experiment, for example, the study sample was
blocked on the sex of the head of the household (male, female) and
ethnicity of household (Black, White, Mexican-American). Thus,
given the number of sub-groups within each blocking category, six
blocks can be formed (2 for sex X 3 for ethnicity = 6 blocks), and
units within each block are randomly assigned a treatment or control
condition. The treatments in this experiment refer to four variants of
an offset tax rate coupled with the provision of manpower training
services. Thus, there is a mixture of treatment conditions (that is,
offset tax rate, manpower training services, combinations of tax rates
and training services) permitting the testing of a number of
hypotheses regarding program impacts. The power in the design lies
in the randomization procedure—that is, the random assignment of
treatments to the different blocks. This procedure serves to control
for virtually all threats to internal validity.

Despite the inherent advantages of the true experiment as a means
of assessing policy impacts, there is some disagreement among policy
analysts as to the general utility of the experimental approach,
disagreement ranging from ethical concerns to methodological
considerations (see Scioli and Cook, 1973). While the ethical
reservations may escape a final resolution, the methodological
disagreements await the further application of the experimental
approach coupled with an assessment of its strengths and limitations
for policy impact analysis.[4]

QUASI-EXPERIMENTAL DESIGN

The second major approach to the problem of internal validity is
subsumed under the general rubric of "quasi-experimental design."
The essential difference between the "true" and the "quasi-experimental" design, relative to the internal validity question, centers on
the randomization principle. In the quasi-experimental design the
researcher does *not* have control over the assignment of experimental
units to the various treatment and control groups. As Campbell and
Stanley (1963: 34) state it:

There are many natural social settings in which the research person can introduce something like experimental design into this scheduling of data collection procedures (e.g., the when and to whom of measurement) even though he lacks the full control over the scheduling of the experimental stimuli (the when and to whom of exposure and the ability to randomize exposures) which makes a true experiment possible. Collectively, such situations may be regarded as quasi-experimental designs.

The methodological linkage between the true and the quasi-experimental design is found in the initial discussion of "plausible rival hypothesis." The quasi-experimental approach rejects the notion that the lack of randomization ipso facto precludes inferences concerning treatment effects (that is, policy impacts). Conversely, the argument is that any experiment is valid until proven invalid through the verification of rival hypotheses. An example of this may be found in terms of the "closure" principle discussed by Hubert Blalock (1967).

Closure refers to the assumption that all *relevant* variables have been included in an analysis. The key word here is "relevant." By this we mean all variables which may affect the main hypothesis (that is, policy activity→policy impact). As Blalock points out, social science research is faced with the problem, at present, of treating the closure problem in an assumptive fashion. The methodology provides no clear-cut means of determining whether all the relevant variables have been included in the research design. He states accordingly:

> Since it will always be possible that some unknown forces may be operating to disturb or to lead us to believe a causal relationship exists when in fact it does not, the only way we can make causal inferences at all is to make simplifying assumptions about such disturbing influences. . . . The basic difficulty is a fundamental one: there seems to be no systematic way of knowing for sure whether or not one has located all of the relevant variables [Blalock, 1961: 13-14].

While true experimental design relies primarily upon randomization and experimental controls to alleviate this problem, the quasi-experimental approach must utilize a different strategy. The basic strategy is that of *specifying* the variables that the quasi-experimental design fails to control and then discounting these potential influences through careful analysis of supplementary data. In effect, the researcher checks off the threats to internal validity in evaluating the validity of his own design. The point to note is that Blalock's argument is a warning to the researcher that excluded variables may affect his results. Similarly, Campbell's threats to internal validity are cautionary signals. Both arguments, while they may serve as sources of rival hypotheses, require empirical confirmation for their acceptance. Invalidation is based on demonstrated effect rather than mere conjecture.

AN EXAMPLE OF A QUASI-EXPERIMENTAL DESIGN

An example which adequately demonstrates the quasi-experimental approach is the multiple interrupted time-series design. This design allows measurement of the impact of a program both in isolation and in comparison with other similar units of analysis.

The basic building block of this design is the interrupted time series. Figures 4A and 4B illustrate the general form of this design. In Figure 4A we see a series of observations on the criterion measure $(O_1 - O_8)$ interrupted by the intervention of the treatment condition (X). The design is most appropriate where the intervention is abrupt; that is, where there is a specifiable point in the $O_1 - O_8$ observation period where the treatment conditions are activated.[5] Figure 4B illustrates that the point of comparison is upon the interruption in the trend of criterion measures occurring at the $O_4 - O_5$ interval. The

---

$$T_{-4} \quad T_{-3} \quad T_{-2} \quad T_{-1} \qquad T_1 \quad T_2 \quad T_3 \quad T_4$$
$$X$$
$$O_1 \quad O_2 \quad O_3 \quad O_4 \qquad O_5 \quad O_6 \quad O_7 \quad O_8$$

```
T_  = Observations Prior To Treatment Inter-
      vention.

T   = Observations Post-Treatment Interven-
      tion.
```

Figure 4A: INTERRUPTED TIME-SERIES DESIGN

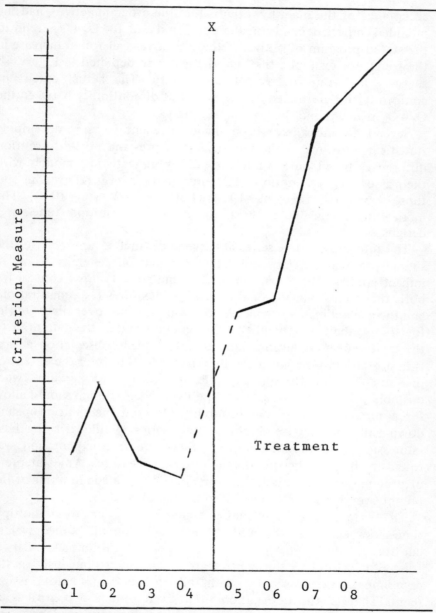

Figure 4B: INTERRUPTED TIME-SERIES DESIGN

acceptance of the main hypothesis that the program activity had the intended impact depends on the conformity of the $O_5 - O_8$ trend to the stated program objective. If the objectives call for an increase in the trend, for example, the hypothetical case depicted in Figure 4B suggests a certain degree of conformity. The actual extent of conformity is determined by the extent of discontinuity between the $O_1 - O_4$ segment and the $O_5 - O_8$ segment.

Several advances have been made in recent years in developing statistical measures of the significance of pre- and post-intervention differences based on a number of different statistical models with their associated assumptions. The interested reader is referred here to those sources (Glass et al., 1972; Gray, 1973; Wilson, 1973). The models are applicable to both the single and multiple time-series designs.

The interrupted time-series has several distinct advantages over the simple pre-treatment/post-treatment comparison generally found in impact studies. The extension of the time period allows control for both the prior behavior of the criterion measures (i.e., maturation) and the general instability in the criterion measures over time. On the first point, the design highlights the general trend of the data prior to the treatment intervention. This pre-intervention observation period is important in providing a baseline from which to infer the extent of program impact. If, for example, the criterion measures were unstable prior to the treatment, the researcher's design should allow for a measurement of the instability. Marked instability (up and down shifts in the trend of the time series) would give the false impression of a program impact where the true explanation was found in the periodic shift in the criterion measures. Any statement of program impact would, therefore, have to be made in terms of the pre-intervention trend in the criterion measures.

The extension of the simple time-series design to a multiple time-series design is achieved through inclusion of "nonequivalent control groups." The nonequivalent control group is similar in conceptualization to the control group discussed previously in the experimental design section, with the exception of random assignment. That is, the designation of a given unit as a control is an ex-post-facto assignment and is not grounded on the randomization principle. Thus, the assumptions based on randomization are excluded from this design. This limitation does not, however, preclude utilization of the design in certain nonexperimental settings.

Figures 5A and 5B depict the design in graphic form. The main utility of the design is similar to that of the random control group design: the provision of a comparison baseline. The previous point on rival hypotheses is relevant here. Admittedly, there are many possible differences between units, nonrandomly assigned to treatment and control conditions, which may affect the policy outcome-impact relationship. If the units in Figure 5 were states, for example, the researcher would have to exercise extreme caution in equating Pennsylvania and Alabama for comparison purposes. The point is, though, that this type of comparison is not *logically* precluded. The acceptance (or rejection) of the comparison is an empirical question best addressed through the framework of Campbell's "threats to internal validity." The work by Campbell and others on the Connecticut Crackdown and the British Breathalizer Test are particularly instructive on this point.[6]

In lieu of established threats to validity, the multiple time-series design shares the advantages of the randomized control group design. It provides a baseline from which we might infer what would occur (relative to the criterion measures—objectives) in the absence of the specific program activity (that is, intervention). The main hypothesis of program impact suggests a significant difference between the time series of the treatment and control units. For example, a significant

	T_{-4}	T_{-3}	T_{-2}	T_{-1}	X	T_1	T_2	T_3	T_4
E	O_1	O_2	O_3	O_4		O_5	O_6	O_7	O_8
C^1	O_1^1	O_2^1	O_3^1	O_4^1		O_5^1	O_6^1	O_7^1	O_8^1
C^{11}	O_1''	O_2''	O_3''	O_4''		O_5''	O_6''	O_7''	O_8''

Figure 5A: MULTIPLE INTERRUPTED TIME-SERIES DESIGN

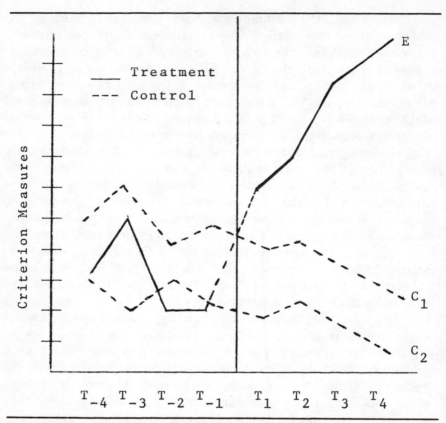

Figure 5B: MULTIPLE INTERRUPTED TIME-SERIES DESIGN

impact might be revealed in a marked difference in the slope of the time-series lines between the treatment and control units.

A cautionary note should be entered here with regard to the selection of control units for comparison with the treatment group. Every effort should be made to obtain groups which are as similar as possible to the treatment group on *dependent* variables (i.e., the impact criteria). This similarity should be evidenced along several observation points *prior* to the intervention of the program action. This serves to indicate that the groups share a similar pattern of fluctuation prior to the program intervention (that is, are similar in their reliability) and arrived at the point of intervention by a similar route. Otherwise, the regression artifact threat becomes a major concern as the between-group differences observed in the post-intervention comparison may be due to dissimilar patterns of unreliability (i.e., instability) prior to the treatment intervention. Also, the less reliable the measurements of impact, the more likely you are to obtain a false positive impact (or negative) due to the presence of a regression artifact in the data.

A similar point can be made when the groups are "matched" prior to the intervention to attain pre-intervention equivalence on variables other than the effectiveness criteria of interest (e.g., demographic variables). Unless it can be demonstrated that the matching variables correlate highly with the effectiveness criteria and the effectiveness criteria are highly reliable when measured over time, an appreciable amount of "slippage" may occur leading to an "under-adjustment" in the matching process. The lower the correlation between matching variables and effectiveness criteria, and the lower the reliability of the effectiveness criteria, the greater the amount of under-adjustment for pre-intervention differences and hence the more plausible is the regression artifact threat. This becomes most pronounced when, for example, an analysis of covariance model is employed.[7]

The most noticeable advantage of the multiple time-series design is its wide applicability to situations where the true experimental design is either not feasible or precluded for a variety of reasons. In the first instance, the researcher may wish to evaluate a program which is already in operation. Thus, random assignment is not possible. Through the use of supplementary data, and various "non-reactive measures" (Webb et al., 1966), he may still be able to conduct the study within a time-series design. In other situations, the true experimental design approach may be precluded on political grounds. That is, those people responsible for administering the program may balk on the question of random assignment, as needy cases may be excluded from treatment. This requires a "non-re-active" design capable of measuring impacts within systematic frameworks of analysis. The quasi-experimental approach appears to provide a promising alternative for research conducted within these types of constraints.[8]

CONCLUSION

Our intention in this paper has been to present alternative approaches—experimental and quasi-experimental—toward measuring the impact(s) of public policy. The crucial question of internal validity was discussed in relation to the specific designs presented. The importance of systematic impact analysis cannot be overstated. Although the attempt to construct explanatory models of policy outputs is an important area of research in its own right, an exclusive emphasis upon what causes policy leaves unanswered the question relevant to the future well-being of a society: to wit, did the policy action have a significant impact upon the target population consistent with objectives of the policy? Until the linkage between policy outputs and policy impacts is forged through systematic impact analysis, that information most vital to the future well-being of society will be lacking.

NOTES

1. For examples of this type of research, see Dye (1966), Sharkansky (1969), and Hofferbert (1974). For an overview of the general area of public policy analysis within political science, see the Autumn 1972 issue of the *Policy Studies Journal.*
2. Statistically speaking, it can be shown that the maximum possible validity of a measure is equal to the square root of the reliability.
3. In the discussion of the threats to validity, and in later discussion, the term "treatment" is to be interpreted as equivalent to "program activity."
4. A forthcoming appraisal may be found in Riecken (1974).
5. As Campbell (1969: 416) points out: "A gradually introduced reform will be indistinguishable from the background of secular change, from the net effect of the innumerable change agents continually impinging."
6. For examples of application of this design, see Campbell and Rose (1968), Glass (1970), and Fisk (1970).
7. For discussion of this, see Lord (1970) and Campbell and Erlebacher (1970).
8. For political science applications of the quasi-experimental approach, see Caporaso and Roos (1973) and Cook (1974).

REFERENCES

BLALOCK, H. M., Jr. (1967) "Causal inferences, closed populations, and measures of association." American Political Science Review 61: 130-136.

――― (1961) Causal Inference in Non-Experimental Research. Chapel Hill: University of North Carolina Press.

BRACHT, G. H. and G. V. GLASS (1968) "The external validity of experiments." American Educational Research Journal 5 (November): 437-474.

CAMPBELL, D. T. (1969) "Reforms as experiments." American Psychologist (April): 409-429.

――― and A. ERLEBACHER (1970) "How regression artifacts in quasi-experimental evaluations can mistakenly make compensatory education look harmful," in J. Hellmuth (ed.) Compensatory Education: A National Debate, vol. 3 of The Disadvantaged Child. New York: Brunner/Mazel.

CAMPBELL, D. T. and H. L. ROSS (1968) "The Connecticut crackdown on speeding." Law and Society Review (August): 33-53.

CAMPBELL, D. T. and J. STANLEY (1963) Experimental and Quasi-Experimental Designs in Research. Chicago: Rand McNally.

CAPORASO, J. A. and L. L. ROOS, Jr. (1973) Quasi-Experimental Approaches. Evanston: Northwestern University Press.

COOK, T. J. (1974) "Review" of J. A. Caporaso and L. L. Roos, Jr., Quasi-Experimental Approaches. Administrative Science Quarterly (June): 278-281.

――― F. P. SCIOLI, Jr. (1974) "Value assumptions underlying evaluation research." Presented at annual meeting of Public Choice Society, March 21-23, New Haven, Conn.

――― (1972) "A research strategy for analyzing the impact of public policy." Administrative Science Quarterly 17 (September): 328-339.

DYE, T. R. (1966) Politics, Economics and the Public. Chicago: Rand McNally.

FISK, D. M. (1970) The Indianapolis Police Fleet Plan: An Example of Program Evaluation for Local Government. Washington, D.C.: Urban Institute.

GLASS, G. V. et al. (1972) The Design and Analysis of Time-Series Experiments. Boulder, Colo.: Laboratory of Educational Research.

GRAY, V. (1973) "The use of time-series analysis in the study of public policy." Policy Studies Journal 2 (Winter).

HOFFERBERT, R. I. (1974) The Study of Public Policy. New York: Bobbs-Merrill.

KELLY, T. F. (1971) "Income maintenance experimentation: a new policy tool." Working Paper 955-2 (April 9). Washington, D.C.: Urban Institute.

KERSHAW, J. A. (1970) Government Against Poverty. Chicago: Markham.

KIRK, R. E. (1968) Experimental Design: Procedures for the Behavioral Sciences. Belmont, Calif.: Brooks-Cole.

LIGHT, R. J. and P. V. SMITH (1970) "Choosing a future: strategies for designing and evaluating new programs." Harvard Educational Review 40 (Winter): 1-28.

LORD, F. N. (1970) "Large-scale co-variance analysis when the control variable is fallible." Journal of the American Statistical Association 55: 307-321.

RIECKEN, H. W. [ed.] (1974) Experimentation as a Method for Planning and Evaluating Society's Programs. New York: Academic Press.

ROSS, H. L., D. T. CAMPBELL, and G. V. GLASS (1970) "Determining the social effects of a legal reform." American Behavioral Scientist (March/April): 493-509.

SCIOLI, F. P., Jr. and T. J. COOK (1973) "Experimental design in policy impact analysis." Social Science Quarterly (September): 271-280.

SHARKANSKY, I. (1969) The Politics of Taxing and Spending. New York: Bobbs-Merrill.

WEBB, E. J. et al. (1966) Unobtrusive Measures. Chicago: Rand McNally.

WILSON, L. A., II (1973) "A review of statistical techniques appropriate for the analysis of time-series quasi-experiments." Policy Studies Journal 2 (Winter).

THE INITIAL IMPACT OF REVENUE SHARING ON THE SPENDING PATTERNS OF AMERICAN CITIES

DAVID A. CAPUTO
Purdue University

RICHARD L. COLE
George Washington University

This paper describes general revenue sharing and its contribution to governmental finances in the United States, describes the results of the study to investigate initial spending patterns, and evaluates this type of policy research.

For the past forty years, federal-state-local relations in the United States have been described in terms of "shared functions"—a term which implies that programs which are financed largely by the national government are implemented and administered by the local governments. The primary vehicle by which this pattern of shared power and responsibility has been fostered and maintained is the system of grants-in-aid. Grants-in-aid, as Michael Reagan (1972: 55)

AUTHORS' NOTE: *This is a revision of a paper prepared for presentation at the 1973 meeting of the Southern Political Science Association. The authors request that any reproduction, duplication, or use of the data and information contained herein be prohibited without their permission.*

defines the concept, provide "money payments furnished by a higher to a lower level of government to be used for specific purposes and subject to conditions spelled out in law or administrative regulations." It is clear that grants-in-aid have had a tremendous impact on federal relationships in the United States and, in the well-known analogy of Morton Grodzins (Grodzins and Elazar, 1966: 7-14), have been the principal device whereby federalism was transformed from a system which may once have been conceived of as a "layer cake" to one which by the mid-1960s could more aptly be described as a "marble cake."

During the 1960s, according to James Sundquist and David Davis (1969: 1), this pattern of intergovernmental relations "entered a new phase." This transformation is described by Sundquist and Davis as involving both quantitative and qualitative aspects. Quantitatively, the rapid increase in both the absolute number of grant-in-aid programs and in the dollar amount of federal funds allocated to such programs during the 1960s is astonishing. In 1960 there were just over 100 federally sponsored grant-in-aid programs; by 1970 there were about 530. In the 1960s the amount of funds transferred through these programs totalled approximately $7 billion; by 1971 the figure was over $30 billion (Reagan, 1972: 4-5; Sundquist and Davis, 1969: 1-2).

Even more important was the qualitative alterations in federal relations occurring in the 1960s. Before 1960, as Sundquist and Davis point out, "the typical federal assistance program did not involve an expressly stated national purpose. It was instituted, rather, as a means of helping state or local governments accomplish *their* objectives." However, grants-in-aid were often used in the 1960s by "the federal government to achieve *its* objectives—national policies defined, although often in very general terms, by the Congress" (Sundquist and Davis, 1969: 3). Clearly, the system of grants-in-aid which has evolved over the past several decades has had a major impact on American federalism and on urban politics. So important has been this impact that Michael Reagan (1972: 57) concludes that grants-in-aid "constitute a major social innovation of our time."

As dramatic as these changes in intergovernmental relationships were in the 1960s, President Nixon's domestic proposals represent potentially an even more significant change in intergovernmental relationships. In outlining his proposal of revenue sharing, a major element in his program of "New Federalism," the President declared in his 1972 State of the Union Address that "Revenue Sharing . . . can help reverse what has been the flow of power and resources toward Washington by sending power and resources back to the States, to the communities, and to the people. Revenue sharing can bring a new sense of accountability, a new burst of energy and a new spirit of creativity to our federal system" (Congressional Quarterly Almanac, 1972: 5-A).

On October 12, 1972, a version of President Nixon's general revenue sharing program was approved by the Congress. In signing the legislation on October 20, the President stated that "The New American Revolution is truly under way . . . what America wants today at the State and local level, at the city level and at the county level, and, I believe, at the federal level is not bigger government but better government, and that is what this is all about" (Washington Post, June 18, 1973). In December 1972, the first checks—totaling $5.7 billion were mailed to the more than 38,000 general-purpose governmental units in the United States.

As passed by the Congress, general revenue sharing is designed to return over $30 billion over a five-year period to the country's general-purpose governmental units. The measure departs significantly from previous grant-in-aid programs in that, except for relatively minor restrictions (revenue sharing funds may not be used as matching funds for federal grant-in-aid programs, for most educational needs, or for projects discriminating on the basis of race, color, or national origin; in addition, federal wage regulations must also be met), the recipient governments are free to spend their revenue sharing money according to their wishes and needs. Most importantly, these needs are to be determined by the local communities themselves, not by Washington administrators.

Although President Nixon (Congressional Quarterly Almanac, 1972: 9-A) stated in early 1972 that his program of revenue sharing enjoyed "overwhelming public support . . . the endorsement of both major political parties and most of the nation's governors and mayors," it is clear that revenue sharing is not without its critics.

There are those, such as Michael Reagan (1972: 83), who argue that the major advantage of grant-in-aid programs—the technical and administrative skills extended to local governments—is absent from the revenue sharing concept. Others (Cannon and Broder, June 18, 1973) contend that the money will be spent largely on frivolous and unnecessary items, largely ignoring social service and welfare needs. Some fear that cities will be unable to resist public pressures to apply the newly acquired money to reduce or stabilize local tax rates and thus ignore a large number of pressing urban problems. Still others (Congressional Quarterly Weekly Report, March 3, 1973: 431) have suggested that, with the possible demise of poverty and Model Cities programs, revenue sharing will not be used by cities to maintain those on-going community action, socially oriented programs.

Finally, some state and urban administrators are fearful that revenue sharing will actually mean a net loss in the return of federal funds to their areas if other categorical grant programs are eliminated. Testifying before Senator Edmund Muskie's Government Operations Subcommittee on Intergovernmental Relations in February of 1973, Mayor Wes Uhlman (Congressional Quarterly Weekly Report, March 3, 1973: 471) of Seattle stated that "the new federalism (including revenue sharing) has turned out to be a Trojan horse for America's cities, a gift left behind by an administration retreating from its basic responsibilities to its citizens."

This study investigates the initial policy implications of President Nixon's general revenue sharing program for metropolitan America. In a conceptual sense, as indicated above, the impact of revenue sharing is self-evident. The legislation does represent a significant shift in the pattern of intergovernmental relations developed over the past several decades and especially as those relationships progressed in the 1960s. However, our concerns in this paper are more specific and more immediate. As will be documented below, there has occurred a great deal of speculation in the press, among public officials, and among private individuals concerning the impact of revenue sharing upon municipal politics. There are those who believe that revenue sharing has been used mainly for income tax reduction, for exotic and unnecessary "hardware" items, and to increase the salaries of public officials. Other analysts have expressed the hope, at least, that the funds will be used to bolster the cities' capabilities to meet pressing social needs.

In this study we are interested in determining the *actual* impact of revenue sharing on spending patterns of local governments, the influence of social and political environments on these spending decisions, the degree to which citizen input in this process has been encouraged and its effect, the probable implications of revenue sharing for on-going categorical grant programs (specifically those funded by Model Cities and OEO grants), and the overall evaluation of revenue sharing by local officials.

In order to assess these concerns, a questionnaire was mailed to the chief administrative officer of every city over 50,000 in the spring of 1973. Table 1 indicates the return rates and distribution patterns of those returning the questionnaire.

As indicated in Table 1, 51.8% of the respondents completed and returned their questionnaires. This response rate compares quite favorably with other studies of comparable scope, such as Carl Stenberg's (1972) study done for the Advisory Commission on Intergovernmental Relations. Stenberg received a 51% return from a

Table 1. RATE AND DISTRIBUTION OF QUESTIONNAIRE RETURNS

Classification	No. of Cities Surveyed (A)	Cities Reporting No.	% of (A)
Total, all cities	409	212	51.8
Population Group			
Over 500,000	26	13	50.0
250,000-500,000	30	19	63.3
100,000-250,000	98	56	57.1
50,000-100,000	255	124	48.6
Metropolitan Type			
Central city	258	138	53.5
Suburban area	151	74	49.0
Form of Government[a]			
Mayor-council	164	75	45.7
Council-manager	212	125	59.0
Other[b]	31	11	35.5

a. One responding city could not be coded on this variable; this accounts for the classification summing to 211.

b. Includes commission, town meeting, and representative town meeting forms of government.

questionnaire mailed to the chief executive officer of every city over 25,000 in the United States. Furthermore, the returns were fairly evenly distributed among the various demographic and political characteristics of the cities.

IMPACT OF REVENUE SHARING ON
URBAN SPENDING PATTERNS

We are concerned in this section with: (1) how cities have allocated their initial revenue sharing checks; (2) the extent to which revenue sharing has altered the spending patterns of American cities; and (3) the extent and effect of citizen involvement in the decision process. It may be found that revenue sharing is being spent in areas previously receiving relatively low priority by urban governments, such as health and welfare concerns, or that the money is being used solely in areas already receiving the largest share of the municipal budget, such as law enforcement and environmental concerns. Alternately, it may be found that revenue sharing is being evenly distributed among the various municipal functions in proportion to previous spending patterns. We are interested in this section, also, in the degree to which citizen input was encouraged in the decision to allocate initial revenue sharing checks and the effect such involvement or lack of it had on decision patterns. Table 2 summarizes the initial expenditure decisions of revenue sharing funds for the responding cities.

Several interesting facts are revealed in Table 2. In the first place, it is apparent that, although our questionnaire was mailed only a few weeks after the first and second waves of revenue sharing checks were issued (the first revenue sharing checks were issued in December 1972 and the second in January 1973; our survey was mailed in March 1973), most of the cities had determined how most of the initial funds were to be spent. In fact, as Table 2 indicates, only 18.8% of the total amount of revenue sharing funds had not been allocated by those responding to the survey. Secondly, it is obvious that, although revenue sharing funds were distributed over a wide variety of functions, the spending was concentrated in a relatively

Table 2. DISTRIBUTION OF INITIAL GENERAL REVENUE SHARING FUNDS

Function	Proportion of Revenue Sharing Funds (%)
Environmental protection[a]	12.7
Law enforcement	11.5
Street and road repair	10.9
Fire prevention	10.4
Parks and recreation	7.4
Miscellaneous capital expenditures	4.8
Building renovation	3.9
Municipal salaries	3.7
Direct tax relief	2.4
Equipment and equipment repair	2.2
Land annexing	1.8
Transit systems	1.7
Social services for the poor and aged	1.6
Debt retirement	1.4
Health services	1.1
Libraries	1.0
Building code enforcement	0.9
Investments	0.3
Extra personnel	0.1
Planning	0.1
Other functions	1.3
Undetermined	18.8

a. This category is broadly defined to include sewage disposal, sanitation, and pollution abatement.

few areas. In fact, five areas—environmental protection, law enforcement, street and road repair, fire prevention, and parks and recreation—received over 50% of the funds. It is apparent, in addition, that the "social service" areas received a relatively small proportion of the initial revenue sharing allocations. As indicated in Table 2, only 1.6% of the total revenue sharing grant was allocated to social services for the poor and aged and only 1.1% was allocated for health services. It is also significant to note that only 2.4% of the total revenue sharing fund was alloted to *direct* tax relief. Of course, this is not to imply that revenue sharing did not prevent an increase in local taxes in some areas by relieving the need for a larger increase in taxes.

Although Table 2 presents an interesting summary of the allocation of revenue sharing funds by functional category, it obviously provides no insight into the actual effect(s) revenue sharing funds had on spending patterns in American cities. That is, there is no way to determine from Table 2 whether revenue sharing funds have been disproportionately allocated to one function or another, and the table may thus mask important deviations from usual expenditure patterns. For example, although only 2.7% of revenue sharing funds were spent on social service and health functions, it is difficult to interpret the significance of this. Thus, it is important to examine not only the overall pattern of the allocation of revenue sharing funds, but also to compare this allocation with the normal expenditure patterns of American cities. Table 3 compares the proportion of the total municipal budgetary allocations for eight categories of municipal expenditures, as reported to the United States Bureau of the Census in 1971, with the proportion of revenue sharing funds allocated for these same functions. In order to provide meaningful comparisons, only those 212 cities responding to this survey were used in the calculation of the proportion of municipal funds normally allocated to the various functions.

The outstanding feature of Table 3 is the degree to which the expenditure of revenue sharing funds parallels the "normal" dis-

Table 3. COMPARISON OF REVENUE SHARING EXPENDITURES WITH
1971 BUDGETARY ALLOCATIONS[a] (in percentages)

Function	Revenue Sharing Expenditure	1971 Budget Allocation
Environmental protection	12.6	11.9
Law enforcement	11.5	13.2
Street and road repair	10.9	11.8
Fire prevention	10.4	10.0
Parks and recreation	7.4	7.5
Social services for poor and aged	1.6	1.2
Health services	1.1	3.6
Libraries	1.0	2.0

a. In both our survey and the Census Bureau data, capital and operating expenditures for each item are combined. Of course, the largest item of municipal expenditures—for public education—is not included in this analysis since the allocation of general revenue sharing funds on education is prohibited.

SOURCE: 1971 budgetary allocations were calculated from data in U.S. Bureau of the Census, *City Government Finances in 1970-71* (Washington, D.C.: Government Printing Office, 1972).

tribution of municipal spending (using 1971 as the basis of comparison). Although this table is not based on all revenue sharing expenditures, it is reasonable to expect only minor variations as the rest of the funds are expended. Although there are some interesting deviations (law enforcement received a smaller proportion of revenue sharing funds and environmental protection a greater proportion than the "normal" allocation), it is apparent that most cities spent their revenue sharing funds in similar fashion as their "normal" expenditure pattern. This finding, we would suggest, has both discouraging and encouraging implications. It is obvious that, contrary to what many had hoped, revenue sharing is not being used solely to bolster the cities' response to pressing health, social, and welfare needs. An examination of Table 3 in fact reveals that a slightly smaller proportion of revenue sharing funds has been allocated to the combined categories of health and welfare needs than that which would be expected in the "normal" budgetary process. At the same time, we cannot conclude that many cities have spent their revenue sharing "bonuses" for frivolous or unimportant items. Of course, there may be individual exceptions to this general rule, but the overall conclusion concerning the initial impact of revenue sharing on the aggregate spending patterns of American cities is that such funds have been allocated in similar fashion as prior expenditure decisions.

It is also of interest to determine the extent and impact of citizen participation in the allocation of revenue sharing funds. Although the expenditure of revenue sharing requires no citizen input, it is clear that many cities accepted President Nixon's (Congressional Quarterly Almanac, 1972: 9-A) challenge that revenue sharing should "send power . . . back to the people" and invited citizen involvement in the initial spending decisions. In fact, as indicated in Table 4, almost half of the cities responding to this survey held public hearings prior to their decisions on revenue sharing allocations.

Table 4 also indicates that city size or metropolitan type made relatively little difference in the decision to hold or not to hold public hearings. Cities in the 100,000 to 250,000 size class and those classified as central cities were somewhat more likely to hold public hearings than were other cities. Still, about half of all cities,

Table 4. PUBLIC HEARINGS AND THE ALLOCATION OF REVENUE SHARING FUNDS

Classification	Holding Public Hearings (%)	Holding Public Hearings (N)	Not Holding Public Hearings (%)	Not Holding Public Hearings (N)
Total, all cities	49.2	96	50.8	99
Population Group				
Over 500,000	45.5	5	54.5	6
250,000-500,000	50.0	9	50.0	9
100,000-250,000	58.8	30	41.2	21
50,000-100,000	45.2	52	54.8	63
Metropolitan Type				
Central city	53.2	67	46.8	59
Suburban area	42.0	29	58.0	40
Form of Government				
Mayor-council	32.8	22	67.2	45
Council-manager	57.6	68	42.4	50
Other	60.0	6	40.0	4

regardless of size or metropolitan type, encouraged citizen involvement in the decision to allocate revenue sharing funds.

Perhaps the most interesting finding of Table 4 is the differing responses by mayor-council and council-manager cities to the question of citizen involvement. Mayor-council cities (32.8%) were much less likely to have held public hearings on these decisions than were council-manager (57.6%) cities. This is, of course, precisely opposite what would be expected, according to Banfield and Wilson (1963: 138-150), given the supposed "professional" biases of council-manager cities. It might be concluded that mayor-council cities are more concerned with encouraging an involved citizenry in decision-making and then being subject to political reprisal if the public's suggestions are not followed. Alternately, one might conclude, as Eisinger (1973: 11-29) maintains, that citizens felt their channels to decision-making were more open in mayor-council cities and that the need for public hearings in these cities was less than in manager cities. In any case, it will be interesting to determine if this trend continues in the future.

Just as important is the determination of whether citizen input appears to have made a noticeable difference in the allocation of initial revenue sharing funds. Table 5 explores this question.

Table 5. EFFECT OF PUBLIC HEARINGS ON THE EXPENDITURE PATTERN OF INITIAL REVENUE SHARING FUNDS (in percentages)

| Expenditures | Total, All Cities (N = 212) | Held Public Hearings?[a] | |
		Yes (N = 96)	No (N = 99)
Environment	12.7	11.7	12.8
Law enforcement	11.5	11.1	12.8
Road repair	10.9	10.3	12.3
Fire prevention	10.4	11.2	10.4
Recreation	7.4	9.4	5.7
Other capital	4.8	6.4	4.0
Building renovation	3.9	4.5	3.7
Salaries	3.7	2.5	5.3
Direct tax relief	2.4	.6	2.2
Equipment and repair	2.2	2.9	2.2
Land annexing	1.8	1.4	2.5
Transit systems	1.7	1.1	2.0
Social services	1.6	1.9	.6
Debt retirement	1.4	1.4	1.3
Health	1.1	1.5	.9
Libraries	1.0	1.0	1.3
Code enforcement	.9	1.7	.1
Investments	.3	.1	.3
Extra personnel	.1	.1	.2
Planning	.1	.1	.1
Other	1.3	1.8	1.1
Undetermined	18.8	17.6	16.9

a. Columns in this and following tables often fail to sum to 100% due to rounding procedures.

Table 5 indicates that citizen participation in the expenditure of revenue sharing funds did not dramatically alter the major spending patterns previously noted; however, some interesting deviations in the overall trends are observed. Cities which did not hold public hearings were more likely to spend their revenue sharing funds for environmental concerns, law enforcement needs, repair of streets and roads, municipal salary increases, land annexing, and—perhaps most interesting of all—direct tax relief. Cities which did encourage public hearings were more likely to spend their revenue sharing funds on parks and recreation needs, social services, and health functions. It is noted also that cities which held public hearings also allocated a smaller proportion of their total revenue sharing funds to any

Table 6. EXPENDITURE PATTERN OF INITIAL REVENUE SHARING FUNDS BY CITY SIZE AND METROPOLITAN TYPE (in percentages)

Expenditures	Total, All Cities (N = 212)	City Size				Metropolitan Type	
		Over 500,000 (N = 13)	250,000-500,000 (N = 19)	100,000-250,000 (N = 56)	50,000-100,000 (N = 124)	Central City (N = 138)	Suburban Area (N = 74)
Environment	12.7	10.4	7.7	14.9	12.5	12.6	12.6
Law enforcement	11.5	22.7	13.5	8.6	11.3	11.2	12.1
Road repair	10.9	8.3	13.6	12.0	10.3	11.0	10.8
Fire prevention	10.4	13.3	14.0	9.0	10.2	12.7	6.2
Recreation	7.4	7.6	4.0	8.1	7.5	6.0	10.1
Other capital	4.8	.4	5.8	6.0	4.6	4.7	5.0
Building renovation	3.9	4.1	2.0	2.5	4.8	3.5	4.7
Salaries	3.7	1.6	9.2	3.7	3.1	3.2	4.7
Direct tax relief	2.4	.0	.0	2.1	3.2	2.7	1.9
Equipment and repair	2.2	.0	1.7	2.0	2.6	2.6	1.4
Land annexing	1.8	1.4	.3	2.3	1.7	1.2	3.0
Transit systems	1.7	4.5	1.2	2.0	1.4	2.4	.6
Social services	1.6	1.7	.7	1.7	1.7	1.4	2.0
Debt retirement	1.4	2.4	.1	2.5	1.0	1.5	1.2
Health	1.1	2.2	1.2	1.9	1.0	1.6	.2
Libraries	1.0	.8	.7	1.6	.9	1.2	1.0
Code enforcement	.9	1.0	.3	.7	1.1	1.1	.6
Investments	.3	.0	.0	.8	.2	.3	.3
Extra personnel	.1	.0	.0	.3	.1	.1	.3
Planning	.1	.0	.1	.1	.1	.1	.0
Other	1.3	.9	.7	1.3	1.5	1.4	1.1
Undetermined	18.8	17.2	26.3	14.1	19.8	18.3	19.4

purpose. Aggregate data, such as that presented in Table 5, do not "prove" that the decisions to hold or not to hold public hearings were responsible for these differences; however, we do find some evidence to indicate that public hearings may have been associated with some slight alterations in the expenditure of revenue sharing funds.

SOCIOECONOMIC CHARACTERISTICS AND
THE ALLOCATION OF REVENUE SHARING FUNDS

It was found in the previous section that cities spent most of their revenue sharing funds in a relatively few functional areas and that the spending of these funds was in very close proportion to the "normal" patterns of municipal spending. Also it was noted that those cities which held public hearings deviated slightly in their spending patterns from those which did not encourage citizen involvement.

In this section we are interested in determining whether a number of demographic variables, often found to be associated with city expenditures, are related to the allocation of revenue sharing funds. In general, it has been found that those factors associated with a city's increasing social needs (such as heterogeneous population, percentage nonwhite, and mean annual income) are associated with increasing municipal welfare expenditures. Hawkins and Dye (1970: 17-24) found, for example, that upper-income cities spend larger proportions of their budgets on such items as police, fire, and library needs, and Lineberry (1969) concludes that lower-income cities and those with larger populations spend a larger percentage of their budgets on social service functions. It will be especially interesting to determine if the allocation of revenue sharing funds appears to be affected by these variables since, as indicated above, many have expressed hopes that these funds will be used by cities with high social needs to fill the gaps in their service programs. Table 6 examines the distribution of revenue sharing funds by population size and city type.

As Table 6 indicates, smaller cities were more likely to spend their revenue sharing money on environmental concerns and for equip-

Table 7. EXPENDITURE PATTERN OF INITIAL REVENUE SHARING FUNDS BY RACE AND INCOME (in percentages)

Expenditures	Total, All Cities (N = 212)	Percent Black and Other Races				Mean Annual Income			
		Less than 2% (N = 50)	2-9% (N = 70)	9-20% (N = 45)	More than 20% (N = 47)	Less than $9,500 (N = 29)	$9,500-10,500 (N = 42)	$10,500-12,500 (N = 95)	More than $12,500 (N = 46)
Environment	12.7	17.4	12.0	11.5	9.8	20.7	8.8	9.8	16.6
Law enforcement	11.5	12.4	9.5	14.4	10.7	12.8	9.9	12.3	10.3
Road repair	10.9	11.2	12.0	8.8	11.0	13.8	11.1	11.5	7.7
Fire prevention	10.4	10.7	7.7	13.2	11.6	5.1	13.6	12.1	7.5
Recreation	7.4	7.4	9.5	4.2	7.1	8.8	5.8	8.8	4.8
Other capital	4.8	6.1	3.4	1.8	8.5	1.1	3.0	5.0	8.4
Building renovation	3.9	3.7	4.6	5.2	1.8	1.1	5.6	3.7	4.6
Salaries	3.7	.0	3.4	5.5	6.4	4.4	5.9	2.0	4.9
Direct tax relief	2.4	4.7	2.1	.0	2.8	1.9	4.1	1.9	2.3
Equipment and repair	2.2	2.5	.7	2.3	4.1	6.2	3.1	1.0	1.4
Land annexing	1.8	2.8	2.2	2.0	1.3	.5	1.5	1.3	4.2
Transit systems	1.7	1.8	1.0	1.2	3.2	.8	3.2	1.5	1.4
Social services	1.6	2.1	1.5	2.1	.9	3.0	1.1	1.0	2.5
Debt retirement	1.4	.5	1.8	.0	3.0	7.0	.0	.9	.1
Health	1.1	.5	1.5	1.2	1.2	.7	1.2	1.0	.9
Libraries	1.0	1.3	1.7	.1	.7	1.1	1.8	1.0	4.1
Code enforcement	.9	.8	1.3	.6	.7	.4	1.0	1.5	.1
Investments	.3	.5	.6	.0	.0	.0	.6	.5	.0
Extra personnel	.1	.0	.4	.0	.0	.5	.3	.0	.0
Planning	.1	.0	.0	.0	.2	.0	.7	.1	.0
Other	1.3	1.4	1.4	.6	1.9	2.5	1.3	.9	1.5
Undetermined	18.8	13.5	21.4	24.3	14.9	6.2	13.5	24.6	19.2

ment and repair than were larger cities. Most interesting is the fact that smaller cities were more likely to use a portion of their revenue sharing funds for direct tax relief than were larger cities. Large cities, on the other hand, were more likely to spend their revenue sharing checks on public safety (law enforcement and fire prevention) functions, on mass transit needs, and on health concerns than were the smaller cities.

Suburban cities were likely to spend a larger portion of their revenue sharing funds on parks and recreation and on land annexing. Central cities were more likely to spend a portion of their funds on fire prevention, transit needs, health concerns, and, interestingly, direct tax relief.

City size and metropolitan type, of course, are not the only indicators of municipal needs. Also important are such variables as percentage nonwhite, mean income, ethnicity, and population growth. Table 7 examines the allocation of revenue sharing funds by race and income characteristics.

Table 7 also presents some interesting relationships. As expected, those cities having the lowest per-capita mean income were more likely to spend their revenue sharing funds on social service functions than were other cities; and, also as anticipated, higher-income cities were more likely to allocate their funds for such functions as land annexing, capital expenditures, building renovation, and libraries. However, those cities with the largest proportions of nonwhite residents were less likely to allocate their funds to social service functions than were those with the least proportion of nonwhite inhabitants. It is interesting to note that the higher the propotion of nonwhite residents, the lower the proportion of revenue sharing spent for environmental functions and that cities with the lowest median incomes were most likely to spend their checks for environmental problems. There is no clear relationship between race or mean income and proportion of funds allocated for law enforcement functions. It is found that the lower the mean income, the more likely is the city to have spent a larger proportion of its revenue sharing check on any category.

In general, those cities with lower mean incomes are more likely to have allocated a larger proportion of their revenue sharing funds,

Table 8. EXPENDITURE PATTERN OF INITIAL REVENUE SHARING FUNDS BY POPULATION GROWTH AND ETHNICITY (in percentages)

Expenditures	Total, All Cities (N = 212)	Population Change (1960-1970)				Foreign-Born			
		Less than .00% (N = 8)	0-20% (N = 73)	20-30% (N = 73)	More than 30% (N = 58)	Less than 6% (N = 49)	6-15% (N = 52)	16-25% (N = 56)	More than 25% (N = 55)
Environment	12.7	7.3	14.0	15.5	15.0	13.4	13.3	10.9	12.9
Law enforcement	11.5	15.0	12.0	7.2	9.1	7.3	9.4	14.0	14.6
Road repair	10.9	11.6	8.4	16.3	11.3	17.6	10.6	7.4	8.9
Fire prevention	10.4	14.2	11.0	4.9	8.1	9.6	9.7	9.6	12.7
Recreation	7.4	4.0	7.8	4.8	11.0	7.0	7.5	9.5	5.4
Other capital	4.8	3.7	6.9	4.8	3.4	3.3	.6	3.1	12.0
Building renovation	3.9	4.1	1.8	2.1	7.1	4.3	4.0	3.5	3.9
Salaries	3.7	7.4	2.5	3.7	1.6	6.8	2.4	2.3	3.6
Direct tax relief	2.4	3.6	2.1	1.4	2.1	.5	3.5	2.1	3.4
Equipment and repair	2.2	1.3	3.6	2.1	1.5	4.3	2.8	.5	1.4
Land annexing	1.8	.9	.9	2.5	3.7	.6	3.5	2.3	.9
Transit systems	1.7	2.0	1.2	1.4	2.3	1.8	2.5	1.1	1.5
Social services	1.6	1.4	1.3	1.3	2.4	1.8	1.0	2.0	1.7
Debt retirement	1.4	3.3	.5	2.4	.1	2.2	.4	.0	1.0
Health	1.1	2.0	.6	.7	1.1	.5	.5	2.1	1.3
Libraries	1.0	1.4	.8	.7	1.0	1.7	.3	1.6	.5
Code enforcement	.9	.7	.2	1.4	1.8	.2	.6	2.3	.4
Investments	.3	.1	.3	1.8	.0	.0	1.3	.1	.0
Extra personnel	.1	.1	.1	.7	.1	.5	.1	.1	.0
Planning	.1	.1	.2	.0	.0	.2	.0	.1	.0
Other	1.3	1.2	1.4	2.4	.8	.9	2.2	1.8	.4
Undetermined	18.8	14.1	22.9	17.2	18.6	15.5	22.0	23.8	13.3

more likely to have spent those funds on social service and environmental functions, and less likely to have spent their funds on such items as land annexing, building renovation, libraries, and other capital expenditures. Thus, we find some evidence to support the conclusion that cities in the lower-income categories will appropriate their funds faster than upper-income cities and are more likely to spend their funds on social service and environmental concerns. Cities with larger proportions of nonwhite residents are also less likely to spend their funds on such functions as building renovation, land annexing, and libraries; however they are less likely to spend their funds on environmental concerns and, surprisingly, are less likely to spend their funds for social service functions. We find no clear relationship between proportion nonwhite and the speed with which cities allocated their initial revenue sharing checks.

Hawkins (1971: 65-72, 79-82) maintains that population change and ethnicity are often associated with differing patterns of city expenditures. Table 8 examines the relationship of these variables to the distribution of revenue-sharing funds.

On a priori grounds, as Lineberry and Sharkansky have noted (1971: 220-221), "one expects a clear and unambiguous positive relationship between spending levels and growth rates: As a community grows it should spend more to meet new service demands." Most of those relationships revealed in Table 8 are consistent with this expectation. As that table indicates, those cities which experienced greater population increases in the past decade were more likely to spend their revenue sharing funds for environmental concerns, for parks and recreation, for building renovation, for land annexing, and for social services. Interestingly, those experiencing less of a population increase were more likely to spend their revenue sharing funds on public safety functions (law enforcement and fire prevention).

Lineberry and Sharkansky (1971: 220-221) and Lineberry and Fowler (1967: 701-716) have found positive relationships between ethnic characteristics and spending for welfare concerns. Those cities responding to this survey with large ethnic concentrations were more likely to spend their revenue sharing funds for health needs, more likely to spend their funds for public safety functions, and less likely to allocate their funds to street and road repair.

SOCIOECONOMIC CHARACTERISTICS AND
THE ALLOCATION OF REVENUE SHARING: A SUMMARY

Summarizing these last two sections, it has been found that most American cities spent most of their revenue sharing funds in five categories. The data suggest that revenue sharing has not been applied primarily (or even largely) to social and welfare concerns, nor has it been used for unusual or frivolous expenditures. For the most part, cities have spent their initial revenue sharing funds as they spent public funds in the past.

Despite these overall trends, cities with particular social and service needs tended to spend their revenue sharing funds for these purposes as noted. Thus, larger cities were more likely to spend a portion of their funds on public safety functions, on mass transit needs, and on health concerns than were smaller cities. Smaller cities were more likely to spend a portion of their revenue sharing money on environmental concerns, equipment and equipment repair, and on direct tax relief. Central cities were more likely to spend a portion of their funds on fire prevention, transit needs, health care, and direct tax relief. Suburban areas were more likely to spend their funds on parks and recreation and on land annexing than were central cities.

Also it was found that cities with lower mean incomes were more likely to have allocated a larger proportion of their revenue sharing checks for any purpose and were more likely to have spent their funds for social service and environmental concerns. Cities with large white populations were more likely to have spent their revenue sharing funds on such items as building renovation, land annexing, and libraries. Cities with rapidly expanding populations were more likely to have spent their funds for environmental concerns, for parks and recreation, for building renovation, for land annexing, and for social services. Cities with large ethnic concentrations were more likely to spend their funds for public safety concerns.

POLITICAL CHARACTERISTICS AND
THE ALLOCATION OF REVENUE SHARING FUNDS

A number of pertinent hypotheses concerning the possible effects of the cities' political characteristics upon their allocation of revenue sharing funds are possible. Martha Derthick (1968: 257) has found, for example, that manager-council cities reach decisions more rapidly than mayor-council cities. It should be of interest to determine if manager-council cities are able to reach decisions concerning the allocation of revenue sharing funds earlier than mayor-council cities. Also, Lineberry and Fowler (1967: 701-716) maintain that those cities displaying "unreformed" political characteristics (mayor-council form of government, partisan ballots, and single-member council elections) are more responsive to socioeconomic cleavages in the population than are "reformed" cities (those with council-manager form of government, nonpartisan ballots, and at-large elections). Table 9 compares the allocation of revenue sharing funds among the various cities by forms of government.

As was the case when considering the effect of socioeconomic characteristics, Table 9 indicates that although the cities were similar in their allocation of initial revenue sharing funds, a number of interesting deviations do appear. As expected, unreformed cities were somewhat more likely to spend a portion of their funds on health and social service functions, although the total amount allocated to these concerns remains quite small. Unreformed cities were much more likely to spend their funds on public safety (law enforcement and fire prevention) functions than were reformed municipalities. Also, unreformed cities were more likely to allocate a portion of their funds for direct tax relief—possibly reflecting their more immediate interest in voter concerns. Reformed cities, on the other hand, were more likely to spend their funds on such concerns as land annexing, libraries, and parks and recreation. Surprisingly, unreformed cities had allocated larger portions of their funds for any purpose than had reformed cities. In general, political characteristics were only slightly related to variations in the spending patterns of initial revenue sharing funds and it is quite possible that those differences which were observed were more directly a function of population characteristics such as city size (unreformed political characteristics are more often found in larger cities) than the political characteristics.

Table 9. POLITICAL CHARACTERISTICS AND THE DISTRIBUTION OF REVENUE SHARING FUNDS (in percentages)

Expenditures	Total, All Cities (N = 212)	Form of Government[a]		Method of Election[b]		Council Representation[b]	
		Mayor-Council (N = 75)	Council-Manager (N = 125)	Partisan (N = 69)	Nonpartisan (N = 133)	Ward (N = 57)	At-Large (N = 140)
Environment	12.7	12.2	13.4	12.0	13.1	14.7	11.5
Law enforcement	11.5	13.3	9.6	14.8	10.0	14.5	10.8
Road repair	10.9	10.8	11.3	13.5	9.8	14.4	9.3
Fire prevention	10.4	17.1	7.0	16.5	7.2	12.8	9.9
Recreation	7.4	5.1	9.0	5.7	8.5	4.7	8.6
Other capital	4.8	4.7	4.4	3.5	4.8	6.0	4.8
Building renovation	3.9	3.3	4.6	2.9	4.7	3.7	4.4
Salaries	3.7	3.3	3.9	1.6	5.1	2.6	4.2
Direct tax relief	2.4	4.9	.4	2.7	1.7	4.4	.4
Equipment and repair	2.2	2.4	2.2	3.0	2.0	2.8	2.2
Land annexing	1.8	.5	2.4	.5	2.7	.7	1.7
Transit systems	1.7	2.1	1.6	2.0	1.7	1.7	1.9
Social services	1.6	2.0	1.4	2.0	1.5	1.7	1.7
Debt retirement	1.4	2.8	.5	2.0	1.2	.6	1.2
Health	1.1	1.4	.9	1.6	1.0	1.4	1.1
Libraries	1.0	.7	1.3	.6	1.2	.3	1.3
Code enforcement	.9	.3	1.0	.5	1.2	.7	1.1
Investments	.3	.0	.2	.1	.5	.0	.5
Extra personnel	.1	.0	.2	.0	.2	.0	.2
Planning	.1	.0	.1	.0	.1	.0	.1
Other	1.3	.4	2.0	.9	1.5	.7	1.5
Undetermined	18.8	10.3	23.7	13.8	21.9	12.7	21.9

a. The remaining cities fell in the "Other" category.
b. Information was missing for a number of cities on these variables. This explains why the totals do not equal 212.

IMPACT OF REVENUE SHARING ON
EXISTING PROGRAMS AND SERVICES

The above discussion has been concerned with the allocation of revenue sharing funds and the degree to which this allocation has been affected by various environmental factors. The survey also solicited information concerning the impact of revenue sharing on existing programs. Specifically, we are interested in this section in the degree to which revenue sharing has encouraged new, innovative programs at the municipal level and the probable effect of revenue sharing on Model Cities and OEO-funded programs if the legislation supporting these activities is phased out.

These concerns, of course, may have very important political consequences. A particularly sensitive issue is the possible effect of the revenue sharing concept on programs such as Community Action Agencies and Model Cities activities. Although President Nixon (Congressional Quarterly Weekly Report, March 10, 1971: 63-A) publicly stated that there was little reason to believe that revenue sharing would mean a dismantlement of these programs, there are those who fear that revenue sharing funds (either general or special) will not be sufficient to maintain these activities should Model Cities and OEO legislation be phased out. Senators Gaylord Nelson (Democrat—Wisconsin) and Jacob Javits (Republican—New York) are among those very much concerned about the future of community action programs and have sponsored legislation which would provide money specifically for mayors to use in support of such programs. An aide to the Senators (Congressional Quarterly Weekly Report, March 10, 1973: 506) is reported as commenting that "The administration is perpetrating a fraud when it says CAAs (community action agencies) can survive revenue sharing."

Our survey asked city officials to indicate whether they would use general revenue sharing funds to support local programs funded by Model Cities and OEO legislation if these two programs were eliminated. Table 10 summarizes the responses.

It is apparent from Table 10 that only a minority of the cities definitely will allocate a portion of their general revenue sharing funds to Model Cities and OEO activities. Perhaps the most

Table 10. USE OF REVENUE SHARING FUNDS FOR OEO AND
MODEL CITIES ACTIVITIES

| | Will general revenue sharing funds be used for OEO and Model Cities activities?[a] | | | | | |
| Classification (Total N = 147) | Yes (N = 29) | | No (N = 59) | | Uncertain (N = 59) | |
	(%)	(N)	(%)	(N)	(%)	(N)
Total, all cities	19.8	29	40.1	59	40.1	59
Population Group						
Over 500,000	20.0	2	20.0	2	60.0	6
250,000-500,000	41.2	7	23.5	4	35.3	6
100,000-250,000	18.6	8	46.5	20	34.9	15
50,000-100,000	15.6	12	42.8	33	41.6	32
Metropolitan Type						
Central city	21.3	24	40.7	46	38.0	43
Suburban area	14.7	5	38.2	13	47.1	16
Form of Government [b]						
Mayor-council	17.6	10	45.6	26	36.8	21
Council-manager	20.5	17	37.3	31	42.2	35

a. Question answered by only those cities receiving funds from these programs.
b. Column totals fail to equal column Ns due to "Other" category.

significant aspect of Table 10 is the large percentage of cities (40.1%) indicating uncertainty about using revenue sharing funds for the Model Cities and OEO programs. These differences did not vary significantly among the various demographic and political categories, except that officials in cities of the 250,000-500,000 size category were much more certain that portions of their revenue sharing funds *would* be allocated to these activities than were officials in any other category, and officials in the 100,000-250,000 and 50,000 to 100,000 size categories were more certain revenue sharing funds *would not* be used for these programs. Undoubtedly, the large proportion of officials reporting a degree of uncertainty to this question reflects their inability to predict the outcome of the President's special revenue sharing proposals, and especially those dealing with "Better Communities." However, the point to be stressed from Table 10 is that most cities do not anticipate the funding of Model Cities and OEO activities from general revenue sharing sources. If those programs are to receive revenue sharing support, it will have to come from the President's special revenue sharing proposals.

We are interested in the degree to which general revenue sharing has encouraged the development of new, innovative programs at the local level. One of President Nixon's (Congressional Quarterly Almanac, 1972: 9-A) arguments in support of revenue sharing was that it would promote more "flexible" local governments and that it would "bring . . . a new spirit of creativity to our federal system." The respondents to this survey were asked to indicate whether initial revenue sharing funds were being used mainly to support new programs or were being applied to existing activities. Table 11 summarizes the responses to this question.

It is apparent that most cities applied their initial revenue sharing funds to existing programs rather than using those funds to support new activities. As indicated in Table 11, only 28.5% of the cities reported spending their funds mainly on new programs. However, some interesting deviations in this pattern are evident. Smaller cities were more likely to use initial revenue sharing funds for new programs than were the larger cities. Likewise, suburban areas and those with council-manager forms of government were more likely to use their revenue sharing money for new programs. In general,

Table 11. USE OF REVENUE SHARING FOR NEW AND EXISTING PROGRAMS[a]

Classification (N = 193)	Revenue Sharing Used Mainly For			
	New Programs (N = 55)		Existing Programs (N = 138)	
	(%)	(N)	(%)	(N)
Total, all cities	28.5	55	71.5	138
Population Group				
Over 500,000	0.0	—	100.0	10
250,000-500,000	5.9	1	94.1	16
100,000-250,000	37.3	19	62.7	32
50,000-100,000	30.4	35	69.6	80
Metropolitan Type				
Central city	22.8	28	77.2	95
Suburban area	38.6	27	61.4	43
Form of Government[b]				
Mayor-council	19.4	13	80.6	54
Council-manager	34.8	40	65.2	75

a. Totals drawn from those responding to the question.
b. Column totals fail to equal column Ns due to "Other" category.

however, it is concluded that most cities spent most of their initial revenue sharing funds for existing programs.

In summary, the previous section explored the functional allocation of revenue sharing funds. In this section, we were concerned with the probable impact of revenue sharing on OEO and Model Cities activities and in its use for new and innovative programs. It was found, as reported above, that most cities probably will not use their general revenue sharing funds for OEO and Model Cities programs. Nor have most cities used their funds for new programs. Rather, most cities have allocated their initial revenue sharing checks to on-going programs. It is emphasized that these conclusions may be significantly altered if special revenue sharing programs are approved by the Congress and as future general revenue sharing checks are received.

ATTITUDES OF MUNICIPAL OFFICIALS
TOWARD REVENUE SHARING

Finally, we are interested in determining the attitudes of local officials toward general revenue sharing. Clearly, a number of local officials have publicly expressed their disappointment in revenue sharing and their disapproval of its effects on local government. Mayor Uhlman's position has been pointed out above. Testifying before the same committee, Mayor Henry Maier (Congressional Quarterly Weekly Report, March 3, 1973: 472) of Milwaukee stated that "we find the cities to be worse off financially than before general revenue sharing was enacted." Expressing a similar view, Mayor Kevin White (The Washington Post, June 17, 1973) has stated that "I am one who fought for the basic tenets of the New Federalism, in the form of general revenue sharing, for the past three years. I find myself chagrined that I don't know now what I have, except that I have less money in the short run and the prospect of less money in the long run."

Although exceptions (Congressional Quarterly Weekly Report, March 3, 1971: 471-473) to these views have been expressed, it is widely reported that mayors are disappointed with the revenue sharing concept and especially because they fear a net reduction in the flow of funds from the federal government to the localities. In order to determine how widespread these attitudes actually are, the survey asked the respondents to estimate the effect general revenue sharing would have on the total amount of federal funds they would receive. Table 12 summarizes their responses.

The most important conclusion supported by the data in Table 12 is that the respondents did not see general revenue sharing funds greatly increasing the total amount of federal funds they would receive. In fact, 53.4% felt that general revenue sharing would have no or only a marginal effect (increase) on the total amount of federal funds they would receive. Cities in the 50,000 to 100,000 and over 500,000 categories were more optimistic about the effect of general revenue sharing funds than the other cities in the population or other two categories.

Approximately one-third (34.5%) of the respondents felt that general revenue sharing funds would lead to a decrease in total federal funds. Cities in the 250,000 to 500,000 group, central cities and mayor-council cities were more likely to feel the effect of general revenue sharing would be a decrease in total federal funds.

Table 12. EFFECT OF GENERAL REVENUE SHARING FUNDS ON TOTAL FEDERAL FUNDS FOR URBAN AREAS

Classification (N = 180)	Greatly Increase (N = 22)		Increase Somewhat (N = 55)		No Effect (N = 41)		Decrease Somewhat (N = 34)		Greatly Decrease (N = 28)	
	(%)	(N)	(%)	(N)	(%)	(N)	(%)	(N)	(%)	(N)
Total, all cities	12.1	22	30.6	55	22.8	41	18.9	34	15.6	28
Population Group										
Over 500,000	0.0	—	60.0	6	10.0	1	20.0	2	10.0	1
250,000-500,000	0.0	—	13.3	2	13.3	2	46.7	7	26.7	4
100,000-250,000	9.6	5	25.0	13	28.9	15	17.3	9	19.2	10
50,000-100,000	16.5	17	33.1	34	22.3	23	15.5	16	12.6	13
Metropolitan Type										
Central city	6.0	7	30.8	36	20.5	24	24.8	29	17.9	21
Suburban area	23.8	15	30.2	19	27.0	17	7.9	5	11.1	7
Form of Government[a]										
Mayor-council	10.0	6	21.7	13	23.3	14	20.0	12	25.0	15
Council-manager	13.8	15	34.9	38	21.1	23	18.3	20	11.9	13

a. Column totals fail to equal column Ns due to "Other" category.

Based on Table 12, it is possible to conclude that the respondents felt general revenue sharing would not have a great effect (either to increase or decrease) total federal funds. Thus, general revenue sharing was not seen as a source of increased revenues for the cities, nor was it seen as a major factor in reducing federal funds.

Related to this question, was the overall evaluation of general revenue sharing by the respondents. Table 13 summarizes the responses to this question.

Contrary to what might have been expected, it is found that those officials responding to this survey are overwhelmingly in support of general revenue sharing. Only 8.5% of the city officials reported a degree of dissatisfaction. There was relatively little difference in this overall response when considering various environmental charac-teristics, except that council-manager cities were somewhat more satisfied with the concept than were mayor-council cities. In general, we find among local officials a high level of satisfaction with the revenue sharing program.

It is observed, then, that a number of cities (although generally a minority) expect a loss of federal revenues resulting from revenue sharing but that most officials are satisfied with the concept at this

Table 13. RESPONDENT SATISFACTION WITH GENERAL REVENUE SHARING

Classification (N = 199)	Very Satisfied (N = 92)		Somewhat Satisfied (N = 64)		Uncertain (N = 26)		Somewhat Dissatisfied (N = 12)		Very Dissatisfied (N = 5)	
	(%)	(N)	(%)	(N)	(%)	(N)	(%)	(N)	(%)	(N)
Total, all cities	46.2	92	32.2	64	13.1	26	6.0	12	2.5	5
Population Group										
Over 500,000	45.4	5	27.3	3	27.3	3	0.0	–	0.0	–
250,000-500,000	37.4	6	25.0	4	31.3	5	0.0	–	6.3	1
100,000-250,000	40.4	21	40.4	21	9.6	5	9.6	5	0.0	–
50,000-100,000	50.1	60	30.0	36	10.8	13	5.8	7	3.3	4
Metropolitan Type										
Central city	45.9	58	30.2	38	15.9	20	5.6	7	2.4	3
Suburban area	46.7	34	35.6	26	8.2	6	6.8	5	2.7	2
Form of Government [a]										
Mayor-council	41.2	28	29.4	20	20.6	14	5.9	4	2.9	2
Council-manager	48.4	58	33.3	40	10.0	12	5.8	7	2.5	3

a. Column totals fail to equal column Ns due to "Other" category.

stage in the program. One possible explanation for the positive reaction to general revenue sharing may be the administrative ease with which cities receive their funds. City agencies do not have to allocate extensive staff time or personnel to meeting regulations or completing applications. Instead, staff can work on program development and implementation. After the often tedious and demanding requirements of the various grant-in-aid programs, city officials may be responding more favorably to the administrative arrangements regarding general revenue sharing than to the program as a source of new and expanded revenues. Again, it will be interesting to determine how these attitudes may change as future revenue sharing decisions are reached.

SUMMARY AND CONCLUSIONS:
THE POLICY IMPLICATIONS OF
REVENUE SHARING FOR METROPOLITAN AMERICA

This paper has investigated numerous policy aspects of general revenue sharing for urban America. Perhaps the outstanding conclusion of this study is that, to date, cities have allocated their revenue sharing funds in a few areas and in close proportion to their ordinary budgetary patterns. As mentioned throughout this paper, we do not find cities allocating large proportions of general revenue sharing funds to health, welfare, and social service functions. At the same time, we cannot conclude that these funds have been spent for unusual or frivolous items. Rather, the effect of general revenue sharing to date has been to increase the cities' financial outlays on *existing* programs and projects. For the most part, the effect of revenue sharing has not been to encourage new and innovative projects at the local level, but has been used instead to bolster the cities' capacities to fund existing programs.

Within this overall conclusion, however, a number of interesting and perhaps significant deviations were noted. It was found that cities with particular needs (as indicated by such variables as per-capita income, city size, ethnicity, and proportion nonwhite) were more likely to allocate their funds for those purposes. Thus, large cities were more likely to allocate their revenue sharing funds for public safety, mass transit, and health concerns. Cities with lower mean annual incomes were more likely to spend their funds for environmental and social service functions. Cities with large white populations were more likely to allocate their revenue sharing checks for such functions as land annexing, libraries, and building renovation; and cities with rapidly expanding populations were more likely to spend their funds for environmental concerns, for parks and recreation, for building renovation, for land annexing, and for social services. These are trends which may be accentuated as future revenue sharing checks are received.

We found the *potential* impact of revenue sharing to be greatest concerning its effect on Model Cities and OEO-funded activities. Most cities indicated that they would not use revenue sharing funds to support these activities if Model Cities and OEO legislation is phased out. Of course, this does not mean that these activities will not be supported in the future, even if they are phased out of the federal budget, since special revenue sharing programs may become available for these purposes. Our findings do indicate that any "transition period" between cutoffs in these categorical grant programs and the passage of special revenue sharing programs would create severe financial problems for such programs and those who benefit from them.

We found that about half the cities had encouraged some form of citizen input in the process of allocating revenue sharing funds; however, there were no dramatic differences in such allocation between those cities which did and those which did not hold public hearings. It was noted that those cities which *did not* hold public hearings were more likely to spend their funds for environmental concerns, law enforcement, street and road repair, land annexing, municipal salary increases, and, unexpectedly, direct tax relief. Those which *did* hold public hearings were more likely to spend their funds on parks and recreation, social service needs, and health concerns. Still, the differences between the two were rather minor. One of the most interesting aspects of the citizen participation question is that, despite no regulation requiring such participation, almost half the cities reported holding public hearings. Perhaps this may be interpreted as a tangible consequence of the recognition of citizen groups which government-sponsored programs such as Model Cities and OEO have encouraged.

We found also that about a third of all cities responding expect revenue sharing to result in a net loss of federal funds received by their cities; however, most officials were satisfied with the revenue sharing concept. If such high levels of satisfaction persist, this would obviously indicate that urban officials may present very formidable political opposition to any attempts to dismantle or to alter drastically general revenue sharing after its initial five-year period.

In conclusion, we find that initial revenue sharing decisions have not resulted in the development of new, creative, and innovative programs at the municipal level and that most cities are spending their funds in close proportion to their previous budgetary patterns. However, we do find a number of interesting deviations in these spending patterns and observe that cities with particular needs are more likely to allocate their funds for those needs. These are trends which we believe could be fruitfully examined in future revenue sharing studies.

EVALUATION

Perhaps one of the most important, yet least emphasized aspects of social science research involves self-evaluation of the methods, research design, findings, and theoretical implications used and reached by policy researchers. This section considers the just-discussed research in such a manner and offers a variety of suggestions for those specifically interested in policy research and analysis.

Methodologically, this research illustrates a number of problems which are both common to policy analysis in general and specific to studies of revenue sharing. In the first place, our survey was conducted shortly after the receipt of initial revenue sharing checks (all cities had received two, and some three, checks prior to returning the questionnaire). Many of the conclusions and trends noted above may be altered by future spending patterns. We plan to continue and expand our research efforts in the area in order to draw conclusions based on longitudinal data. Secondly, as we have emphasized throughout, this is an aggregate study of the impact of revenue sharing and is not an in-depth examination of revenue sharing decisions of any single city. It is quite possible that some individual cities may deviate significantly from the trends reported above. Some may well have spent large portions of their initial checks for municipal salaries, health concerns, social services, or other items which received a relatively small proportion of the total general revenue sharing allocation. This latter problem, of course, is shared by all those contemplating survey research strategies and we concluded that the benefits of aggregate survey results outweighed the advantages of a case study approach.

In addition, studies of revenue sharing present unique methodological problems to the policy analyst. Revenue sharing funds are allocated with almost no spending restrictions. Although recipient cities are required to file with the Office of Revenue Sharing reports indicating both planned and actual uses of these funds, there is no "guarantee" that the funds have been dispersed in the reported manner. Since revenue sharing is treated as part of the general fund by most cities, it is possible that city officials themselves may be unable to pinpoint the precise financial impact of revenue sharing funds any more easily than they could trace the precise distribution of revenue generated by property taxes, sales taxes, income taxes, and so forth. Thus, in policy studies of the impact of new sources of revenue, and especially of revenue sharing funds, the researcher is particularly dependent on the honesty and judgment of the responding official.

This research also illustrates a number of problems of research design which must be faced by the policy analyst. In this case, there were three basic constraints which influenced our research design and strategy. In the first place, we decided in early fall 1972 that it would be both interesting and important to monitor and investigate the impact of the general revenue sharing legislation if it were passed. This meant that there was *not* a great deal of time available for detailed and exhaustive discussions concerning the pros and cons of various approaches. Instead, a variety of decision rules were set. It was decided that outside funding would be impossible, at least initially, to obtain prior to actually conducting the research. Rather than delay the research, it was decided that we would meet expenses from a small research grant we had from the university and from our personal resources. Thus, we immediately realized the financial parameters we had to deal with and we decided that the research effort would not be broadened to include other units of government and that the case study approach, while attractive in many respects, would not meet our research needs.

Once these decision rules had been set it became easier to organize and decide other matters. Our research interest was in the urban use of general revenue sharing funds and it was decided, given what we assumed our response rate would be, to include all cities over 50,000 population in our survey. Other factors in reaching this decision included the greater availability of demographic and political data for cities over 50,000 population and, of course, the fact that a substantial portion of general revenue sharing funds was allocated to these cities.

A final factor entered into our decisional calculus. We were interested not only in how cities spent their revenue sharing funds, but also in the procedures followed in reaching those decisions and the attitudes of public officials toward general revenue sharing. It was felt that both of these areas were important to any under-standing of the impact of general revenue sharing and future support for the program.

These restrictions and overall guidelines enabled us to set clear priorities; when we received a 51.8% response rate on our initial mailing we decided not to send out a follow-up. Again several factors were involved in that decision. First, the response rate is generally considered acceptable by most methodologists and we did not feel it was atypical in any respect. Second, we planned to do follow-up investigations for the next three years and did not want to increase the possibility of nonresponse in the future.[1]

These elementary, yet critical restrictions were also competing with several major theoretical concerns. In the first place, we were not interested in studying the impact of a policy decision in a post facto manner. If anything, policy analysis and policy research has been too narrowly construed on this point. It was decided that important and useful research could be done on a program which was just beginning and which had important social and political implications for those involved. Secondly, it was decided that another major shortcoming of much policy research is the lack of significant longitudinal dimensions; thus, conclusions based on shifts and trends over time are usually difficult or impossible. Finally, the lack of a comparative emphasis in a great deal of contemporary policy analysis prompted us to select the survey approach rather than the case study, in-depth approach. It was decided that comparisons across a variety of structural, size, regional, and demographic characteristics would be of extreme value for the social scientist interested in the study of general revenue sharing.

Certainly, the reader has his own impressions and conclusions about our success or lack of it which may conflict with ours; however, we would like to summarize briefly our feelings. We believe our findings are quite representative not only of cities over 50,000 in general, but also fo specific demographic and structural categories of cities. Our findings will be useful in developing trends and analyzing shifts over time among these various categories of cities.

In addition, the findings provide a useful base for additional research. We have already repeated our survey and anticipate doing so at least one more year. Given the nature of the responses, our anticipation is to be able to discuss in considerable depth and with greater confidence the revenue-sharing decisions reached and the attitudes held by the city officials (see Caputo and Cole, 1974). With our initial data, trends and changes should be more readily observed and it should be possible to uncover any specific variable which might account for that change. Finally, attitudinal information may provide some insights as to the nature and extent of probable reform measures in congressional consideration of the legislation in the next two years.

In sum, then, the findings provide useful summary information as well as an important base from which informed projections may be possible. This would seem to be the very essence of policy research.

In closing, we would like to offer four specific recommendations for those interested in engaging in such research. First, be aware of the trade-offs when considering what you want to do with what you are capable of doing. If objectives are clearly stated prior to undertaking research efforts, the researcher will not only have a better focus for that research, but will find himself eliminating a great deal of the waste and inefficiency associated with trying to stretch scarce resources too thin.

Second, be aware of the weaknesses and limitations in your research. Where possible, correct them. Where not, decide if they are critical. If in fact they are crucial, redesign your efforts. Perhaps a useful way of doing this is to critically review the proposal as if you are a referee for a journal. If you do not find serious difficulties with the data or methodology involved and if the conclusions you may draw appear justified, then do not worry.

Third, the complexity or resource demands should not keep you from undertaking research. Individual ingenuity and hard work are important substitutes for financial resources. In addition, many types of research can be redesigned to cut costs yet still retain the essential aspects of the design.

Finally, do not be discouraged when critics contend your conclusions are unfounded or poorly supported. In most cases, they neither have access to better data nor possess any better understanding of the peculiarities of the subject under investigation. While criticism is always disconcerting, it should not be debilitating if the three previously recommended steps have been followed. In fact, you are probably in a position to make a unique, and difficult to refute, contribution to the understanding of public policy and its analysis if you have followed the prior steps. This is the best possible justification for this type of policy research.

NOTE

1. The questionnaire asked the respondent if he wanted to receive a copy of the final results. We mailed summary results to over 95% of the respondents and to all the nonrespondents. Our anticipation was that this might increase the response rate in future mailings.

REFERENCES

BANFIELD, E. C. and J. Q. WILSON (1963) City Politics. New York: Alfred A. Knopf.
CANNON, L. and D. S. BRODER (1973) "Nixon's 'New Federalism': struggle to prove itself." Washington Post (June 17): 1.
CAPUTO, D. A. and R. L. COLE (1974) Urban Politics and Political Decentralization: The Case of Federal Revenue Sharing. Lexington, Mass.: D.C. Heath.
Congressional Quarterly Almanac (1972) Washington, D.C.: Congressional Quarterly, Inc.
Congressional Quarterly Weekly Reports (March 3 and 10, 1973; March 10, 1971) Washington, D.C.: Congressional Quarterly, Inc.
DERTHRICK, M. (1968) "Intercity differences in administration of the public assistance program: the case of Massachusetts," in J. Q. Wilson (ed.) City Politics and Public Policy. New York: John Wiley.
EISINGER, P. (1973) "The conditions of protest behavior in American cities." American Political Science Review 67 (March): 11-29.
GRODZINS, M. and D. ELAZAR [eds.] (1966) The American System. Chicago: University of Chicago Press.
HAWKINS, B. (1971) Politics and Urban Policies. Indianapolis: Bobbs-Merrill.
––– and T. DYE (1970) "Metropolitan 'fragmentation': a research note." Midwest Review of Public Administration (February): 17-24.
LINEBERRY, R. (1969) "Community structure and planning commitment: a note on the correlates of agency expenditures." Social Science Quarterly (December).
––– and E. P. FOWLER (1967) "Reformism and public policies in American cities." American Political Science Review (September): 701-716.
LINEBERRY, R. and I. SHARKANSKY (1971) Urban Politics and Public Policy. New York: Harper & Row.
REAGAN, M. (1972) The New Federalism. New York: Oxford University Press.
STENBERG, C. (1972) The New Grass Roots Government? Washington, D.C.: Advisory Commission on Intergovernmental Relations.
SUNDQUIST, J. and D. DAVIS (1969) Making Federalism Work. Washington, D.C.: Brookings.
Washington Post (1973) June 17, 18, and 19.

6

CHOOSING AMONG ALTERNATIVE PUBLIC POLICIES

STUART S. NAGEL

University of Illinois

The purpose of this article is to provide an introduction to a basic methodology which can be used for testing the effects of alternative public or legal policies. The testing methodology depends mainly on whether the legal policies involve (1) making legal or illegal some activity like capital punishment, or (2) deciding how to allocate governmental funds to alternative activities like subsidizing low-rent public housing versus home ownership for the poor.

Other examples of controversial legal policies involving the issue of whether something should be made legal or illegal include legalizing marijuana, prohibiting malapportioned legislatures, legalizing medical abortions, or providing for elected rather than appointed judges. Other examples of controversial legal policies involving the allocation of scarce governmental resources include allocating funds between

AUTHOR'S NOTE: *This research is one of a series of policy science studies on measuring and achieving effects of alternative legal policies partly financed by the National Science Foundation grant GS-2875. The writer also thanks Duncan MacRae for his suggestions.*

Table 1. DECISION RULES FOR ADOPTING OR PREFERRING NONEXPENDITURE POLICIES

Problem Situation	Policies or Means (X's)	Goals or Ends (Y's)	Adopt X_1 (where there is only one policy under consideration) if:	Prefer X_1 over X_2 if:
One	X_1	Y_a	$R_{X_1Y_a} \cdot z$ is greater than zero.	
Two	X_1 and X_2	Y_a		$R_{X_1Y_a} \cdot z$ is greater than $R_{X_2Y_a} \cdot z$.
Three	X_1	Y_a and Y_b	$[(R_{X_1Y_a} \cdot z$ times $W_{Y_a})$ plus $(R_{X_1Y_b} \cdot z$ times $W_{Y_b})]$ is greater than zero.	
Four	X_1 and X_2	Y_a and Y_b		U_{X_1} is greater than U_{X_2}, where U_{X_1} = the expression in brackets under situation three.

Meaning of Symbols:

$R_{X_1Y_a} \cdot z$ = the correlation or slope between X_1 and Y_a holding constant intervening variables z.

W_{Y_a} = the value weight of goal a.

U_{X_1} = the rank-order utility of policy 1.

X, Y, and z can be dichotomous attributes or interval-measured variables.

X, Y, and z can be static (i.e., one point in time) or dynamic (i.e., Δx, Δy, and Δz, where Δ = change in).

Numbered subscripts differentiate policies, and alphabetic subscripts differentiate goals.

[154]

busing versus compensatory education in improving educational opportunities for poor children, between anti-pollution water enforcement programs versus water clean-up facilities, and allocating funds between fair employment enforcement activities versus manpower training to provide better employment opportunities to minorities.[1]

CHOOSING AMONG NONEXPENDITURE POLICIES

THE GENERAL PROBLEM AND THE ILLUSTRATIVE DATA

Table 1 summarizes the decision rules involved for adopting or preferring nonexpenditure policies. Each row in the table illustrates a different problem situation. The first situation involves one policy and one goal, and the problem is to decide whether or not to adopt the policy in light of its relation to the one goal. The second situation involves two policies and one goal, and the problem is to decide which policy to prefer if they both cannot be adopted. Situation three involves one policy and two goals, and the problem (like the first problem) is to decide whether or not to adopt the policy in light of its relation to the two goals. Situation four involves two policies and two goals, and the problem there (like the second problem) is to decide which policy to prefer if they both cannot be adopted.

In order to better understand the decision rules, it is helpful to have a concrete example. One concrete example that can be used is the problem situation of deciding what to do to decrease the occurrence of illegal searches by the police. One alternative that the courts have adopted is to exclude or throw out illegally obtained evidence from courtroom proceedings in criminal cases on the theory that doing so will deter the police from using illegal methods to obtain evidence. Prior to 1961 the U.S. Supreme Court allowed the state courts and legislatures to decide themselves whether to adopt this exclusionary rule. In 1961 the Supreme Court in the case of *Mapp v. Ohio* declared that the fourth amendment required that illegally seized evidence be inadmissible in all American criminal cases, at least when objected to by defense counsel.

In 1963 a mailed-questionnaire survey was made of one randomly selected police chief, prosecuting attorney, judge, defense attorney, and ACLU official in each of the 50 states to determine, among other things, their perceptions of changes in police behavior before and after *Mapp v. Ohio*. The experiment was aided by virtue of the fact that 24 of the 50 states had already adopted the exclusionary rule before *Mapp v. Ohio*, and respondents from those states could thus serve as a control group; 23 were newly forced to adopt the rule at that time, and respondents from those states could thus serve as an experimental group; and three states which were not used in the analysis had partially adopted it.

Table 2 shows that 57% of the respondents from the control group of states reported an increase in police adherence to legality in making searches since 1961; whereas 75% of the respondents from the experimental group of newly adopting states reported an increase. This 18 percentage points difference (or, roughly speaking, a correlation of +.18) cannot be readily attributed to a chance fluke in the sample of respondents since there is less than a five out of 100 probability that one could distribute 104 respondents over the six cells in Table 2 purely by chance and come out with a +.18

Table 2. THE RELATION BETWEEN ADOPTING THE EXCLUSIONARY RULE AND INCREASED POLICE ADHERENCE TO LEGALITY IN MAKING SEARCHES

		Exclusionary Rule		
		Had All Along (Control Group)	Newly Adopted (Experimental Group)	
Police Adherence to Legality	Increase since 1961	57%	75%	+18 percentage points difference
	No change	34%	21%	
	Decrease	9%	4%	
	Number of Respondents	48	56	104

correlation. This +.18 correlation is also not readily attributable to a misperception of the reality on the part of the respondents since there was such a high correlation among the different kinds of respondents from the same state or type of states on the empirical question of police adherence to legality, even though there was great disagreement on the normative question of the desirability of the exclusionary rule.

The +.18 correlation between newly adopting the exclusionary rule and increased police adherence to legality in searches seems to be largely attributable to the fact that the states that newly adopted the exclusionary rule also disproportionately reported an increase in programs designed to educate the police as to search-and-seizure law, which in turn correlates highly with increased police adherence to legality. States that already had the exclusionary rule also often underwent an increase in police adherence to legality possibly because of the stimulus of the publicity given in *Mapp v. Ohio,* and because of long-term public opinion trends demanding higher standards of police behavior. (For further discussion of the problem of increasing police adherence to legality in making searches, see Oaks, 1970; LaFave, 1965; Nagel, 1965.)

THE FOUR DECISION SITUATIONS

Figure 1 shows the relation between alternative policies and alternative goals involved in the problem of increasing police adherence to legality in making searches, and can be nicely used to illustrate the decision rules in Table 1. The top part of Figure 1 shows that the exclusionary rule (X_1) should be adopted (in light of the decision rule for problem situation one) if increased police adherence to legality (Y_a) is one's only goal, since there is a positive correlation between X_1 and Y_a.

Many judges and others (including Felix Frankfurter in his dissenting opinion in *Mapp v. Ohio*) have argued that tort or criminal actions against the police are far more effective than adopting the exclusionary rule as a means of increasing police adherence to legality. The questionnaire asked the respondents how often tort or criminal actions had occurred against the police in their communities for making illegal searches. If one divides the respondents into those

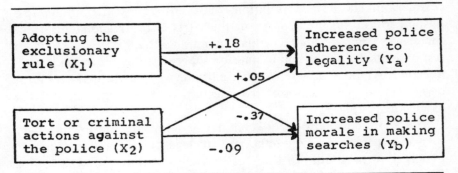

Figure 1: ALTERNATIVE POLICIES AND GOALS INVOLVED IN INCREASING
POLICE ADHERENCE TO LEGALITY IN MAKING SEARCHES

relatively few who said there had been at least one such action in recent years versus those who said there had been none, then there is only a +.05 correlation between the occurrence of such actions and increased police adherence to police legality. The low correlation and the low occurrence of such actions may be attributable to the fact that prosecutors are reluctant to prosecute the police who have been aiding them, and searched individuals are reluctant to sue because of the time, cost, embarrassment, unsympathetic juries, police discretion, and difficulty of assessing collectible damages. Thus, the exclusionary rule (X_1) should be preferred (in light of the decision rule for problem situation two) over tort or criminal actions (X_2) if increased adherence to legality (Y_a) is one's only goal (and the decision-maker cannot adopt both policies), since there is a greater positive correlation between X_1 and Y_a than there is between X_2 and Y_a.

An additional goal one might have in dealing with the problem of increasing police adherence to legality in making searches is the goal of simultaneously increasing police morale, or at least not decreasing it. The mailed questionnaire asked the respondents about changes in police morale before and after *Mapp v. Ohio*. The correlation between being a respondent from a state that had newly adopted the exclusionary rule (X_1) and reporting increased police morale (Y_b) in making searches was a $-.37$. The negative correlation may be attributable to the fact that when evidence is thrown out which the police have worked hard to obtain through what they may have considered a lawful search, this is demoralizing to their enthusiasm for making future searches. If the correlation between X_1 and Y_b had been positive, like the correlation between X_1 and Y_a, then it would be easy to decide in favor of adopting X_1. However, since the correlation between X_1 and Y_b is negative, one must decide whether that negative correlation is enough to offset the positive correlation between X_1 and Y_a.

The matter is not resolved simply by noting that the X_1 and Y_b correlation is greater than the X_1 and Y_a correlation. This is so because it is unlikely that one would weight the Y_a and Y_b equally. If the Y_a goal has a weight 3 times or more the Y_b goal, then the $-.37$ correlation would not be enough to offset the $+.18$ correlation in view of the fact that 3 times .18 is greater than 1 times .37. On the other hand, if the Y_a goal has a weight 2 times or less the Y_b goal, then the $-.37$ correlation would be enough to offset the $+.18$ correlation. In other words, if the correlation of X_1 and Y_a (times the weight of Y_a) plus the correlation of X_1 and Y_b (times the weight of Y_b) is greater than zero, then X_1 should be adopted in light of the decision rule for problem situation three is Y_a and Y_b are one's only goals. (On the methodology of weighting goals, see Guilford, 1954: 154-301; Churchman et al., 1957: 136-154.)

The most complicated problem situation involves both multiple policies and multiple goals, but even this situation is simple to resolve conceptually after going through the first three problem situations. Suppose the weight of Y_a is 3 times greater than the weight of Y_b as determined by a scientific psychological survey of public, legislative, or judicial opinions. Note also that the correlation between the occasional occurrence of tort or criminal actions against the police and increased police morale was a negative $-.09$. Thus, the exclusionary rule (X_1) should be preferred (in light of the decision rule for problem situation four) over tort or criminal actions (X_2) if increased adherence to legality (Y_a) and increased police morale (Y_b) are one's only goals (and the decision-maker cannot adopt both policies) since in Figure 1: $+.18$ x 3 plus $-.37$ x 1 is greater than $+.05$ x 3 plus $-.09$ x 1. In other words, .54 plus $-.37$ is greater than $+.15$ plus $-.09$.

VARIATIONS AND ALTERNATIVES TO THE BASIC RULES

Instead of using the correlation coefficients between the variables shown in Figure 1 in order to make the policy choices shown in Table 1, one could use the regression slopes between the policy and goal variables when a line is fitted to the dots on a graph of the variables. The dots are generated by plotting the positions of the communities of the respondents. Whether regression or correlation measures are more meaningful is a somwhat disputed issue among social scientists (Blalock, 1972a: 73-152; Blalock, 1964: 50-52). Correlation coefficients are simpler and not influenced by the units of measurement used, but unlike regression coefficients they are not capable of being used to predict how many additional units of Y can be obtained by an increase in units of X. Correlation coefficients should be favored in this decision-making context because each one can be used to indicate the amount of variation on Y_a and Y_b accounted for by X_1 and X_2 respectively. Regression weights cannot be used in this comparative context because they can be increased or decreased by changing the units of measurement (for example, from dollars to pennies) without changing how closely the variables vary together (Blalock, 1972: 361-385, especially 383-385).[2]

The decision rules in Table 1 can be logically extended to cover more policies. For example, three or more policies and one goal is analogous to situation two. One policy and three or more goals is analogous to situation three. Likewise, analogous to situation four is (1) two policies and three or more goals, (2) three or more policies and two goals, or (3) three or more policies and three or more goals. Additional policies concerning the problem of illegal police searches might relate to police training and police selection practices. Additional goals might relate to decreasing the crime rate and decreasing the unsuccessful prosecution rate.

The methodology can also be extended to other areas of controversy like marijuana, malapportionment, abortion, and judicial selection, provided that one can obtain data on the relations between adoption of the controversial policy (and alternative policies) and the goals (on which there is some mutual agreement). In the American federal system where states and cities do experiment with alternative approaches to given social problems, this kind of data can often be obtained provided one has (1) some financial support and (2) some cooperation from knowledgeable persons. Even if solid data cannot always be fully obtained, use of the conceptual approach outlined can often be helpful in clarifying and making more effective governmental policy analysis.[3]

The correlation approach just presented is closely related to benefit-cost analysis in that for each situation, benefit-cost analysis says make the following decisions:[4]

Situation one. Adopt X_1 if the benefits of X_1 are greater than the costs of X_1.

Situation two. Prefer X_1 if the B–C of X_1 is greater than the B – C of X_2.

Situation three. Adopt X_1 if B of X_1 is greater than C of X_1, where $B = B_{Y_a} + B_{Y_b}$.

Situation four. Prefer X_1 if the B – C of X_1 is greater than the B – C of X_2, where B is figured as in situation three.

Determining such benefit minus cost differences is often less meaningful than the correlation approach for three reasons. First, the B – C approach does not consider the correlation or probability that X will achieve Y unless one resorts to a complicated system of probability calculations.[5] Second, the B – C approach does not measure X in interval units but just as present or absent, unless one resorts to a complicated system of marginal analysis. Third, the B – C approach requires B and C to be measured in the same units, unless one resorts to a complicated system of exponent weights. (For further discussion of benefit-cost analysis, see Prest and Turvey, 1965; Black, 1968: 37-118; Miller and Starr, 1960: 33-102.)

The correlation approach can also be distinguished from the matrix decision theory approach for choosing among nonexpenditure policies. In the matrix decision approach to the problem of increasing police adherence to legality, there is one state-of-nature or Z variable, unless one wants to distinguish between rural and urban police or some other possibly significant intervening variable. There are four alternative policies since there are two positions on X_i^* and two positions on X_2. There are nine possible payoff alternatives since there are three positions on Y_a and three positions on Y_b. This yields a matrix with one column and four rows. In each cell of the matrix, one shows the average payoff score (with ranks from 1 to 9) for each of the four alternative strategies. The strategy to choose using this approach is simply the one with the highest payoff score.[6]

This matrix decision approach, however, will not work relative to the correlation approach if one X or means variable is measured on a continuum rather than broken into a few discrete subpositions. If an X variable is continuous, then theoretically there are an infinity of alternatives. If the X variables yields a manageable 10 to 15 alternative strategies, then the drawback exists that the strategy with the highest payoff may be one that exists in only a few communities; but by small-sample coincidence, those few communities may have undergone an increase in both police adherence and police morale. In other words, the decision matrix approach can lead to faulty decisions if the sample size is not substantial for the empirical occurrences of each alternative strategy, whereas the correlation approach mainly requires a substantial sample only for the overall sample size. (For further discussion of matrix decision theory, see Richmond, 1968: 501-560; Miller and Starr, 1960: 55-100.)

One of the goals that can be included (in the correlation analysis) is to keep costs down. However, when trying to decide how to allocate scarce financial resources among diverse policy activities, it may be more meaningful to use a kind of linear programming approach about to be described rather than the correlation approach which we have just presented. (For further discussion of some important aspects of the correlation approach to making nonexpenditure policy choices, see Campbell, 1969; Blalock, 1964; Nagel, 1966.)[7]

CHOOSING AMONG EXPENDITURE POLICIES

THE GENERAL PROBLEM AND THE ILLUSTRATIVE DATA

To illustrate on a very simple level what is involved in applying linear programming concepts to choosing among alternative expenditure polices, let us take the problem of allocating $10 in campaign expenditure money to media dollars and precinct organization dollars. Suppose we are in a congressional district in which 39 votes are expected to be cast among the two candidates running, which means our candidate needs 20 votes to win. (For further discussion of the problem of rationally allocating campaign expenditures, see Kramer, 1966; Agranoff, 1972; Nagel and McCarthy, 1974.)

There may be some combination of media and precinct dollars that will enable us to get our 20 votes while spending substantially less than the $10 we have available. Finding that combination is the cost minimization problem. Likewise, there may be some combination of media and precinct dollars that will enable us to get as many votes as possible above 20 votes while spending no more than the $10 we have available. This is the benefit maximization problem. Linear programming is an excellent method for determining what combination of expenditures will minimize costs while achieving at least a minimum benefit level or determining what combination will maximize benefits while keeping within a maximum cost level.

Linear programming or optimizing can be defined as a procedure whereby one finds the optimum allocation of funds or some other scarce resource between two or more alternatives in light of a given minimizing or maximizing goal and in light of given constraints or conditions. In order to be linear rather than nonlinear programming, the relations between the resources and the goals must be straight-line or constant-return relations rather than curved-line or diminishing-return relations.

Suppose that we have obtained (1) data from the Federal Communications Commission showing how much money was spent by each of the approximately 800 congressional candidates in 1972 on television and radio, (2) data from the General Accounting Office showing how much money was spent in total by each of the candidates, and (3) data from the *Congressional Quarterly* showing how many votes were obtained. If we substract the FCC media expenditures from the GAO total expenditures, we should have a rough estimate of precinct organization expenditures for each candidate. If we then do a regression analysis with media dollars (M) and precinct dollars (P) as the independent variables and votes obtained as the dependent variable, we should be able to come up with a roughly accurate empirical equation between these variables, which might read something like Votes Obtained = 5 + 2M + 1P. The 5 in this equation indicates the number of votes likely to be obtained without any expenditure of funds. The 2 and the 1 indicate the relative weights of media dollars and precinct dollars in determining the number of votes obtained. (On doing a regression analysis between policy alternatives and goals, see Blalock, 1960: 273-285; Draper and Smith, 1966.)

In our illustration there are basically only two constraints. One relates costs to our two activity variables; the other relates benefits to our two activity variables. The first says the sum of media dollars and precinct organization dollars must be less than or equal to $10. This is our maximum cost constraint. The second constraint says 20 Votes = 5 + 2M + 1P. This is our minimum benefits constraint.

GRAPHING THE SOLUTION

To understand better what is involved in finding optimum expenditure combinations through linear programming, it is helpful to make a graph depicting our constraints. Figure 2 shows the maximum cost line as a straight line connecting (1) the point at which $0 is spent for precinct organization and $10 is spent for media to (2) the point where $0 is spent for media and $10 is spent for precinct organization. Every point on that line involves a combination of M and P that adds up to $10, which is why it is also called an equal cost line.

Figure 2 also shows the minimum benefits line as a straight line connecting (1) the point at which $0 is spent for precinct organization and $7.50 therefore has to be spent for media (in order for 5 + 2M + 1P to add up to 20) to (2) the point at which $0 is spent for media and $15 therefore has to be spent for precinct organization (in order for 5 + 2M + 1P to add up to 20). Every point on that line involves a combination of M and P that produces 20 votes, which is why it is also called an equal benefit line or an indifference line.

Regardless of whether we want to minimize costs or maximize

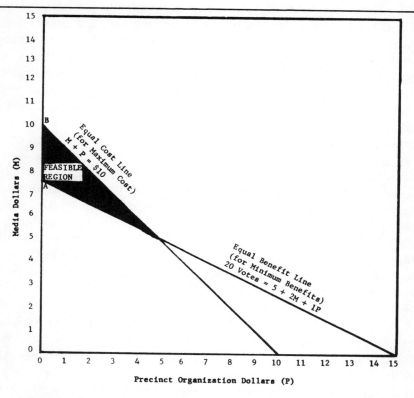

Point A is where total cost is minimized while providing at least 20 votes.
M = $ 7.50   P = $0   TC = $ 7.50   Votes = 20

Point B is where votes are maximized while not spending more than $10.
M = $10.00   P = $0   TC = $10.00   Votes = 25

Figure 2: ALLOCATING MEDIA DOLLARS AND PRECINCT DOLLARS TO MINIMIZE
COSTS OR MAXIMIZE VOTES (with constant returns to dollars spent)

benefits, the ideal combination has to be below the maximum cost
line. Likewise, it has to be above the minimum benefit line. This
means the ideal combination has to be a point somewhere in Figure 2
within the area marked "feasible region" since that is the only area
where both constraints are satisfied simultaneously.

Point A (where M = $7.50 and P = $0) is the point where total
cost is minimized while providing at least 20 votes. This is so because
that is the point farthest away from the maximum cost line that is

still within the feasible region. By only spending $7.50, we save $2.50 for the next election or for other worthwhile causes. Point B (where M = $10 and P = $0) is the point where votes are maximized while not spending more than $10. This is so because that is the point farthest away from the minimum benefit line that is still within the feasible region. At that point, 25 votes will be obtained since the number of votes obtained equals 5 + 2M + 1P. One may wish to obtain these extra votes as insurance against miscalculation or in order to claim a mandate for an aggressive political program or for ego gratification.[8]

Note that the minimum benefits line represents a binding constraint on cost minimization in the sense that if we did not need to get at least 20 votes we could save additional money. The money we are not saving by virtue of that constraint can be considered an opportunity cost. Likewise note that the maximum cost line represents a binding constraint on benefit maximization in the sense that if we did not need to limit ourselves to $10 we could obtain additional votes up to 39 votes. The votes we are not obtaining by virtue of that constraint can also be considered an opportunity cost.

An alternative way of interpreting the optimizing in Figure 2 is to use concepts from production and consumption economics. With those concepts one recognizes that point A is the cost minimization point because there is a family of parallel equal cost lines with one for every possible total cost, and point A is the point where the lowest equal cost line is located which just touches the minimum benefit line. This point can be thought of as the point where the producer of votes minimizes his total costs in allocating his budget to two factors of production, namely, media dollars and precinct organization dollars, analogous to labor and capital. Likewise, point B is the benefit maximization point because there is a family of equal benefit lines for every possible total vote, and point B is the point where the highest equal benefit line is located which just touches the maximum cost line. This point can be thought of as the point where the consumer purchasing media and precinct organization units maximizes his total utility by optimally allocating his budget between these two consumer goods, analogous to food and clothing.

VARIATIONS AND ALTERNATIVES TO THE BASIC SCHEME

It should be noted that one cannot in our illustration maximize: benefits minus costs. This is so because we do not know how many dollars we or our candidate considers a given vote to be worth. If one vote is worth $1, then point B maximizes benefits minus costs better than point A since 25 votes x $1 (minus $10 in costs) is more than 20 votes x $1 (minus $7.50). If, however, one vote is worth only $0.45, then point B maximizes benefits minus costs *worse* than point A since 25 votes x $.45 (minus $10 in costs) is *less* than 20 votes x $.45 (minus $7.50 in costs). Unless one can somehow convert a non-monetary benefit like votes into monetary units, one may have to choose between the goals of minimizing total costs or maximizing total benefits rather than trying to combine these two goals together.

Although one cannot (1) simultaneously minimize costs and maximize benefits or (2) maximize benefits minus costs, one can arrive at a compromise position between minimizing costs and maximizing benefits. Thus, with the data from Figure 2, one can choose an M of $8.75, which is the midpoint between $7.50 (the cost minimization position) and $10.00 (the benefit maximization position). Doing so will mean a midpoint or compromise P of $0, TC of $8.75, and 22.5 votes.

In some linear programming problems, the activity variables cannot be allowed to go as low as $0 as we allowed them to do here. For example, in our problem, perhaps our candidate might insist on a minimum expenditure of $2 for precinct organization in order to preserve the precinct machinery which is needed for liaison work with his constituents between elections. This would mean drawing a vertical line in Figure 2 up from the $2 precinct organization point to the top of the graph, thereby narrowing the feasible region and shifting it to the right. If such a constraint existed in our problem, then the new cost minimization point would be to spend $2 for precinct organization and $6.50 for media. The $6.50 is needed to bring the total expenditure up high enough to obtain 20 votes in light of the equation, 20 votes = 5 + 2M + 1P. Likewise, if such a constraint existed in our problem, the new benefit maximization point would be to spend $2 for precinct organization and $8 for media. Such a combination will mean spending our full $10 in order to obtain 23 votes in light of the equation, votes obtained = 5 + 2M + 1P.

An alternative way of expressing the same ideas shown in Figure 2 (that is more like the nonexpenditure correlation analysis model previously presented) is to plot four separate graphs for the two goal variables and the two policy variables.[9] The first graph would show total cost as a goal or dependent variable on the vertical axis and precinct dollars as a policy or independent variable on the horizontal axis. One would then plot the relation TC = 7.5 + .5P, which follows from the fact that TC = M + P and M = (20 − 5 − P)/2. Doing so indicates total cost is at a minimum at $7.50 with 20 votes where P - $0. The second graph would show total cost against media dollars by plotting the relation TC = 15 − M, which follows from TC = M + P and P = 20 − 5 − 2M. Doing so also indicates that total cost is at a minimum at $7.50 where M = $7.50, provided neither P nor M can be negative. The third graph would show total votes against precinct dollars by plotting Votes = 25 − P, which follows from Votes = 5 + 2M + 1P and M = 10 − P. Doing so indicates that total votes are at a 25-vote maximum when $0 are spent for P, which means the whole $10 is being spent for M. The fourth graph would show total votes against media dollars by plotting Votes = 15 + M, which follows from Votes = 5 + 2M + 1P and P = 10 − M. Doing that also indicates total votes are at a maximum of 25 when M = $10.

To make our expenditure allocation problem somewhat more realistic, although somewhat more complicated, we could change the minimum benefit line to reflect the fact that incremental expenditures of either media or precinct organization dollars do not bring equally incremental votes. Instead, additional dollars spent tend to produce additional votes at a decreasing rate by virtue of the fact that additional votes, at least beyond a certain point, become harder to get. (For an analysis of some aspects of curvilinear correlation, see Nagel, 1963.) A minimum benefit equation reflecting this phenomena (and at the same time indicating that media dollars are more potent vote getters than precinct organization dollars) would be 20 votes = $5 \cdot \sqrt[2]{M} \cdot \sqrt[3]{P}$.

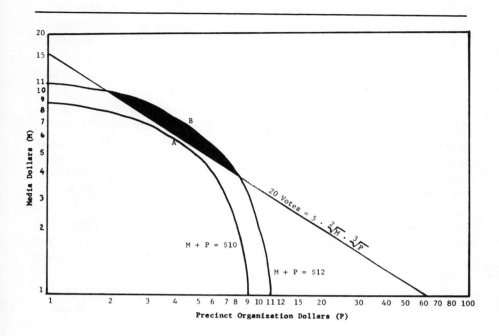

Point A is where total cost is minimized while providing at least 20 votes.
    M = $6.20   P = $4.15   TC = $10.35   **Votes = 20**

Point B is where votes are maximized while not spending more than $12
    M = $7.23   P = $4.77   TC = $12.00   **Votes = 23**

Figure 3: ALLOCATING MEDIA DOLLARS AND PRECINCT DOLLARS TO MINIMIZE COSTS OR MAXIMIZE VOTES (with diminishing returns to dollars spent)

Figure 3 shows this new diminishing-returns minimum benefit line as a straight line because it is drawn on logarithmic interval paper rather than equal interval paper. The $10 maximum cost line comes out to be a curved line rather than a straight line on logarithmic interval paper. Logarithmic interval paper is used because it converts the equation $20 = 5 \cdot \sqrt[2]{M} \cdot \sqrt[3]{P}$ into a straight line which makes it much easier to plot. Note that there is no point on the $10 maximum cost line which touches the minimum benefit line and therefore, there is no combination of M and P adding up to less than $10 which will achieve 20 votes with this new minimum benefit line.

In order to create a feasible region, a $12 maximum cost line is also shown. The feasible region is then logically at or beneath the $12 maximum cost line and also at or above the 20-vote minimum benefit line. The cost minimization point A is at the point on the minimum benefit line furthest away from the $12 cost line or closest to the $10 cost line. It just so happens that this is the point where $6.20 is spent for media and $4.15 is spent for precinct organization. This exact allocation was determined by using simple differential calculus, but one can make an accurate enough estimate by carefully examining the graph, especially if more detailed one-cycle logarithmic graph paper is used. The benefit maximization point B is at the point on the maximum cost line furthest away from the minimum benefit line. This is the point where $7.23 is spent for media and $4.77 is spent for precinct organization. This exact allocation was also determined by using differential calculus, but again, one can make a reasonably accurate estimate from the graph or a more detailed version of it.[10]

To ease the work involved in linear programming, there are now available many canned computer routines that only require a simple statement of the constraints to satisfy and the goals to optimize in order to calculate the optimum allocation points for two or more expenditure alternatives. Unfortunately, such computer routines are not so readily available for the diminishing returns or nonlinear programming problem, but it can often be handled either graphically or with the aid of an electronic calculator for doing the calculus arithmetic involved. Computer routines for doing linear and non-linear regression analysis are helpful for determining the benefit constraint equations. (For further discussion of the linear programming approach to making expenditure policy choices, see Laidlaw, 1972; Baumol, 1965: 70-102; Nagel, 1973b.)

THE NEED FOR REFINEMENTS AND APPLICATIONS

In many expenditure policy problems, the goal or benefits variable is not as easy to measure as votes are. Nevertheless, there are a number of imaginative ways to measure psychological satisfaction or other goal variables. (On measuring benefits and costs of public policies, see Black, 1968: 37-89; Dorfman, 1964; Alberts, 1970; Guilford, 1954: 154-301.) Goal measurement problems are involved in both expenditure and nonexpenditure policies. They are generally not as difficult to handle as the broader problem which this article has emphasized of relating means or policies to goals in making policy choices.

Many further refinements can be developed on the basic methodological techniques presented here for choosing among nonexpenditure and expenditure policies. What is especially needed, however, is not so much additional methodological refinements, but rather the application of these existing methodologies to more public policy controversies by social scientists, policy appliers, and policymakers.

NOTES

1. The distinction between legalization policies and expenditure policies made in this article is closely related to the distinction between regulatory and distributive policies made by Lowi (1964) and the distinction between legal and economic policies made by Szanton (1973). This distinction is also partly one between policies that are primarily dichotomous versus those that are measured on a continuous interval scale.

2. Unstandardized regression weights statistically hold constant the influence of other variables, but so do partial correlation coefficients and standardized regression weights (Blalock, 1972b: 429-458). The difference between the two upper percentages in Table 2 is closer to the regression weight of X (as the independent variable) and Y (as the dependent variable) in the table than the correlation coefficient of X and Y (Blalock, 1972b: 294, 385). The correlation coefficient equals the regression weight if both variables have the same spread or dispersion (Blalock, 1972b: 384). The closer the standard deviations of the two variables, the more useful the *correlation* is for predicting Y from X, but not the correlation squared although it more accurately indicates the percent of variation on Y accounted for by X (Mueller et al., 1970: 315-319).

3. For another more concrete, less abstract example of the use of the correlation approach in making nonexpenditure policy choices, see Nagel (1973a).

4. Wherever the equations use $B - C$, one can substitute B/C if the benefit and costs are not measured in the same units. The $B - C$ calculation, however, is more meaningful if the same units are used, since one is more interested in maximizing total profits (that is, $B - C$) than in maximizing the profit rate (that is, B/C). See McKean (1966: 35-37, 46-47).

5. The correlation coefficients or regression weights can be treated roughly, as probabilities are in decision theory under risk. In the regression approach, $Y = a + bX$ where a linear relation is present, and $\text{Log } Y = \text{Log } a + b\text{LogX}$ where a nonlinear relation is present.

In the probability approach, EU or expected utility equals the probability of the occurrence (or nonoccurrence) of some crucial intervening Z event times the +X payoff (or −X payoff). EU is like Y, probability like b, and the X payoff is like X.

6. In situation 1, our decision choices are to choose $+X_1$ or $-X_1$. If the percentage of $+X_1$ places which are $+Y_a$ is greater than the percentage of $-X_1$ places which are $+Y_a$, then choose $+X_1$. Those percentages stated as decimals can be considered the payoffs. In situation 2, the choices are $+X_1$ $+X_2$; $+X_1$ $-X_2$; $-X_1$ $+X_2$; and $-X_1$ $-X_2$. Choose whichever one of those four choices gives the highest percentage of $+Y_a$. Alternative one, however, is impossible if we cannot have both X_1 and X_2. Alternative four is also impossible if we cannot reject both X_1 and X_2. Alternative two says prefer X_1, and alternative three says prefer X_2. In situation 3 we have to choose between $+X_1$ and $-X_1$ as in situation 1. Choose $+X_1$ if the $+X_1$ places have a higher average score on $W_a \cdot Y_a + W_b \cdot Y_b$ or on $Y_a^{W_a} \cdot Y_b^{W_b}$ than the average score of the $-Y_1$ places on those same dependent variable measures. The same payoff approach is used in situation 4 as in situation 3 except the decision choices are the same as those in situation 2.

7. The Nagel (1966) article mainly deals with the statistical manipulation of dichotomous policy and goal variables that have been coded 1 for present and 0 for absent.

8. If the regression weight of P were greater than the regression weight of M, then the minimum benefits line would intersect the vertical axis above the maximum cost line rather than below it. In other words, the minimum benefits line would be substantially steeper, thereby showing that just a little change in P is needed to offset a relatively big change in M to hold votes constant. In Figure 2, however, just a little change in M is needed to offset a relatively big change in P to hold votes constant. The consequences of such a shift in the relative slopes and positions of the linear constraints are to (1) shift the feasible region to the lower portion of the hourglass figure, (2) shift minimization point A to the intersection of the P axis with the minimum benefits line, and (3) shift the benefits maximization point B to the intersection of the P axis with the maximum TC line.

9. Graphing a goal variable against a policy variable (rather than graphing the policy variables against each other as in linear programming) is what might be referred to as an optimum level rather than an optimum mix approach. The optimum level approach especially lends itself to the use of differential calculus (where curved line relations are involved) for finding the slope of the goal variable with respect to the policy variable, setting this slope equal to zero, and then algebraically solving to find the optimum position on the policy variable.

10. To make a calculus determination of M at the cost minimization point, find the slope of the equation $TC = M + P$, with $(20/(5 \cdot \sqrt[2]{M}))^3$ substituted for P. Then set the expression for the slope equal to zero, and solve for M. To make a calculus determination of M at the votes maximization point, find the slope of the equation $V = 5 \cdot \sqrt[2]{M} \cdot \sqrt[3]{P}$, with $10 - M$ substituted for P. Then set the expression for the slope equal to zero, and solve for M (Richmond, 1968: 40-66 and 577).

REFERENCES

AGRANOFF, R. (1972) The New Style in Election Campaigns. Boston: Holbrook.
ALBERTS, D. (1970) A Plan for Measuring the Performance of Social Programs: The Application of Operations Research Methodology. New York: Praeger.

BAUMOL, W. (1965) Economic Theory and Operations Analysis. Englewood Cliffs, N.J.: Prentice-Hall.

BLACK, G. (1968) The Application of Systems Analysis to Government Operations. New York: Praeger.

BLALOCK, H. (1972a) Causal Models in the Social Sciences. Chicago: Aldine.

——— (1972b) Social Statistics. New York: McGraw-Hill.

——— (1964) Causal Inferences in Nonexperimental Research. Chapel Hill: University of North Carolina Press.

——— (1960) Social Statistics. New York: McGraw-Hill.

CAMPBELL, D. (1969) "Reforms as experiments." American Psychologist 24: 409-429.

CHURCHMAN, C. W., R. L. ACKOFF and E. L. ARNOFF (1957) Introduction to Operations Research. New York: John Wiley.

DORFMAN, R. (1964) Measuring Benefits in Government Investments. Washington, D.C.: Brookings.

DRAPER, N. R. and H. SMITH (1966) Applied Regression Analysis. New York: John Wiley.

GUILFORD, J. P. (1954) Psychometric Methods. New York: McGraw-Hill.

KRAMER, G. (1966) "A decision-theoretic analysis of a problem in political campaigning." Mathematical Applications in Political Science. Arnold Foundation.

LAFAVE, W. (1965) "Improving police performance through the exclusionary rule." Missouri Law Review 30: 391.

LAIDLAW, C. (1972) Linear Programming for Urban Development Plan Evaluation. New York: Praeger.

LOWI, T. (1964) "American business, public policy, case studies, and political theory." World Politics 16: 677-715.

McKEAN, R. (1966) Efficiency in Government Through Systems Analysis. New York: John Wiley.

MILLER, D. and M. STARR (1960) Executive Decisions and Operations Research. Englewood Cliffs, N.J.: Prentice-Hall.

MUELLER, J., K. SCHUESSER and H. COSTNER (1970) Statistical Reasoning in Sociology. Boston: Houghton Mifflin.

NAGEL, S. (1973a) Comparing Elected and Appointed Judicial Systems. Beverly Hills, Calif.: Sage Professional Paper in American Politics 04-001.

——— (1973b) Minimizing Costs and Maximizing Benefits in Providing Legal Services to the Poor. Beverly Hills, Calif.: Sage Professional Paper in Administrative & Policy Studies 03-011.

——— (1966) "Optimizing legal policy." University of Florida Law Review 18: 577-590.

——— (1965) "Testing the effects of excluding illegally seized evidence." Wisconsin Law Review 1965: 283-310.

——— (1963) "Simplified curvilinear correlation." (mimeographed paper available from the author)

——— and J. McCARTHY (1974) "Rationally allocating campaign and governmental expenditures among geographical districts." (mimeographed paper available from the author)

OAKS, D. (1970) "Studying the exclusionary rule in search and seizure." University of Chicago Law Review 37: 665-757.

PREST, A. R. and R. TURVEY (1965) "Cost-benefit analysis: a survey." Economics Journal 75: 683-735.

RICHMOND, S. (1968) Operations Research for Management Decisions. New York: Ronald Press.

SZANTON, P. (1973) "Public policy and law: legal training as 'perverse' preparation for policy-making role in government." Antitrust Law and Economics Review 6: 51-66.

PART III

APPLICATIONS TO CRIME CONTROL

7

PROBLEMS IN THE USE OF EVALUATION IN LAW ENFORCEMENT AND CRIMINAL JUSTICE

JOHN A. GARDINER

University of Illinois,
Chicago Circle

Since 1968, as substantial federal funding has started to flow to state and local government agencies to improve law enforcement and criminal justice, interest has grown in the development of methods to determine the effectiveness of crime control programs. Funding sources, both public and private, are becoming increasingly interested in identifying the effects of their programs and projects and in estimating the relative merits of alternative approaches to basic problems. The tool of evaluation has yet, however, to play a major role in the management of criminal justice programs. (For an analysis of the varying forms and levels of evaluation used in 1972 by the state planning agencies which allocate LEAA—that is, Law Enforcement Assistance Administration—crime control funds, see Kimberling and Fryback, 1973. A general description of practices as of 1974 is provided in LEAA Evaluation Policy Task Force, 1974.) Explanations for this limited role vary: in part it reflects our limited understanding of the nature of crime and of the relationship between crime and the programs designed to reduce it. Lacking accepted models on which to judge program performance, managers tend to seek only simpler indicators of the operational characteristics of their programs. In at least equal measure, however, the nonutilization of evaluation can be explained by the relatively minor role played by goal orientations in criminal justice management: preoccupied with day-to-day managerial duties and responses to crises, managers are seldom disposed to invest in in-depth reviews of programmatic successes and failures. (For illustrations of the conflicts which can develop between police administrators and program evaluators, see Bloch, 1973.)

The three articles which follow deal in different ways with fundamental issues in the evaluation of criminal justice programs. By way of introduction, let me briefly describe several basic problems confronting researchers and agency leaders working in this area of evaluation.

(1) *What are the goals of criminal justice agencies?* Evaluation of a government agency or program must be in terms of its performance against some set of expectations or goals, whether stated or unstated, whether those of the evaluator or of the agency.[1] In the case of almost every criminal justice program, goals are vague, overlapping, and frequently contradictory. At the broadest level, the results or *outcomes* of programs, police agencies are expected to prevent or reduce crime, provide various social services, protect individual liberties, and increase the public's sense of security. The judicial system—courts, prosecutors, and defense attorneys—is expected to protect the innocent, convict the guilty, and generally observe concepts of fairness and justice. The goals of correctional agencies relate to both society at large (put dangerous criminals out of circulation, prevent future recidivism, and vindicate social mores) and the individual offenders under their control (provide medical, psychological, and training services, rehabilitate offenders, and act justly and fairly).

In addition to these outcome goals, criminal justice agencies have a set of product or *output* goals—arrests made, traffic tickets written, service calls made, indictments issued, convictions and acquittals, and the like.[2] Finally, each agency has a set of *input* and *process* goals concerning the way it conducts its activities. In addition to basic questions of costs and manpower, measures have been developed relating to police response time (the time between the reporting of a crime and the officer's arrival at the scene), trial delay, training standards, provision of counsel, and so on.

It is readily apparent that there will often be conflicts among these goals, both among different levels of goals (outcomes, outputs, and the like) and among different goals at each level. A patrol program designed to reduce crime might take manpower away from answering service calls; a "stop and frisk" policy to increase arrest rates may well increase charges of police brutality. For the person attempting to evaluate a criminal justice program, the point is *not* that he should attempt to find a clear and unambiguous set of goals in the program being studied, but rather that he must be sensitive to the varying effects of the program along many different lines.

(2) *What are the indicators of program success or failure?* Once the evaluator has selected a set of goals against which to evaluate an agency or program, he must select indicators which will reflect the degree to which these goals are being met. For many reasons, as will be illustrated in the articles which follow, this is particularly difficult in the field of criminal justice. First, at least as compared with such policy areas as housing or employment, there is less data available for use in research or evaluation in the criminal justice area; what data is available has often been collected for basic managerial purposes and cannot easily be adapted to answer evaluation questions. (Until managers recognize evaluation as a valuable management tool, of course, it is unlikely that they will start to collect useful data.)

A second obstacle to the development of useful program indicators lies in the fact that many relevant events only become known if someone chooses to report them.[3] In the area of "victimless" crime, the volume of gamblers, drug users, and clients of loan sharks and prostitutes is unknown unless they are arrested. Victims of more serious crimes are unknown unless they report the offense to the police;[4] the President's Commission on Law Enforcement and Administration of Justice (1967) and the recent LEAA victimization surveys estimate that approximately one-half of all major crimes are never reported to the police. Similarly, when we attempt to measure the success of correctional programs, we only learn of those recidivists who are arrested by the police, an unknown proportion of the total number of recidivists among program graduates. If we witness a rise in reported crime or in re-arrests of former offenders, therefore, it is virtually impossible to tell whether this represents a real increase in crime or recidivism (suggesting program failure) or merely more accurate reporting of a stable (or possibly even declining) problem. Indeed, it has been argued that increased reporting of crime or police brutality and corruption may be a sign of program *successes,* at least in the sense of increased public confidence in the willingness and ability of the system to act.

A third limitation on indicators in criminal justice is that some goals are essentially unquantifiable. Progress toward such goals as civility, fairness, justice, decency, and humanity cannot be readily scored on data sheets. In a desire to focus on "objective" and machine-readable "events," we often omit the sounds, smells, sights, atmospheres, and other minutiae which are part of real-life situations. Pedestrian as they may sound, among the most desirable changes in criminal justice may be the re-introduction of courtesy in official contacts with citizens; reduction of noise levels in courtrooms so that defendants, witnesses, and others can hear what is happening; diminution of the oppressive fear of violence (guard against inmate, inmate against guard, inmate against inmate) which pervades prisons, and so on. Unless program evaluations capture the aura of these perceptible but unquantifiable phenomena, they rapidly run the danger of substituting measurable but minor indicators for unmeasurable indicators of more important issues.[5]

(3) *What is the contribution of criminal justice agency activities to the attainment of criminal justice goals?* Even after we establish sets of goals, indicators of progress toward those goals, and indicators of agency or program inputs, a major conceptual as well as methodological problem remains in developing causal models on the basis of which we can attribute changes in outcome levels (crime rates, recidivism rates, and the like) to the effects of particular

programs. Simply stated, the efforts of criminal justice agencies constitute only a few of many factors affecting crime rates or other outcome measures. Other factors which are assumed to contribute to these rates include biological and psychological characteristics of the population, family stability, housing conditions, employment opportunities, the weather, cultural patterns, and steps taken by individuals to reduce their potential for victimization. Not only do we know little about the separate contributions of each of these factors to aggregate outcome indicators; there is also some evidence that they have differential impacts on various types of offenders (Glaser, 1973). If the crime rate in the central business district declines after the police introduce a new patrol system, it is seldom safe to rule out the alternative possibilities that some or all of the decline was caused by a drug treatment program, a changing job market, new streetlights, or a television campaign to persuade store owners to install burglar alarms. If the graduates of a correctional program are not returned to prison, is it because the program changed their outlook on life, because they were able to find a satisfactory job, because they were now too old to hustle success- fully, or were they simply not apprehended by the police? While much can and has been done to rule out spurious correlations and reduce the number of alternative explanations available (see, e.g., Glaser, 1973; Maltz, 1972; Zimring, 1973), often the most that can be said is that we cannot rule out the possibility that the program reduced crime.[6]

The three articles which follow apply a variety of techniques to cope with these issues. In "Complementary Measures of Police Performance," Roger B. Parks utilizes both official statistics and citizen surveys to estimate police performance levels in 45 neighbor- hoods in the St. Louis metropolitan area. In the second article, Solomon Kobrin and Steven G. Lubeck address problems involved in the specification and measurement of the goals of crime control, the responses of criminal justice agencies, and the predictive contri- butions of social and demographic characteristics of the jurisdictions being studied. Finally, Michael Kelly considers problems inherent in the evaluation of pre-trial release programs and the weaknesses of available quantitative data as guides to the institutional realities of lower court activities.

NOTES

1. This is not to say that individual agency leaders are necessarily guided by these goals. Some may articulate different goals; others may be guided more by constraints of personal or organizational survival.

2. For a review and analysis of problems involved in measuring the outputs of *court* systems, see Eisenstein and Jacob (1973). Output and outcome measures for *police* programs are summarized and analyzed by Maltz (1972 and 1973) and Ostrom (1973).

3. In some cases, as when the purposes of the evaluation can be served by less than comprehensive data bases, it is feasible for the evaluator to go out and collect his own data relating to these events. Gardiner (1969), Reiss (1971), Rubinstein (1973), and Wilson (1968), for example, make extensive use of participant observation as a basis for characterizations of the behavior of police agencies.

4. This problem will to some extent be alleviated by the LEAA-sponsored victimization surveys being conducted by the Bureau of the Census. While these surveys will give a more accurate picture of true rates of common crimes on a national level, sample sizes generally are not adequate for evaluations of neighborhood-level crime control programs, but offer extensive data at the city level for Atlanta, Baltimore, Chicago, Cleveland, Dallas, Denver, Detroit, Los Angeles, Newark, New York, Philadelphia, Portland (Oregon), and St. Louis.

5. The most effective portrayals of these matters can be found in the documentary films which have been made in the last five years on police, court, and prison life. Rubinstein (1973) offers the most effective verbal portrayal to date of the working environment of policing.

6. For a thoughtful discussion of the use of experiments and demonstrations to test these issues in the police area, see Lewis (1972).

REFERENCES

BLOCH, P. B. (1973) "Implementing police programs to determine their effectiveness: the cases of team policing and policewomen." Presented at the annual meeting of the American Political Science Association, September 4-8, New Orleans.

EISENSTEIN, J. and H. JACOB (1973) "Measuring performance and outputs of criminal courts." Presented at the annual meeting of the American Political Science Association, September 4-8, New Orleans.

GARDINER, J. A. (1969) Traffic and the Police. Cambridge: Harvard University Press.

GLASER, D. (1973) Routinizing Evaluation: Getting Feedback on Effectiveness of Crime and Delinquency Programs. Washington, D.C.: Government Printing Office.

KIMBERLING, W. C. and J. T. FRYBACK (1973) "Systematic evaluation of criminal justice projects: a state of the art in the United States." Journal of Criminal Justice 1 (Summer): 145-160.

LEAA Evaluation Policy Task Force (1974) Report. Washington, D.C.: Law Enforcement Assistance Administration.

LEWIS, J. H. (1972) Evaluation of Experiments in Policing: How do you Begin? Washington, D.C.: Police Foundation.

MALTZ, M. D. (1973) "Output measures for crime control programs." Presented at the annual meeting of the American Political Science Association, September 4-8, New Orleans.

––– (1972) Evaluation of Crime Control Programs. Washington, D.C.: Government Printing Office for the National Institute of Law Enforcement and Criminal Justice.

OSTROM, E. (1973) "On the meaning and measurement of output and efficiency in the provision of urban police services." Journal of Criminal Justice 1 (Summer): 93-112.

President's Commission on Law Enforcement and Administration of Justice, Task Force on Assessment (1967) Crime and its Impact—An Assessment. Washington, D.C.: Government Printing Office.

REISS, A. J., Jr., (1971) The Police and the Public. New Haven: Yale University Press.

RUBINSTEIN, J. (1973) City Police. New York: Farrar, Straus & Giroux.

WILSON, J. Q. (1968) Varieties of Police Behavior. Cambridge: Harvard University Press.

ZIMRING, F. (1973) Deterrence: The Legal Threat to Crime Control. Chicago: University of Chicago Press.

8

COMPLEMENTARY MEASURES OF
POLICE PERFORMANCE

Indiana University

The provision of public goods and services is a multi-billion dollar industry in contemporary America. In fiscal 1971 local governments alone spent over $100 billion in providing goods and services to their citizenry (Bureau of the Census, 1971: 21). The public nature of these goods and services poses very serious difficulties for the analyst

AUTHOR'S NOTE: *An earlier version of this article was presented at the 1973 annual meeting of the American Political Science Association in New Orleans. The research upon which this article is based was funded by the Center for Studies of Metropolitan Problems of the National Institute of Mental Health under Grant 5 RO1 MH 19911-02. The Urban Affairs Center of Indiana University provided additional funding. A research grant from the National Science Foundation (RANN) has provided the opportunity to pursue the multiple indicator approach further. The author is most appreciative of this support. The merits of this article are due to a large extent to the comments and criticisms of John Hamilton, James McDavid, Nancy Neubert, Elinor Ostrom, Dennis Smith, Virginia Fielder, and Patti Goldammer, and to Vincent and Elinor Ostrom who brought all of us together in the Workshop in Political Theory and Policy Analysis at Indiana University. Additional comments which have helped in clarifying this revision were provided by Stephen L. Wasby.*

who wishes to evaluate such industries or individual firms (local governments) within them.[1] Public goods and services are demanded and supplied in the context of a variety of institutional arrangements—arrangements which are designed to compensate for the weakness or failure of market decision-making arrangements when confronted with situations of joint supply and/or consumption (Bator, 1958; Buchanan, 1968; V. Ostrom, Tiebout and Warren, 1961). Problems are posed on the demand side, both to the provider and the analyst, by (1) possible distortions in the communication of demands to suppliers, (2) the necessity to aggregate disparate demands, and (3) potential incentives to falsify preferences for goods and services endemic to such arrangements (Bowen, 1943; Buchanan, 1968). On the supply side, to which this article is addressed, serious questions arise as to the identification of the product or products and the measurement of the quantity and quality of such products when identified (Hirsch, 1968; E. Ostrom, 1971; Ridley and Simon, 1938).

In the study of agencies providing a physical output (water supply, for example) or performing an observable and quantifiable operation (refuse collection) one may apply many of the analytic tools of economics and management science directly to questions of how much output is produced, what quality of service is provided, and at what cost (Hirsch, 1968: 478-479; E. Ostrom, 1971; Blair and Schwartz, 1972). The raison d'etre of program budgeting systems has been to foster such application (Joint Economic Committee, 1969). However, in dealing with more complex services such as police, one must obtain a series of indicators to identify the products and to deal with questions of the quantity, quality, and cost of these products (Shoup and Mehay, 1971; Operations Research Task Force, 1972).

This article focuses upon multiple indicators of the quantity and quality of outputs of agencies providing neighborhood police services. "Policing" provides an excellent illustration of the problems of measurement in the public sector; it is a highly complex congeries of activities, with little agreement upon the identification of outputs or upon measures of quantity and quality. The restriction to neighborhood police services—patrol, criminal investigation, response to service calls, and other activities of police in predominantly residential neighborhoods—provides a common perspective. This comparable unit of analysis enables one to analyze the activities of departments varying widely in scale of operation, degree of special-ization, availability of resources, and other distinguishing charac-teristics. It is safe to say that most local police departments, regardless of other activities in which they engage, allocate a large portion of their efforts to providing police services to residential neighborhoods.

In a recent study of police services provided to residential neighborhoods in the St. Louis, Missouri, metropolitan area (E. Ostrom, Parks, and Smith, 1973), operational measures of police performance were obtained from a variety of sources, for a variety of indicators of police output.[2] Sources included central record-keeping systems, municipal police and budgetary files, published statistics, and interviews conducted with more than 700 police officers and almost 4,000 residents. Measures included (1) those directly related to crime (crime and clearance rates, rates of warrant issuance by prosecutors), (2) "style" measures with implied per-formance consequences (officers' training and education, special-ization of department), (3) "input" measures often used as output proxies (full-time officers per 1,000 population, expenditures per capita), (4) direct measures of police activities (calls for service answered per 1,000 population, "density" of patrol provided, extent of follow-up to reported crimes), and (5) measures derived from citizen-consumer experiences with the police in their neighborhoods and their perceptions and evaluations of the services provided by those police.

These are not all indicators of a common product. If they were, they should be highly correlated and thus only one or two could be chosen for convenience. Rather they are indicators of different facets of policing, some closely related and others not so. This diversity of indicators can help to avoid the problem of goal distortion which arises from over-measurement of only a few aspects of organizational performance. As Etzioni (1964: 9-10) notes:

> Curiously, the very effort—the desire to establish how we are doing and to
> find ways of improving if we are not doing as well as we ought to

do—often has quite undesired effects from the point of view of organizational goals. Frequent measuring can distort the organizational efforts because, as a rule, some aspects of its outputs are more measureable than the others. Frequent measuring tends to encourage over-production of highly measureable items and the neglect of less measurable ones. . . . The distortion consequences of over-measuring are larger when it is impossible or impractical to quantify the more central, substantive output of an organization, and when at the same time some exterior aspects of the product, which are superficially related to its substance, are readily measurable.

Since the operational measures are gathered from a variety of independent sources, they can contribute to the avoidance of pathologies of goal displacement inherent in self-measurement (Likert, 1961; Etzioni, 1964; Skolnick, 1966; Hoffman, 1971; E. Ostrom, 1971). They can help to prevent an organization from turning inward upon activities of primarily internal relevance (Selznick, 1943). They will be somewhat less likely to encourage organization members to engage in activities which may improve their "score" on internal measures at some expense to organization output (Peter and Hull, 1969: 43-44; Hoffman, 1971: 11).

A final consideration supports the use of varied indicators, and principally of multiple measures within each type of indicator. Public sector performance indicators are generally quite complex conceptually. Operational measures developed for such indicators will have various degrees and types of error, if not due to inherent biases, then to the vagaries of the measurement process itself. Faced with this, the analyst is forced to rely upon the simultaneous use of a series of such error-prone measures.

. . . the operational implication of the inevitable theoretical complexity of every measure . . . calls for multiple operationism, that is, for multiple measures which are hypothesized to share in the theoretically relevant components but have different patterns of irrelevant components. . . . If a proposition can survive the onslaught of a series of imperfect measures, with all their irrelevant error, confidence should be placed in it [Webb et al., 1966: 3].

In the pages to follow, a brief discussion of the research base for this analysis will be presented. This will be followed by a discussion of each of the types of indicators, the operational measures obtained for those indicators, and the relationships among those operational measures. This may contribute to an appreciation of the complexity of police output and will suggest where better operational measures are necessary (Clark, 1972).

RESEARCH BASE

In the spring and summer of 1972 a research group headed by Elinor Ostrom of Indiana University conducted an extensive study of police services provided to a number of neighborhoods in the St. Louis Metropolitan Area.[3] That research and the underlying design have been described at length elsewhere (E. Ostrom, Parks, and Smith, 1973). The discussion here is intended only to present the context in which the operational measures were obtained and to establish some boundaries for warrantable generalization of the findings.

Forty-five neighborhoods were included in the St. Louis study. These neighborhoods consisted of (1) separately incorporated municipalities providing their own police service or contracting for service, (2) census tracts within larger municipalities in St. Louis County, (3) Planning Areas within the City of St. Louis, and (4) urban places within unincorporated areas of St. Louis County. The neighborhoods were predominantly residential in character, of a lower-middle to middle-income status. The 45 neighborhoods were served by 29 different primary police jurisdictions, ranging in size from a low of 2 part-time men to a high of more than 2,200 full-time officers. Their budgets ranged from $14,000 to over $30 million.

An immediate question is whether or not the wide range of variation among police departments allows valid comparison. While this range of variation is found when focusing upon the police departments, the neighborhoods themselves were carefully selected to ensure their comparability. The choice of neighborhoods within a single state and metropolitan area removed many possible sources of variation. Further restrictions were imposed upon the set of all potential sample neighborhoods. At least 60% of the dwelling units had to be owner-occupied, median value of owner-occuped housing

Median Housing Value	Independently Incorporated Communities				St. Louis Neighborhood Planning Areas	St. Louis County	
	500-4,999	5,000-15,999	16,000-28,900	28,901-66,000[c]		Unincorporated Neighborhoods	Communities with Contract Police
$20,900 to $24,999 and $15,000 to $19,999 with rent ≥ $120	1.1 N^a = 275 SA^b = 3	1.2 N = 594 SA = 6	1.3 N = 192 SA = 2	1.4 N = 378 SA = 4	1.5 None in this cell	1.6 N = 79 SA = 1	1.7 N = 81 SA = 1
$10,000 to $14,999 and $15,000 to $19,999 with rent < $120	2.1 N = 178 SA = 2	2.2 N = 276 SA = 3	2.3 N = 409 SA = 4	2.4 N = 333 SA = 4	2.5 N = 589 SA = 7	2.6 N = 108 SA = 2	2.7 N = 309 SA = 4
Less than $10,000	3.1 None in this cell	3.2 N = 115 SA = 2	3.3 None in this cell	3.4 None in this cell	3.5 None in this cell	3.6 None in this cell	3.7 None in this cell

a. = number of respondents interviewed.
b. = number of sample areas included.
c. Neighborhoods were the units of analysis in this community population category.

Figure 1: DISTRIBUTION OF CITIZEN INTERVIEWS

had to be below $25,000, and the resident population could not be highly skewed toward either the old or the young.[4] Neighborhoods remaining after application of these criteria were then stratified into clusters of "similar systems" (Przeworski and Teune, 1970: ch. 2) by considering factors of wealth, size of jurisdiction, and type of organizational arrangements for policing (whether the neighborhood contracted for police services or not). Variations within clusters were minimized with a single exception. We dichotomized neighborhoods within cells into those with greater than 30% black population in 1970 and those with less than that percentage. Sensitivity to this dichotomy in the choosing of sample neighborhoods ensured—to the extent allowed by the existence of appropriate neighborhoods—that we would include a significant sample of black respondents.

Having determined those neighborhoods which were of interest, we proceeded to choose among them on the basis of contiguity in clusters of neighborhoods. This was felt to have been a particular strength in previous research (E. Ostrom, Baugh, Guarasci, Parks, and Whitaker, 1973) and we wished to duplicate it in St. Louis. These considerations allowed the choice of 45 sample areas such that meaningful variations along the dimensions of size and organization for provision of police service, individual wealth within the community, and presence or absence of a sizable black population could be obtained while maintaining the "most similar systems" research design.

Nearly 4,000 interviews were obtained from residents of the neighborhood sample areas. Seven hundred and twelve police officers in departments serving the neighborhoods were interviewed. Extensive budgetary, crime, and calls for service data was obtained from these departments and from central record-keeping sources.[5] The data base constructed from this research effort should prove most valuable in addressing issues of police performance in residential neighborhoods. The distribution of sample neighborhoods and the number of interviews obtained with residents of those neighborhoods are presented in Figure 1.

POLICE PERFORMANCE INDICATORS

The indicators and their operational measures are clustered into five groups. These are (1) the direct crime-related measures, (2) "style" measures, (3) input proxy measures, (4) direct activity measures, and (5) citizen-consumer measures. Throughout the discussions of the operational measures and their interrelationships, their relationship to size of jurisdiction measured in terms of population served will also be presented, providing a common reference for all measures.

DIRECT CRIME-RELATED MEASURES

Traditionally, police activity has been measured in relation to crime. The most prevalent measure of this type is the crime "rate," the number of "Part I" or "index" crimes per 100,000 population (FBI, 1972). Other conventional measures are the clearance rate, the percentage of Part I crimes "cleared by arrest," and the arrest rate, defined on either a population or a per-officer base. A succinct discussion of these three measures can be found in a recent LEAA publication, *Evaluation of Crime Control Programs* (Maltz, 1972: ch. 6).

There are serious problems with these measures, problems which have been documented at length (Sellin and Wolfgang, 1964; Biderman, 1966; E. Ostrom, 1971; Maltz, 1972; Richardson, 1973). With respect to the crime rate, inflation and increasing prosperity contribute to almost certain increases in the amount of property-related crime (Biderman, 1966; Task Force on Assessment, 1967; Jenkins, 1970). Many serious and prevalent crimes are excluded from the index and many that are included go unreported. This leads to biased interpretations of the incidence of both victimization and criminal activity among various social groupings (Wolfgang, 1968; Schur, 1969; E. Ostrom, 1971). The rates computed from the number of index crimes are computed on a population base rather than on a base of number of targets and potential offenders (Boggs, 1965; Maltz, 1972). Increases in the reported crime rate may reflect increased identification with the norms of society or increased belief in police efficacy rather than increases in the extent of crime (Biderman, 1966; Jenkins, 1970; E. Ostrom, 1971; Maltz, 1972). The rate has been shown to be very sensitive to procedural changes (Task Force on Assessment, 1967). Emphasis placed upon the crime rate may provide an incentive to record incidents in such a way as to score well on that measure, an incentive consistent with Etzioni's observation quoted above (Maltz, 1972; Seidman and Couzens, 1972). Use of clearance rate as a measure can lead to similar incentives to detectives to score well, resulting in their bargaining with suspected criminals or offering reduced sentences in return for confessions which result in multiple clearances (Skolnick, 1966: 174-176). This can produce an inverse relationship between amount of crime committed (or admitted) and punishment received. The standard method of computing the clearance rate has been shown to be incorrect, rendering it of questionable usefulness in measuring the probability of apprehending offenders (Hoffman, 1971). Similar problems are found with the arrest rate (Maltz, 1972).

In spite of these difficulties, crime, clearance, and arrest rates continue to be used to measure police activity and police perform-ance (American Bar Association, 1972: 57). Police officials and others often point out that the police cannot be held solely responsible for all crimes that are committed (O. W. Wilson, 1963: 322; J. Q. Wilson, 1968a: 59-60), yet the police are quick to claim credit for reductions (see, as an example, St. Louis Board of Police Commissioners, 1972: 3; or any other police department's reports in years of reductions in rate). The press contributes to the use of falling crime rate as a measure of police success as well as pointing to police failures when the rate increases (St. Louis Post-Dispatch, January 23, 1972, and August 13, 1972, for example). Detectives continue to be judged on their ability to clear cases. Patrolmen often find that a high arrest rate is an asset when seeking promotion.

In the St. Louis neighborhoods studied, there were wide variations in two of the operational measures obtained, crime rate and clearance rate. The number of Part I crimes reported per 100,000 population in the neighborhoods varied from a low of less than 350 to a high of nearly 13,000. Clearance rates reported for Part I crimes ranged from zero to 47%. Obviously, given the discussion above, some of this variation can be attributed to reporting differences and other factors; the measures are imperfect.[6]

Examination of FBI Uniform Crime Reports has shown, generally speaking, that the larger the jurisdiction, the higher the reported crime rate (Wolfgang, 1968: 270; E. Ostrom and Parks, 1973: 377). It has been suggested that these figures are misleading and that one should examine neighborhood crime rates rather than city-wide rates (Jacob, 1973: 24). Using the data from the St. Louis sample neighborhoods,[7] the positive relationship between size of jurisdiction and crime rate found when entire cities are compared is also found when neighborhood crime rates are examined. The positive relationship is only a moderate one ($\gamma = +.36$),[8] but does provide some evidence that, even in comparable neighborhoods, the reported crime rate is higher in those which are part of larger jurisdictions. When size is measured in terms of police manpower rather than population, the association is also moderately positive ($\gamma = +.42$) and slightly stronger, which seems consistent with the common-sense explanation that, other things held equal, jurisdictions with relatively more reported crime will hire relatively more police.

While the positive relationship between reported crime and size of jurisdiction found at the city level is also found when focusing upon neighborhood crime figures, these relationships do not necessarily imply any causal link between size of jurisdiction and the extent of crime. Many alternative explanations would need investigation before any such conclusion might be found warrantable. Yet it is important to note that many of those who argue that larger jurisdictions are needed to fight the growing crime wave in America (for example, CED, 1972, and MLEAC, 1972) use FBI crime rates to document this crime problem, neglecting to mention that these crime statistics indicate that it is precisely in the larger jurisdictions that crime (reported) is most serious. The point here is not to debunk such advocates but rather to suggest further evidence of the need for multiple measures in complex situations.

Another aspect of "crime fighting" is measured by the clearance rate. Here the relationships are quite different. There is a moderate positive association between the clearance rate for Part I crimes and the size of the jurisdiction ($\gamma = +.30$). Looking at clearance rate for property crimes only (burglary, larceny, and auto theft), the positive relationship to jurisdiction size is very strong ($\gamma = +.84$). The same relationships hold when size is measured by number of officers.

These measures and their relationship to size of jurisdiction are consistent with a relationship found in an earlier study of police services in the Indianapolis area (E. Ostrom, Baugh, Guarasci, Parks, and Whitaker, 1973). There it was suggested that a department serving a large jurisdiction expended proportionately higher efforts on after-the-fact activities (criminal investigation) and departments serving smaller jurisdictions expended relatively more on preventive activities (assigned patrol). This was characterized as a difference in "production strategy," with the larger department utilizing a more specialized, task-oriented strategy, and the smaller ones, a patrol-oriented strategy. Of course, most departments are heavily engaged in both, but the direction of emphasis in the St. Louis area seems to be similar to that found in Indianapolis. In St. Louis the association between size of jurisdiction and percent of manpower assigned to patrol activities is substantial ($\gamma = -.65$).

Another operational measure in the direct crime-related set was obtained by computing the number of warrant issuances by prosecutors' warrant offices as a percentage of the applications for such warrants made by officers serving the sample .neighborhoods. This, too, is an imperfect measure. Two different warrant offices interact with the police departments studied, the St. Louis County Prosecutor's with the municipal and county departments and the St. Louis Circuit Attorney's with the police serving the City neighborhoods. Discussions with representatives of these two offices, including the County Prosecutor and the Circuit Attorney themselves, indicate quite similar standards for issuance, yet differences may exist. Other factors, uncontrollable or only partially controllable by the police (the willingness of witnesses to testify is an example), also affect this measure (Smith and Ostrom, 1973). Yet, as with other imperfect measures, it can be used to provide us with additional information about policing.

There is a moderate negative association ($\gamma = -.32$) between number of full-time officers in a jurisdiction and percent of applications for which a warrant was issued. This holds true when

Table 1. DIRECT CRIME-RELATED MEASURES AND
SIZE OF JURISDICTION

	Neighborhood Clearance Rate	Neighborhood Warrants (% Issued)	Size of Jurisdiction (Population Served)
Neighborhood Crime Rate	−.26[a] (37)[b]	−.05 (42)	+.36 (43)
Neighborhood Clearance Rate	−	−.10 (37)	+.30 (37)
Neighborhood Warrants	−	−	−.30 (44)

a. Relationship measured by gamma.
b. Number of neighborhoods for which data was available.

population served is used to measure size ($\gamma = -.30$). On this measure, as on the crime rate measure, large departments are scoring less well than the medium-sized departments. The smaller departments are scattered across the scale from low to high on these measures. Table 1 summarizes the relationships among the measures discussed so far and their relationships to size of jurisdiction measured in terms of population served.

The low or negligible relationships among the three direct crime-related measures suggest that while all three can be thought of as measures of conventional police crime-related output, they are measures of different facets of that activity, providing different information about the quantity and quality of police output.

"STYLE" MEASURES

Measures of the style of police services are of two dominant types. One has to do with the size of the police jurisdiction and with the degree of specialization within the department serving that jurisdiction. Size is generally seen as a prerequisite to higher levels of specialization, which in turn are assumed to be positively related to police output[9] (CED, 1972; McCausland, 1972). Larger jurisdictions are assumed necessary to deal in particular with crime which is "no respecter of antique jurisdictional frontiers" (President's Task Force on Suburban Problems, 1968: 17-18; President's Commission on Law Enforcement and Administration of Justice, 1967). Size of jurisdiction is used as a common reference in this article and will be treated as such here.

The other style measures fall under the rubric of professionalization, principally that of the individual officers within a department. The term professionalization has a variety of meanings ranging from neatness of appearance to extensive training in police-specific skills (Smith, 1971 and forthcoming, discusses the various meanings at length). Here it will be approached operationally by two measures which are generally presumed to be a significant factor in professionalization—extent of police-specific training and extent of college education among police officers serving a jurisdiction (Saunders, 1971; Bittner, 1970; for a different view on college education for police, see J. Q. Wilson, 1968b).

Size of jurisdiction and percent of officers with high police-specific training have a very strong positive relationship ($\gamma = +.74$). This strong relationship is not surprising as it is only in the past two years that all new police officers in most of the departments in St. Louis County have been required to have at least 600 hours of police training (McNary, 1971: 55). Prior to that many officers in County municipalities attended two-week training sessions at the Missouri Highway Patrol Academy, while the City of St. Louis and St. Louis County maintained their own academies with longer periods of training. Officers who were employed in the municipalities at the time of institution of the 600-hour requirement have been permitted to remain under a "grandfather" clause.

The relationship between size of jurisdiction and percent of officers with high amounts of college education is negligible ($\gamma = -.06$). Officers in virtually all of the departments encompassed by our study were encouraged to obtain some college education. The local colleges and junior colleges have been providing police-related college courses for these men and federal funding has been made available to help defray the cost of this education. No relationship exists between percent of officers with a high amount of police-specific training and percent of officers with a high level of college education.

Given the very strong association between size of jurisdiction and training noted here, it is not surprising that similar relations (although in two instances, weaker) are found between percent of officers with high police-specific training and neighborhood crime rate ($\gamma = +.27$), neighborhood clearance rate ($\gamma = +.16$), and success in obtaining warrants ($-.39$). Of perhaps more interest are the directions of the (admittedly low) associations between the percent of a given department's officers with a high level of college education, the crime rate in neighborhoods served by that department ($\gamma = -.27$), and the clearance rate achieved in those neighborhoods ($\gamma = +.15$). There is no association between this education measure and the department's success in obtaining warrants.

INPUT MEASURES

Level of expenditure and expenditures per capita have been employed extensively as measures of public agency output by political scientists and economists (see discussion and citations in Jacob and Lipsky, 1968; Hirsch, 1968; and Bahl, 1969). The ways in which higher expenditures are related to greater output are rarely made explicit in such arguments. Yet the implication is clearly present in many discussions of policing that higher expenditures (and the corollary, more manpower) represent higher output. To the extent that marginal returns do not become negative, this assertion is unimpeachable. But those who so argue rarely use this obvious argument. Rather they imply that marginal returns are positive throughout. A recent statement by the Missouri Law Enforcement Assistance Council deploring lower expenditures and manpower in suburban areas asserts that "in the final analysis, the taxpayer typically gets only what he pays for and this applies to police protection and law enforcement services as well. The compromises made by taxpayers in suburbia have led to low levels of service . . ." (1972: 48). The President's Commission on Law Enforcement and the Administration of Justice (1967: 172) claimed to have seen

impressive evidence that in many cities there are too few policemen . . . it is apparent that more police are needed and that municipalities must face up to the urgency of that need and provide the resources required to meet it if crime is to be controlled.[10]

Expenditures and/or manpower figures are used in many cases because of a superficial comparability which they give to analyses across cities and across time. Their use is most often justified by referring to the inadequacies of any other measures of output for public services. Yet the problems inherent in the use of such fiscal indicators are highlighted by noting that "few citizens or leaders are interested in city expenditures per se; they are more concerned with the level and type of service which the funds can purchase" (Clark, 1972: 11), and that "as administrators sadly know, high expenditures may have little impact" (Jacob and Lipsky, 1968: 516). In order to use expenditures, manpower, or other input measures as reasonable proxies for output and/or performance, it would be necessary to know the production functions for various facets of police activity. These are not well known at present (Shoup and Mehay, 1971; Chapman and Sonenblum, 1972; Votey and Phillips, 1972).

Operational measures of input derived from the St. Louis study are (1) the number of full-time officers per 1,000 residents serving the sample neighborhoods and (2) the per-capita expenditures made in those neighborhoods by departments which serve them. In deriving these measures from police budgets and manpower data, allocation formulae developed in earlier studies were used (E. Ostrom, Baugh, Guarasci, Parks, and Whitaker, 1973). These formulae are quite similar to formulae used in a recent study of manpower and expenditure allocation to sub-areas served by the Los Angeles' County Sheriff (Shoup and Rosett, 1969).

Total departmental expenditures are first allocated to categories of assigned patrol, criminal investigation, and supportive services. The assigned patrol expenditure allocated to a neighborhood is simply the sum of salaries paid to men patrolling that neighborhood. Criminal investigation expenditure is allocated to a neighborhood on the basis of the percentage of city-wide Part I crime reported in that neighborhood. Supportive services expenditures are first allocated to patrol and investigation forces city-wide in the proportion which expenditures for these latter items occupy in the budget and then are allocated to neighborhoods in the same manner as the direct patrol and investigation expenditures. This method of expenditure allocation generally yields estimates lying between those which would be made with either an allocation based strictly on percent of reported crime or one based strictly on percent of calls for service—at least in residential neighborhoods (E. Ostrom, Baugh, Guarasci, Parks, and Whitaker, 1973: 53-57).

Per-capita expenditures ranged from a low of $7 to a high of $53 in the sample neighborhoods. Full-time officers assigned to these neighborhoods varied between zero and 3.5 officers per 1,000 residents. The budget of most police departments is dominated by salary and wage expenditures and so it is not surprising to find a very strong association between these two measures ($\gamma = +.72$). Per-capita expenditure has a substantial positive association with size of the jurisdiction ($\gamma = +.54$), while the positive relationship with manpower assigned is low ($\gamma = +.29$). This would seem to indicate that as jurisdictions increase in size, proportionately less resources are devoted to manpower on the street (at least in residential neighborhoods), a finding consistent with the earlier discussion of production strategies.

Table 2 presents the relationships between those two measures of input and the crime-related output measures discussed above. Both input measures have very strong or substantial positive associations with neighborhood crime rates, low positive relationships with

**Table 2. INPUT MEASURES, CRIME MEASURES, AND
SIZE OF JURISDICTION**

Neighborhood Inputs	Neighborhood Crime Rate	Neighborhood Clearance Rate	Neighborhood Warrants (% Issued)	Size of Jurisdiction (Population Served)
Full-time officers per 1,000 residents	+.79[a] (43)[b]	+.11 (37)	−.04 (44)	+.29 (45)
Expenditures per capita	+.66 (43)	+.21 (37)	−.07 (44)	+.54 (45)

a. Relationship measured by gamma.
b. Number of neighborhoods for which data was available.

clearance rates, and negligible negative associations with warrant issuance. An explanation consistent with these findings is that police departments allocate much of their resources on the basis of reported crimes (although many are now moving to much more complex allocation models: see Larson, 1972; Operations Research Task Force, 1972). Such allocation is seen to have only a minor or negligible effect on other measures of crime-related police activities.

DIRECT ACTIVITY MEASURES

Another approach to identification and measurement of output quantity and quality is to attempt to quantify the amounts of specific activities of various kinds in which a police department is observed to engage. These activities in one sense are the *outputs* of the department; the results obtained from such activities may then be conceptualized as *outcomes* (Clark, 1972). These outcomes are a function of both the activities and the environment in which they are performed (Bradford, Malt, and Oates, 1969), and are therefore only partially amenable to control by the police (Hoffman, 1971).

The two operational measures of direct activity are the average number of patrol officers on duty per 1,000 residents in the sample neighborhoods, a measure of the "density" of patrol activity, and the number of calls for service per 1,000 residents responded to by the police in the neighborhoods. Other direct measures not considered here include the level of traffic control provided and the level of investigative follow-up. Because the focus is on neighborhood level police services, traffic control is of relatively lesser importance. The level of investigative follow-up could not be easily determined from police records. In one sense the clearance rate is a measure of the level of follow-up provided, yet a moment's reflection will show that it is not a direct activity measure but rather the result of direct activities and other factors not subject to police control.

Patrol has been described as the most important activity of a police department (O. W. Wilson, 1963: 231). Patrolling is assumed to contribute significantly to "crime fighting" and to such other "goals" of policing as "order maintenance" and "public service."[11] Recently some questions have been raised as to the extent of patrol efficiency in "crime fighting" (American Bar Association, 1972; Police Foundation, forthcoming; Larson, 1972: 34), with suggestions that this ought to be carefully researched in well-designed experiments. But there is no controversy over whether patrolling is an appropriate activity for police.

There are those who have argued that responding to most calls for service is not proper police activity, that this might better be done by, for example, "Emergency Services, Inc." (J. Q. Wilson, 1968a: 5). Others have noted that response to general service calls represents a large percentage of the activities in which police engage (Bercal, 1970; Parks, 1971), that it would be very costly and on some grounds infeasible to separate out these general service responses from "real police work" (American Bar Association, 1972), and that the police response to general service calls can have positive spillovers into other areas of policing (O. W. Wilson, 1963: 228-289; Terris, 1967). Response to calls for service is viewed here objectively as a significant portion of police activity. For that reason the number of responses per 1,000 residents is taken to be a valid operational measure of police activity.

A key consideration in responding to service calls is response time. Many studies have indicated that very rapid response is a significant factor in police crime-fighting activities (Institute for Defense Analyses, 1967; Operations Research Task Force, 1972). Rapid response would seem equally desirable for other police activities. Unfortunately, in spite of the general agreement that rapid response is a very important aspect of police service, many departments, including large departments, have not kept response-time records (Parks, 1971). Many of the St. Louis area departments do not maintain such records and thus it cannot be addressed at this point. Citizen perceptions of police response were obtained, however, and will be considered in the following section.

The association between the direct measures is low ($\gamma = +.26$). Some departments (including the St. Louis City police) have taken steps to separate a part of the patrol force from the immediate response force, assigning this part specifically to crime prevention (St. Louis Police Department, 1968). This results in a higher patrol density than that required to handle expected calls for service. Calls for service exceeding those for which an immediate response unit is available are queued awaiting such availability.

Table 3 summarizes associations between these direct activity measures, the crime-related measures, and size of police jurisdiction. The very strong positive relationship between patrol density and crime rate can be read as the result of allocation formulae used by police departments. The substantial but weaker relation between response to calls and crime rate is consistent with the discussion of specific crime prevention patrol when viewed in light of the very strong association just noted. In high crime areas a portion of the high "density" patrol effort is devoted to crime prevention only, leaving less of the patrol force to respond to service calls.

The negative, low to moderate associations between the direct activity measures and the clearance rate initially appear to be a result of the choice of a more patrol-oriented strategy, with these direct measures merely reflecting that choice. This is found not to be the case for patrol density, however, which has a negligible association with percentage of manpower engaged in assigned patrol activities ($\gamma = +.01$) and only partially so for response to calls for service, where a low but positive association is found ($\gamma = +.20$).

Success in obtaining warrants is positively associated with the direct activity measures. From these data we can see that while

Table 3. DIRECT ACTIVITY MEASURES, CRIME-RELATED MEASURES, AND SIZE OF JURISDICTION

Direct Activity Measures	Neighborhood Crime Rate	Neighborhood Clearance Rate	Neighborhood Warrants (% Issued)	Size of Jurisdiction (Population Served)
Patrol "density"— average patrol force per 1,000 residents in neighborhood	+.82[a] (43)[b]	−.12 (37)	+.13 (44)	+.02 (45)
Calls for service answered per 1,000 residents in neighborhood	+.51 (43)	−.34 (37)	+.17 (43)	−.22 (45)

a. Relationship measured by gamma.
b. Number of neighborhoods for which data was available.

departments scoring higher on direct measures of patrol "density" and response to calls are achieving somewhat lower rates of "clearance by arrest," they appear able to have the relevant Warrant Office concur in the arrests which they do make with slightly more success.

Size of jurisdiction bears a negligible relation to one direct measure, patrol "density." The low negative relation found with response to service calls is consistent with the suggestion above that the latter is partially a measure of a more patrol-oriented strategy, found more frequently in departments serving smaller jurisdictions (E. Ostrom, Baugh, Guarasci, Parks, and Whitaker, 1973).

CITIZEN-CONSUMER MEASURES

Direct activity measures provide us with information about what police are doing; measures obtained from properly designed surveys of residents can help to determine what the effects of that "doing" are; in Clark's (1972) terms, what "outcomes" result from police "outputs." Researchers at the Urban Institute have found that "Many quality aspects of government services cannot be measured in any practical way other than through citizen surveys. For many local government services, citizen perceptions constitute a major aspect of service effectiveness" (Webb and Hatry, 1973: 17). Residents of neighborhoods are, in a very real way, an integral factor in the production of police services in those neighborhoods. For example, police officers are quick to report that without citizen cooperation in reporting suspicious circumstances, the likelihood of police patrols deterring criminal activity would drop significantly. The experiences, perceptions, and evaluations reported by citizen-consumers pertaining to the service which they receive from their police departments (or other local government agencies, for that matter), when gathered in well-designed surveys and properly analyzed, can provide information about the quantity and quality of the output of such agencies which is generally unobtainable from any of the measures previously discussed.

Citizen surveys have been utilized to determine the extent and distribution of criminal victimization in America. While there are problems involved in such surveys (Biderman, 1967), it is clear that they provide a more accurate picture of victimization than do crime statistics (Ennis, 1967). Reports of experiences obtained from citizens can be used to determine the level of follow-up to reported crime provided by departments (E. Ostrom, Baugh, Guarasci, Parks, and Whitaker, 1973). Surveys can be used to determine the extent to which police are providing general, noncrime-related services to citizens—services which are not accounted for by most departments (Bercal, 1970; Parks, 1971). Use of surveys allows one to gather information on the extent to which departments are stopping their own citizenry to enforce traffic and other laws, and to relate the evaluations of police services made by citizens to their having had the experience of being stopped by their own force. This allows one to approach the testing of the hypothesis that neighborhood police forces (particularly "community controlled" forces) may be lax in enforcing the law against local residents, thus accounting for higher evaluations by such residents. James Q. Wilson (1968a: 288), for one, seems to fear that neighborhood control would result in such laxity.

Citizen perceptions of police behavior can provide an important check on direct activity measures. For example, asking citizens how often the police patrol their neighborhoods, or how rapidly the police respond when they are called in a neighborhood, allow an independent assessment of level of patrol and response-time measures.

Larson indicates that citizen perceptions of police responsiveness gathered in a recent survey "seemed to coincide quite closely with the judgments of experienced researchers of U.S. police" (1972: 35). Whether or not citizens perceive crime to be increasing in their neighborhoods, and the types of crime they worry about, can provide a check on crime rates and can guide the police in allocation of crime-fighting resources. Asking citizens whether they know of any mistreatment of individuals by their police may elicit information not available through formal complaint channels (Chevigny, 1969).

Given the necessity for citizen cooperation in the production of police services and the likely prerequisites to such cooperation, citizen perceptions of police honesty, courtesy, and the extent to which the police offer equal treatment to all citizens can be important measures. Citizens' general evaluations of the police services they receive, the confidence that they have in the ability of their police, and their assessment of the degree of professionalism of their police are also important. The necessity for such cooperation aside, measures of this nature are of vital importance to those with a normative commitment to citizen sovereignty.

Gathering police performance measures through the use of population surveys permits the analysis of the degree of equity in provision of police services to a variety of groups and areal units (Shoup, 1964). Surveys can provide much more representative channels of feedback to government officials than are normally found in most communities (Webb and Hatry, 1973). This feedback in turn can facilitate better matching of police output to citizen preferences, with attendant practical and normative benefits (E. Ostrom, 1971).

While surveys can provide valuable measures, there are limitations to the use of surveys and to the measures obtained. Surveys are often costly and time-consuming to design and conduct (for techniques which can reduce field costs, see Hockstim, 1967); the proper design and conduct of a probability sample survey requires skills not generally available in most police departments—or in many academic research operations (Kish, 1965; Lazerwitz, 1968); the analysis of responses is time-consuming, preventing the rapid supply of information often deemed necessary for police operations; and the valid conversion of survey responses into measures of activity or output is a particularly perplexing problem. In many cases, however, the benefits to be obtained will outweigh the costs of surveys and the analytic problems they may generate. This is particularly true for obtaining measures of police services, where many of the activities in which police engage do not appear to be amenable to valid measurement in any other fashion. Even in instances where specific activities can be otherwise measured, measures derived from surveys provide essential cross-checks.

The citizen appraisal measures presented here are of three types—first, citizen-reported experiences; second, citizen perceptions; and third, citizen evaluations of their police.

Citizen-Reported Experiences

Operationally, the experience measures are the percent of households in a neighborhood where the respondent answered that someone in their household had been the victim of criminal activity in that neighborhood within the past year, the percent of households where someone had been assisted by the neighborhood police, and the percent where someone had been stopped by those police.[12] Within the sample neighborhoods, reported victimization of at least one household member ranged from a low of only 4% of the households in one neighborhood to over 30% in another. Percentage reporting an assistance varied from 3% to 24%, and the percent stopped from zero to 23%. These measures are related to one another, to the crime-related measures, and to size of jurisdiction as shown in Table 4.

The positive relationship between citizen-reported victimization and crime rate in the neighborhoods is substantial, yet at first thought not as strong as one might expect. It should be noted that while the neighborhoods were predominantly residential, some

Table 4. CITIZEN-REPORTED EXPERIENCES, CRIME-RELATED MEASURES, AND SIZE OF JURISDICTION

	Experiences in Neighborhood		
	Victimization	Assisted by Own Police	Stopped by Own Police
Assisted by own police	−.21[a] (45)[b]	—	—
Stopped by own police	+.31 (45)	+.51 (45)	—
Neighborhood crime rate	+.59 (43)	−.28 (43)	+.18 (43)
Neighborhood clearance rate	+.14 (37)	+.18 (37)	+.38 (37)
Neighborhood warrants (% issued)	−.17 (44)	+.25 (44)	−.45 (44)
Size of jurisdiction (population served)	+.13 (45)	−.33 (45)	−.19 (45)

a. Relationship measured by gamma.
b. Number as neighborhoods for which data was available.

business activity was found in most of them. Since our household survey did not elicit any information about crimes against neighborhood business and the crime-rate data include such crimes, the size of the relationship is not surprising.[13] The substantial positive association between percentage assisted and percentage stopped by the police may be representative of higher police patrol-oriented activity. The associations with size indicate that smaller departments are stopping residents slightly more frequently and providing somewhat more assistance to those residents.

The moderate positive association between percentage stopped by their police and the clearance rate is perhaps reflecting routine checking for "warrants and wants" which many departments have adopted as a policy when stopping a motorist. This association is consistent with the intent of such policies. The negative relationships of crime rate and victimization to percent assisted are consistent with earlier discussion of the assignment of a substantial portion of the patrol force exclusively to prevention duties in higher-crime areas. Officers so assigned are removed from the pool of manpower available to assist residents, whether at their own initiation or in response to a service call.

Citizen Perceptions

The citizen-perception measures reported here are of the speed of police response (percentage reporting "very rapid"), and of the crime trend in their neighborhood (percentage responding "increasing"). Their perceptions of frequency of police patrol cannot be examined at this time due to minor data inconsistencies. The lowest percentage of a neighborhood's respondents reporting "very rapid" police response was 13%, the highest, 80%. Neighborhoods where the percent stopped by police is higher are somewhat more likely to have a higher percentage reporting "very rapid" ($\gamma = +.22$). Respondents reporting the crime trend as increasing ranged from 7% to 52%. The association with percent stopped was low but positive ($\gamma = +.10$). Table 5 presents the associations between these perception measures, the two remaining experience measures, the direct crime-related measures, and size of jurisdiction.

Table 5. CITIZEN PERCEPTIONS AND EXPERIENCES, CRIME-RELATED MEASURES, AND SIZE OF JURISDICTION

	Perceptions of:	
	Police Response Rate in Neighborhood (% very rapid)	*Neighborhood Crime Trend (% increasing)*
Victimized in own neighborhood	$-.12^{a}$ $(45)^{b}$	+.70 (45)
Assisted by own police	+.54 (45)	−.26 (45)
Neighborhood crime rate	−.18 (43)	+.79 (43)
Neighborhood clearance rate	+.39 (37)	−.08 (37)
Neighborhood warrants (% issued)	+.46 (44)	0 (44)
Size of jurisdiction (population served)	−.40 (45)	+.23 (45)

a. Relationship measured by gamma.

b. Number of neighborhoods for which data was available.

The moderate positive associations between the clearance rate and warrant issuance measures and the percentage reporting very rapid response are consistent with data from other sources indicating significantly higher arrest probabilities with faster responses (Operations Research Task Force, 1972). More rapid response when called has a low but negative association with crime rates and percentage victimized, further suggesting that rapid response is beneficial. Rapid response bears a substantial relationship to percentage reporting instances of police assistance.

As could be expected, the percentage reporting that crime is increasing in their neighborhood is very strongly related to the neighborhood crime rate and to the percentage reporting victimization. Preliminary analyses conducted at the individual respondent level indicate that this is substantially attributable to the experience of being victimized. That is, respondents reporting someone in their household victimized within the past year are considerably more likely to report that crime is increasing in their neighborhoods. This seems a natural response—analysis is currently underway to determine differential effects, if any, attributable to various police activities in the neighborhoods.

The Missouri Law Enforcement Assistance Council has called for a definition of "acceptable levels of professionalism and quality in the provision of (police) services" and argued that a "two-minute response time" must be included as a standard (1972: 3). In this same report "the provision of police services in the suburban fringe is somewhat compromised by the fragmentation of jurisdictions and responsibilities" (1972: 34). The association between reported response rate and size of jurisdiction indicates that, on the only indicator of professionalism and quality specifically delineated by the Council, smaller departments are providing better service.

Citizen Evaluations

The operational measure of citizen evaluations used here is the percentage of respondents in a neighborhood stating "outstanding" when asked to rate the quality of police service provided to their neighborhood. This percentage ranged from a low of only 2% to a high of 59%. In the sample as a whole, 26% of those interviewed gave this response. This range of variation across neighborhoods that in many other respects were quite similar is an indication that citizens are able to discriminate the quality of service which they receive to a considerably greater extent than many scholars have been willing to admit.

The hypothesis that higher evaluations will be received by police who are lenient in enforcement against their own citizenry is not supported by the data. The association between the percentage who reported being stopped by their own police and the percentage reporting outstanding police service is negligible ($\gamma = -.04$).

This operational measure of citizen-consumer evaluations bears a moderate negative relationship to percentage reporting victimization in their household ($\gamma = -.40$) and to the percentage reporting crime increasing ($\gamma = -.31$). It has a low negative association with neighborhood crime rate ($-.29$). Higher citizen evaluation has a moderate positive association with the percentage reporting assistance in the neighborhood ($\gamma = +.35$). A very strong positive association is found between percent of a neighborhood sample rating their police outstanding and the percentage reporting that their police respond very rapidly when called (γ = +.80). Response rate would seem to be an important determinant of citizen evaluations of their police service. Citizen ratings of the service provided by their police exhibit only low associations with the clearance rate (γ = +.16) and with size of the jurisdiction providing service (γ = −.11).

The citizen-consumer measures discussed here are an important source of information bearing upon police performance. As with all of the measures presented, they should not be employed alone.

> Merely tabulating and publishing the responses [to surveys] is not sufficient to make fully productive use of survey information. . . . Pertinent information obtained from other regular sources of government information such as government records should be considered along with survey information. Only through such analysis can survey information be placed into proper perspective with other types of information to provide accurate and comprehensive guidance to government officials for their decision and policy making [Webb and Hatry, 1973: 4] .

However, their use in conjunction with other indicators provides an independent cross-checking capability not found when reliance is placed solely upon agency records.

CONCLUSION

A variety of different indicators of the output of neighborhood police agencies have been discussed and operational measures of those indicators presented. The relationships among these operational measures have been analyzed within, and to some degree, across indicator types. Citizen appraisals have been shown to be of importance, used in conjunction with police and other agency records. It is the author's hope that such appraisals will be made a regularly accepted tool in the analyst's bag of measuring devices, leading to a phasing out of the "what do they know, anyway?" reactions of some scholars and police officials when confronted with responses from citizen surveys.

Employment of multiple indicators, gathered from multiple sources, is necessary to match the complexity of what we simply call "police performance." Such employment has the additional benefits of improving the accuracy of individual measures through the availability of other measures with different imperfections. The synergistic combination of indicators bearing upon the same or different facets of policing will provide much deeper insight into police performance than is possible with single indicators, no matter how accurate they may be. Confronted as we are today with a wide range of suggestions for reforming local police service delivery, such insight is a necessary prerequisite to predicting the likely consequences of proposed reforms, and to evaluating the consequences of reforms which are adopted.

NOTES

1. The classic statements on public goods and services are those of Bowen (1943) and Samuelson (1954 and 1955). More recent sources dealing with public goods and services in the context of local government are V. Ostrom, Tiebout, and Warren (1961), Williams (1966), and Buchanan (1968). The advantages of conceptualizing the production of public goods and services in terms of firms and industries are suggested by V. Ostrom and E. Ostrom (1965) and V. Ostrom (1969).

2. "Indicators" is used here to mean the way to classify variables, that is, input proxies, direct crime related, style, direct activity, and citizen-consumer measures. "Measures" is the term used for operational definitions of the indicators.

3. The success of this research effort was founded upon the excellent cooperation afforded us by police chiefs, police officers, and citizens in the St. Louis area. Without that cooperation the study would have been impossible. A special debt is owed to our interview teams, comprised primarily of undergraduate and graduate students from Indiana University. These fine people demonstrated intelligence, dedication, and an active interest in research which, we believe, made them the equivalent of, and in many ways superior to, the best professional survey researchers in the United States.

4. The 60% owner-occuped criterion was relaxed slightly to include one black and one racially-mixed neighborhood. Neighborhoods with median value of housing over $25,000 were excluded to allow us to concentrate our research upon neighborhoods of more general interest, that is, facing resource constraints more typical of most residential areas. Previous research had indicated age of individual respondent to be of some significance in determining attitudes toward the police (E. Ostrom, Baugh, Guarasci, Parks, and Whitaker, 1973). To reduce the confounding effect of this variable in our analysis, we excluded neighborhoods where more than 20% of the residents were over 65 years of age or where more than 45% were under 21.

5. In St. Louis County the Central Police Records Center, within the County government structure, collects and maintains crime statistics from all municipalities in the County. Mr. Orville Thiel of the St. Louis County Police Data Systems Bureau was kind enough to allow us access to these records for our sample areas in the County and to provide us with extensive calls for service data from those departments which contract with the County for radio dispatch. City clerks and police officials of all jurisdictions were equally helpful in providing these data.

6. The St. Louis Police Department has relied upon an independent auditing agency to validate their records of reported crime. The County Central Police Records Center and the municipalities which report to it have not adopted this procedure.

7. In the analysis presented here, the sample neighborhoods are used as the unit of analysis. The direction and strength of the relationships among the operational measures are of principal interest. For this purpose all measures have been trichotomized into low, medium, and high categories with the exception of per-capita expenditures where a more natural four-way division seemed appropriate. Goodman and Kruskal's gamma will be used as the measure of association here, due to the interpretability of this coefficient (Goodman and Kruskal, 1954; Costner, 1965). As T. P. Wilson (1971) argues, the use of ordinal measures places serious limitations on the statements one can make about relationships. But he goes on to note that such measures can serve important heuristic functions, which make them appropriate for present purposes.

8. The phraseology used here to describe the strength of relationships is taken from that suggested by Davis (1971: 49). A gamma with an absolute value over 0.7 will be said to indicate a very strong association; one from 0.5 to 0.69, a substantial association; 0.3 to 0.49, a moderate one; 0.1 to 0.29, a low one; 0.01 to 0.09, a negligible association; and zero, of course, no association. These are, as Davis notes, essentially arbitrary choices made for the sake of consistency.

9. Degree of specialization will not be addressed in this section. Consistent operationalization of this is a difficult task which has been postponed to later analyses.

10. On the same page, however, the Commission admitted that "There appears to be no correlation between the differing concentrations of police and the amount of crime committed, or the percentage of known crimes solved, in the various cities" (1967: 272).

11. The quotation marks at this point are indicative of the author's uncertainty over such "goals" as useful concepts. Bittner (1970: 2) notes that ". . . we are often told that the role of the police is supposed to center around law enforcement, crime control, and peacekeeping. The principal import of such statements is not to inform, but to maintain the pretense of understanding and agreement . . . such statements of function are abstract and do not restrict the interpretations which can be given to them." These "roles" are often suggested as police "goals," "objectives," or "functions" (see J. Q. Wilson, 1968a, for example), similarly maintaining a pretense of agreement over what we wish the police to be doing, where operationally there may be none.

12. Many of the advantages of survey data can best be captured by analysis at the level of individual respondent. In further work, both individuals and neighborhoods will be considered units of analysis. Questions of equity in nongeographic terms, for example, will require the direct use of individual responses.

13. The association between per-capita retail sales in a neighborhood and percent of respondents reporting someone in their household victimized in the neighborhood is a negligible negative one ($\gamma = -.09$). However, per-capita retail sales and the neighborhood crime rate show a low positive association ($\gamma = +.27$).

REFERENCES

American Bar Association, Advisory Committee on the Police Function (1972) Standards Relating to the Urban Police Function. New York: American Bar Association.

BAHL, R. A. (1969) Metropolitan City Expenditures. Lexington: University of Kentucky Press.

BATOR, F. M. (1958) "The anatomy of market failure." Quarterly Journal of Economics (August): 351-379.

BERCAL, T. (1970) "Calls for police assistance: consumer demands for governmental service." American Behavioral Scientist 13 (May/August): 681-691.

BIDERMAN, A. D. (1967) "Surveys of population samples for estimating crime incidence." The Annals 374 (November): 16-33.

——— (1966) "Social indicators and goals," pp. 68-153 in R. A. Bauer (ed.) Social Indicators. Cambridge: MIT Press.

BISH, R. L. and V. OSTROM (1973) Understanding Urban Government: Metropolitan Reform Reconsidered. Washington, D.C.: American Enterprise Institute for Public Policy Research.

BITTNER, E. (1970) The Functions of the Police in Modern Society. Washington, D.C.: Government Printing Office, DHEW Publication No. (HSM) 72-9103.

BLAIR, L. H. and A. I. SCHWARTZ (1972) How Clean is Our City? Washington, D.C.: Urban Institute.

BLALOCK, H. M., Jr. (1969) Theory Construction. Englewood Cliffs, N.J.: Prentice-Hall.

BOGGS, S. L. (1965) "Urban crime patterns." American Sociological Review 30 (December): 899-908.

BOWEN, H. R. (1943) "The interpretation of voting in the allocation of resources." Quarterly Journal of Economics (November): 27-43.

BRADFORD, D. F., R. A. MALT, and W. E. OATES (1969) "The rising cost of local public services: some evidence and reflections." National Tax Journal 22 (June): 185-202.

BUCHANAN, J. M. (1968) The Demand and Supply of Public Goods. Chicago: Rand McNally.

Bureau of the Census (1971) Governmental Finances in 1970-71. Washington, D.C.: Government Printing Office.

CHAPMAN, J. I. and S. SONENBLUM (1972) A Police Service Production Function. Los Angeles: Institute of Government and Public Affairs, University of California, Los Angeles, Report MR-175.

CHEVIGNY, P. (1969) Police Power. New York: Pantheon.

CLARK, T. N. (1972) "Community social indicators." New Haven: Center for the Study of the City and its Environment, Yale University, Working paper W2-26.

Committee for Economic Development (1972) Reducing Crime and Assuring Justice. New York: Committee for Economic Development.

——— (1970) Reshaping Government in Metropolitan Areas. New York: Committee for Economic Development.

——— (1966) Modernizing Local Government. New York: Committee for Economic Development.

COSTNER, H. L. (1965) "Criteria for measures of association." American Sociological Review 30 (June): 341-353.

COX, K. R. (1972) "The neighborhood effect in urban voting response surfaces," in D. C. Sweet (ed.) Models of Urban Structure. Lexington, Mass.: D. C. Heath.

DAVIS, J. A. (1971) Elementary Survey Analysis. Englewood Cliffs, N.J.: Prentice-Hall.

ENNIS, P. H. (1967) Criminal Victimization in the United States: A Report of a National Survey. Field Surveys II. Report Submitted to the President's Commission on Law Enforcement and Administration of Justice. Washington, D.C.: Government Printing Office.

ETZIONI, A. (1964) Modern Organizations. Englewood Cliffs, N.J.: Prentice-Hall.

Federal Bureau of Investigation (1971) Uniform Crime Reports. Washington, D.C.: Government Printing Office.

GLASER, B. G. and A. L. STRAUSS (1967) The Discovery of Grounded Theory. Chicago: Aldine.

GOODMAN, L. A. and W. H. KRUSKAL (1954) "Measures of association for cross classifications." Journal of the American Statistical Association 49 (December): 732-764.

HIRSCH, W. Z. (1968) "The supply of urban public services," pp. 435-476 in H. S. Perloff and L. Wingo (eds.) Issues in Urban Economics. Baltimore: Johns Hopkins University Press.

HOCHSTIM, J. R. (1967) "A critical comparison of three strategies of collecting data from households." Journal of American Statistical Society 62 (September): 976-989.

HOFFMAN, R. B. (1971) "Performance measurements in crime control." Buffalo: State University of New York, School of Management, Working paper No. 112.

Institute for Defense Analysis (1967) Task Force Report: Science and Technology. Washington, D.C.: Government Printing Office.

JACOB, H. (1973) Urban Justice. Englewood Cliffs, N.J.: Prentice-Hall.

––– and M. LIPSKY (1968) "Outputs, structure, and power." Journal of Politics 30 (May): 510-538.

JENKINS, H. (1970) Keeping the Peace. New York: Harper & Row.

Joint Economic Committee, U.S. Congress (1969) The Analysis and Evaluation of Public Expenditures: The PPB Systems (3 vols.). Washington, D.C.: Government Printing Office.

KATZMAN, M. T. (1971) The Political Economy of Urban Schools. Cambridge: Harvard University Press.

KISH, L. (1965) Survey Sampling. New York: John Wiley.

LARSON, R. C. (1972) Urban Police Patrol Analysis. Cambridge: MIT Press.

LAZERWITZ, B. (1968) "Sampling theory and procedures," pp. 278-328 in H. M. Blalock, Jr. and A. B. Blalock (eds.) Methodology in Social Research. New York: McGraw-Hill.

LIKERT, R. (1961) New Patterns of Management. New York: McGraw-Hill.

MALTZ, M. D. (1972) Evaluation of Crime Control Programs. Washington, D.C.: Government Printing Office for the National Institute of Law Enforcement and Criminal Justice.

McCAUSLAND, J. L. (1972) "Crime in the Suburbs," pp. 61-64 in C. H. Haar (ed.) The End of Innocence. Glenview, Ill.: Scott, Foresman.

McNARY, G. (1971) 1971 Annual Report of the Prosecuting Attorney. St. Louis: St. Louis County Prosecutor's Office.

Missouri Law Enforcement Assistance Council (1972) Criminal Justice System Description 1973. St. Louis: Missouri Law Enforcement Assistance Council, Region 5.

Operations Research Task Force, Chicago Police Department (1972) Allocation of Resources in the Chicago Police Department. Washington, D.C.: Government Printing Office.

OSTROM, E. (1973) "On the meaning and measurement of output and efficiency in the provision of urban police services." Journal of Criminal Justice 1 (June): 93-112.

——— (1971) "Institutional arrangements and the measurement of policy consequences." Urban Affairs Quarterly (June): 447-474.

——— and R. B. PARKS (1973) "Suburban police departments: too many and too small?" in L. Masotti· and J. Hadden (eds.) The Urbanization of the Suburbs. Beverly Hills, Calif.: Sage.

——— and D. C. SMITH (1973) "A multi-strata, similar systems design for measuring police performance." Delivered at the annual meeting of the Midwest Political Science Association, May 2-5.

OSTROM, E., W. H. BAUGH, R. GUARASCI, R. B. PARKS, and G. P. WHITAKER (1973) Community Organization and the Provision of Police Services. Beverly Hills, Calif.: Sage Professional Paper in Administrative and Policy Studies 03-001.

OSTROM, V. (1973) The Intellectual Crisis in American Public Administration. University: University of Alabama Press.

——— (1969) "Operational federalism: organization for the provision of public services in the American federal system." Public Choice 6: 1-17.

——— and E. OSTROM (1965) "A behavioral approach to the study of intergovernmental relations." The Annals 359 (May): 137-146.

OSTROM, V., C. M. TIEBOUT, and R. WARREN (1961) "The organization of government in metropolitan areas: a theoretical inquiry." American Political Science Review 55 (December): 831-842.

PARKS, R. B. (forthcoming) "Production of police services in the St. Louis metropolitan area." Ph.D. dissertation. Indiana University.

——— (1971) "Measurement of performance in the public sector: a case study of the Indianapolis police department." Bloomington: Department of Political Science, Indiana University. (mimeo)

PETER, L. J. and R. HULL (1969) The Peter Principle. New York: William Morrow.

Police Foundation (forthcoming) Report on the Kansas City Reactive-Proactive Patrol Experiment. Washington, D.C.: Police Foundation.

President's Commission on Law Enforcement and Administration of Justice (1967) The Challenge of Crime in a Free Society. Washington, D.C.: Government Printing Office.

President's Task Force on Suburban Problems (1968) "Final Report Excerpt," in C. M. Haar (ed.) The End of Innocence. Glenview, Ill.: Scott, Foresman.

PRZEWORSKI, A. and H. TEUNE (1970) The Logic of Comparative Social Inquiry. New York: John Wiley.

RICHARDSON, E. (1973) "Richardson calls for measure of crime" quoted by Margaret Gentry in Louisville Courier Journal, August 6.

RIDLEY, C. E. and H. A. SIMON (1938) Measuring Municipal Activities. Chicago: International City Managers Association.

St. Louis Board of Police Commissioners (1972) Annual Report. St. Louis: St. Louis Board of Police Commissioners.

St. Louis Police Department (1972) "Statistical evaluation of complaint evaluation program during 1971." Internal memo from Planning and Development Division to Colonel Eugene J. Camp, February 11.

——— (1968) Allocation of Patrol Manpower Resources in the St. Louis Police Department. Volumes 1 and 2. St. Louis: St. Louis Police Department.

St. Louis Post-Dispatch (1973a) "Major crimes up in areas in county." August 13.

——— (1973b) "Serious crimes down in city again in '71." January 23.

SAMUELSON, P. A. (1955) "Diagrammatic exposition of a theory of public expenditures." Review of Economics and Statistics 37 (November): 350-356.

——— (1954) "The pure theory of public expenditures." Review of Economics and Statistics 36 (November): 387-389.

SAUNDERS, C. B. (1971) Upgrading the American Police. Washington, D.C.: Brookings Institution.

SCHUR, E. M. (1969) Our Criminal Society. Englewood Cliffs, N.J.: Prentice-Hall.

SEIDMAN, D. and M. COUZENS (1972) "Crime, crime statistics, and the great American anti-crime crusade: police misreporting of crime and political pressures." Delivered at the annual meeting of the American Political Science Association, Washington, D.C., September 5-9.

SELLIN, T. and M. E. WOLFGANG (1964) The Measurement of Delinquency. New York: John Wiley.

SELZNICK, P. (1943) "An approach to a theory of bureaucracy." American Sociological Review 8 (December): 785-791.

SHOUP, C. S. (1964) "Standards for distributing a free governmental service: crime prevention." Public Finance 19 (Winter): 383-392.

SHOUP, D. C. and S. L. MEHAY (1971) Program Budgeting for Urban Police Services. Los Angeles: Institute of Government and Public Affairs, University of California, Los Angeles, Report MR-154.

SHOUP, D. C. and A. ROSETT (1969) Fiscal Exploitation of Central Cities by Overlapping Jurisdictions: A Case Study of Law Enforcement in Los Angeles County. Los Angeles: Institute of Government and Public Affairs, University of California, Los Angeles, Report MR-135.

SKOLNICK, J. H. (1966) Justice Without Trial. New York: John Wiley.

SMITH, D. C. (forthcoming) "Police professionalization and performance: an analysis of public policy from the perspective of police as producers and citizens as consumers of police services." Ph.D. dissertation. Indiana University.

——— (1971) "Political implications of police professionalism." Bloomington: Department of Political Science, Indiana University. (mimeo)

——— and E. OSTROM (1974) "The effects of training and education on police attitudes and performance," in H. Jacob (ed.) The Potential for Reform of Criminal Justice. Beverly Hills, Calif.: Sage.

Task Force on Assessment, President's Commission on Law Enforcement and Administration of Justice (1967) Task Force Report: Crime and Its Impact—An Assessment. Washington, D.C.: Government Printing Office.

TERRIS, B. (1967) "The role of the police." The Annals 374 (November): 58-69.

VOTEY, H. L., Jr. and L. PHILLIPS (1972) "Police effectiveness and the production function for law enforcement." Journal of Legal Studies 1 (June): 423-436.

WEBB, E. J., D. T. CAMPBELL, R. D. SCHWARTZ, and L. SECHREST (1966) Unobtrusive Measures. Chicago: Rand McNally.

WEBB, K. and H. P. HATRY (1973) Obtaining Citizen Feedback. Washington, D.C.: Urban Institute.

WILLIAMS, A. (1966) "The optimum provision of public goods in a system of local government." Journal of Political Economy (February): 18-33.

WILSON, J. Q. (1968a) Varieties of Police Behavior. New York: Antheneum.

——— (1968b) "Dilemmas of police administration." Public Administration Review 28 (September/October): 407-417.

WILSON, O. W. (1963) Police Administration, second ed. New York: McGraw-Hill.
WILSON, T. P. (1971) "A critique of ordinal variables." Social Forces 49 (June): 432-444.
WOLFGANG, M. E. (1970) "Urban crime," in J. Q. Wilson (ed.) The Metropolitan Enigma.
    New York: Anchor Books.

9

PROBLEMS IN THE EVALUATION OF CRIME CONTROL POLICY

SOLOMON KOBRIN
STEVEN G. LUBECK

University of Southern California

The problems encountered in the evaluation of policy are in general well known. They include the need to specify the goals of policy in terms that permit measurement of the extent to which they are attained; the reduction of abstract statements of policy to the concrete operations through which it is implemented; the requirement that these operations be accessible to systematically recorded observation; and the linking of variation in goal attainment to variation in policy. In less abstruse terms, policy evaluation requires that we know clearly where we want to go, what we do to get there, and whether in fact any headway is being made. Each step in this sequence poses substantial problems. Moreover, these problems differ in their content in different substantive policy areas, posing greater

AUTHORS' NOTE: *This is a revised version of a paper presented at the 1973 annual meeting of the American Political Science Association, New Orleans, September 4-8.*

or less difficulty with respect to each of the requirements for adequate evaluation. In general, the greatest difficulty is encountered in connection with the evaluation of social programs that aim at the reduction of undesirable behavior, or that seek to foster constructive change in attitude and behavior. The latter is exemplified by the War on Poverty conducted by the federal Office of Economic Opportunity; the former, by programs of crime control.

Any effort to evaluate crime control policy faces difficulties unique to this problem area with respect to each of the requirements for adequate evaluation. Three issues are here considered in some detail, with the possibilities of their treatment illustrated by a recent study based on data from the state of California (Kobrin et al., 1972). The first of these concerns specification of the goal of crime control; the second takes up the question of the type and scope of the information required for the evaluation of policy; and the third considers the methodological and measurement problems encountered in making optimal use of data reflecting the operations of criminal justice agencies.

THE GOAL OF CRIME CONTROL

A major concern in the assessment of crime control policy is the special role of criminal justice as one in the complement of instrumentalities for the implementation of social control. Without some clarification and specification of the distinctive contribution of criminal justice to the more general enterprise of social control there is scant prospect of arriving at a realistic determination of the aim of crime control policy.

The thesis to be presented with respect to this problem may be briefly summarized in the following propositions. First, the main deterrent effect of crime control is accomplished without specific relationship to crime control policy, but simply as a consequence of the activity of the agencies of criminal justice. In any society which is not in a state of imminent disintegration, the prevalence and incidence of acts in violation of law constitute an extremely small proportion of the total activity of the population, whatever the alarm these criminal offenses may provoke. Second, the criminal behavior that does occur, and to which there is wide and enduring opposition, tends on the whole to be endemic to particular segments and strata of the population, so distributed as to form varying proportions in the populations of different jurisdictions. Among these segments and strata the propensity for law violation has its major source in the failure of deterrent effect on the part of social control institutions unrelated to crime control agencies. The latter are without either the mandate or the resources to compensate for such failures. Third, what remains possible for criminal justice agencies is to deploy their distinctive resource, the imposition of punitive sanction, to reduce the incidence of offense within the relatively narrow band of variation whose average magnitude has been determined by factors lying outside its control. On this view, the reasonable and realistic aim of crime control policy can be none other than reduction in the incidence of offense to its lowest feasible level, rather than to a level determined by ideal prescription.

THE MAJOR SOURCE OF CRIME CONTROL EFFECTIVENESS

Some detailed justification of these assertions is clearly in order. The first proposition asserts that the main deterrent effect of criminal justice is accomplished without reference to the specific content of crime control policy. This is to say that, irrespective of the character of crime control policy, criminal justice exerts a massive deterrent effect by virtue simply of representing in actual and symbolic ways the demands of the normative order. A strictly sociological analysis of crime, that is, an account of the role of criminal behavior in the social process, would hold, as Durkheim (1960) and others did, that human groups establish and reaffirm their unity and solidarity by excluding, punishing, or destroying those who would violate their sacred norms. So far as the criminal exemplifies forbidden behavior by his offending acts, he serves to mark the outer limits of the moral space inhabited by the group, and provides thereby an important, not to say essential, means of fixing the value orientations of its members. In this paradoxical sense, then, the criminal offender becomes a useful member of his society, serving, some would say, an important "function" as he opens himself to punitive reprisal.[1] Only in the act of punishing the offender can conforming members of the society confront the existential reality of their rules of conduct. This fact has been assimilated into the legal doctrine that a proscription without sanction is without effect.

An implication of this "functional" view of crime is that the concept of a crimeless society becomes an empirical impossibility not, as is frequently asserted, because of unavoidable failures in socialization, or culture conflicts, or inability to learn and appreciate the legal norms due to some defect of personal capacity. Beyond these mundane reasons, and lying at a more fundamental level of the social process, a crimeless society is an impossibility because human groups define their distinctive human character as residing in rules of conduct specific to their cultures. Since rules tend to favor the interests of some but not of others, their legitimacy is continuously exposed to incipient or overt challenge. The recurrent need to assert the validity of social rules, to re-establish their legitimacy in the operational form of social action, can take no other form than the imposition of disability, i.e., some form of punishment, on rule violators. Whatever the effect of punishment may be in reducing the incidence of crime, its dependable consequence is to communicate to those who are customarily law-abiding the positive virtues of the codes which their conformity supports. The punishment of the offender communicates more than just the threat of painful consequences that awaits the malefactor. It serves, more importantly, as the symbolic expression of the legitimacy of the norms by which the law-abiding person regulates his conduct. A recognized consequence of sanction directed to the violator is the reinforcement of conformity to law by the vast majority. Some writers have labeled this effect "general deterrence," suggesting that the activity of crime control is a significant factor in the "moral education" of the populace.[2]

The prevailing tendency to conform to the legal norms is as little related to a situation of mild as it is to one of harsh punishments. Indeed, it is generally true that the law-abiding layman has somewhat vague notions respecting the precise punishments which are legally mandated for specific crimes (criminal homicide excepted). There is, however, no urgent reason why he should have such knowledge. As a circumspect citizen he has little occasion, other than the infrequent traffic violation, for acquiring a working knowledge of the criminal justice system, and most particularly of its success in bringing offenders to book. But where ignorance is, there is fantasy, and in this case in a form distinctively useful for deterrence.

The assumption that fills the vacuum of ignorance is that enormous risk of detection and punishment attends the commission of crime. There is little familiarity with the fact, for example, that on the average the probability of imprisonment for a felony offense which is reported to the police is approximately 5%, and less than that if unreported felonies are included. A number of recent studies have demonstrated that law-abiding persons as compared to law violators overestimate substantially the risk of detection, conviction, and incarceration for a criminal act.[3]

Such faith in the guardians of the law rests in all likelihood on little more than his knowledge that the institution of criminal justice exists as a fixed feature of the social landscape, however remote it may be from his daily concerns. The faith is regularly refreshed by having it brought to attention by the communication media that the machinery of justice engages unremittingly in the apprehension, conviction, and punishment of offenders. These activities are for him their own warrant for his faith in the basic effectiveness of crime control, except, perhaps, on the infrequent occasions when he or those known to him are victimized. Ordinarily, however, no more is needed than this knowledge of retribution-in-being to shore up his avoidance of criminal offense and, consequently, to keep him effectively deterred.

THE SOCIAL ECOLOGY OF CRIME

The second assertion of the thesis under review holds that the type of offenses to which general opposition is least equivocal tends to be endemic to particular segments and strata of the population. It is a staple of every elementary course in criminology that rates of crime have been distributed historically in association with urbanization, sex, age, socioeconomic status, and ethnicity.[4] The relationship between these population characteristics and crime rates has been relatively constant throughout the urban-industrial era. Urban jurisdictions have typically exhibited substantially higher crime rates than do rural jurisdictions. Measures of crime are on the average consistently higher in jurisdictions whose populations contain higher proportions of young male members of the low-income, devalued status, ethnic and racial groups. It is by virtue of these facts that the order of magnitude of the crime problem that confronts the agencies of criminal justice in any jurisdiction has been determined for them by the social ecology of crime.[5]

The question thus arises respecting a reasonable expectation as to the scope of control that may be exercised by agencies of criminal justice. It would seem evident that their mission of crime prevention is of necessity limited to what has been called special deterrence, that is, the use of punitive sanction in a manner calculated to reduce the probability of criminal acts by persons with an established proclivity for crime. This category includes not only those already punished for past offenses, for whom there is high likelihood of recidivism, but also by those who may be marginally likely to commit an offense.[6] It is the number in this category that is most immediately responsible for the magnitude of a jurisdiction's crime rate.

SPECIFICATION OF POLICY OBJECTIVES

Thus, the third proposition asserts that what remains possible as a goal of crime control policy is the deployment of punitive threat in a manner that reduces the crime rate of any given jurisdiction to the lowest level possible within the range of variation whose average magnitude has been determined by factors lying outside the control of its criminal justice agencies. The perspective here offered on the aim of crime control policy brings into focus the role of social factors in generating crime. It does this by establishing the lower limit of possible crime reduction by justice agencies as fixed by the magnitude of the jurisdiction's crimogenic potential. In so doing it directs attention to the intermittantly recognized fact that substantial and sustained effort in crime reduction must be directed to the amelioration of conditions known to foster high crime rates.

Public controversy with respect to this matter may be readily understood. The view of crime control as the exclusive province of police, courts, and corrections reflects in all likelihood an interest-bound commitment to the prevailing pattern of resource allocation, and a disinclination to accept the costs of their reallocation, presumably in money but certainly in power and status. Those who hold this view are demanding for the solution of an enormously complex problem a procedure entailing minimal costs in terms of basic social rearrangements such as, for example, might lead to the disestablishment of the urban racial ghettos. Indeed, the monetary costs of such policy may well be below the high and continuously rising costs of a crime control policy that places the entire burden of responsibility on agencies of criminal justice. Moreover, since the crime control performance demanded of the justice agencies is impossible of realization, there is entailed the further serious cost of a reduction of public confidence in the validity and vitality of the law.[7] The case for the importance of keeping in view the involvement of social factors in crime control may be clarified by a brief note on the sociology of social control.

It is commonly accepted and endlessly repeated that those laws are most effective which have the most complete support in public sentiment. The statement has the surface appearance of a tautology, since it would seem that any rule that enjoyed complete support in public sentiment would be, so to speak, self-enforcing, with the provision of sanction for its violation rendered superfluous. But the appearance of tautology is deceptive, for it may be asserted that in the nature of the case, there can be no such thing as a self-enforcing rule, except in a highly metaphorical sense. Social control in the constructive sense of noncoercive, autonomously initiated conformity to normative prescription is a collective product. It has its source simultaneously in subjective disposition and in the externalized representation of that disposition in a stably institutionalized form. The inculcation of inner control through socializing procedures, that is, the incorporation of cultural norms into the structure of personality is, in fact, a process of internalizing the imperatives enunciated by concrete actors functioning as agents of the normative structure. In the paradigmatic case the imperatives are transformed into sentiments, providing a subjective concordance with objectively existing arrangements designed to implement their observance. As piety is commonly linked to ritual practice conducted by appropriate functionaries, so sentiments requiring conformity to law are linked to the acts of agents of criminal justice.

But the paradigmatic case exists only in analytic abstraction, and residually in the fantasies of the cultural determinists. In the empirical case the processes of acculturation, themselves far from coherent or unitary in content, are intersected by the realities of social structure in a manner commonly productive of discontinuity between subjective disposition and the prescriptions of legal norms.[8] Even if there are grounds for assuming a unitary content of cultural transmission respecting the legal norms for the alienation of property and for the violability of the person (a challengeable assumption), location in the social structure becomes a relevant factor in the differential importance of these norms for various occupational and social class categories. For example, blue-collar workers who steal tools and materials from the workshops of the impersonal corporations who employ them are likely to redefine the law of theft in ways that reduce the subjective dissonance of the act. Corporation executives who engage in price fixing are likely to place a low value on the virtues of competition (Smith, 1970). Young lower-class males who confirm their manhood by assaulting rivals challenging their territorial dominance regard the norms of personal inviolability as having less than absolute validity.[9] In brief, the cogency of normative *proscription* expressed in formal legal statues, that is, the degree to which they are subjectively "self-enforcing," appears to bear a direct relationship to their concordance with interests having their source in the structural location of various population groups. Such locations afford competitive advantages or disabilities, either of which the legal norms may unavoidably intensify, with consequent differences in the degree to which their support is interest-bound.[10]

Hence, while the task of criminal justice in the social control process is to provide for the institutional "objectivation" of sentiments supportive of normative prescription, its capacity to do so is limited by the scope of counternormative interests. The source, character, and prevalence of such interests lie outside the purposes of the present analysis.[11] But so far as such crimes as burglary, robbery, homicide, assault, and rape are concerned, the available evidence indicates that they are endemic to those segments of urban populations which suffer massive disabilities. These have been associated with an intensification of counternormative interests, whose reduction or transformation may be addressed primarily through programs of resource reallocation. Failure to provide the conditions which foster internalized control cannot be remedied by attempts to increase the efficiency of external controls. To the degree that there is reliance solely on crime control activities to accomplish the purposes of social control, to that degree is criminal justice constrained to resort to coercive repression.

Thus, to define the aim of crime control policy in a manner that postulates its limited contribution to social control is to increase the likelihood of a focus on the need for adjunctive policy directed to the more basic determinants of social control. This is not to say that the policies of criminal justice agencies are irrelevant to the task of crime reduction, but only that the potential of such reduction is sharply limited. The difference in crime rates between middle-class and lower-class urban communities is very large. The difference in crime rates between a lower-class urban community with exemplary enforcement and adjudication and one highly deficient in these respects is relatively small. The importance of the latter difference for those who have escaped victimization is not to be denied, and it remains the legitimate aim of crime control policy to reduce to its lowest possible limit the number of victims. But some conception of that limit, open to operational definition, becomes essential if policy is to be evaluated meaningfully.

This mode of evaluation is not, however, without its problems. Its main requirement is the determination of the average incidence of criminal acts that may be expected in any given jurisdiction on the basis of its population characteristics. This requirement may be met in principle although, as will be noted later, substantial work beyond that accomplished in the California study remains to be done.

Order of Magnitude of Crime Predictive Social Factors	Deviation of Observed from Expected Crime Rate	
HIGH	+	Case 1
	0	Case 2
	−	Case 3
INTERMEDIATE	+	Case 4
	0	Case 5
	−	Case 6
LOW	+	Case 7
	0	Case 8
	−	Case 9

Key: +, 0, − = above, commensurate with, and below expectation

Figure 1: PARADIGM FOR THE EVALUATION OF THE "SUCCESS" OR "FAILURE" OF CRIME CONTROL POLICY

However, assuming that a valid measure of a jurisdiction's "natural" crime rate is established, the issue then arises of the criteria for "success" or "failure" in its crime control policy.[12]

Figure 1 represents a paradigm of possible policy output in the form of nine hypothetical cases of crime rate levels relative to three categories of crimogenic potential. For purposes of simplification a single time period is assumed, of sufficient duration to permit crime rates to reflect control policy. "Failure," or deficiency in crime control policy, may be judged to have occurred not only in Case 1, which would presumably represent the highest observed crime rate in the array, but in Cases 4 and 7 as well. Similarly, in Case 3, whose observed crime rate is likely to exceed that in both Cases 4 and 7, the judgment of failure would be unwarranted, since it lies in fact below expectation for the category of jurisdictions of which it is a member.

In proposing this paradigm it is, however, important to note that it is a drastically simplified model of the reality it purports to represent. The fact is that the crimogenic potential of any jurisdiction is likely at any moment to be in process of change in conjunction with transformations in its population composition and social organization, such that its crime predictive social factors may be in process of increasing or decreasing in magnitude. It is consequently necessary to complicate the model by employing diachronic, or time-series, data with reference to the justice system, the social system, and crime measures.

On the other hand, the "success" of jurisdictions having strikingly low crime rates in relation to the predicted magnitude (for example, Cases 3, 6, and 9) may be ambiguous. Criminal justice agencies are entirely capable of reducing the incidence of crimes substantially below its "natural" level by employing repressive enforcement measures and by imposing harsh punishments on those convicted of crime. Massive intimidation together with the removal of crime-prone persons from the community for long periods of time will do wonders for the crime rate. Apart from draconian measures, the tenuous judgments that must be made respecting selection for detaining, arresting, and charging the "marginally deterrable" group in the population, that is, "those next most likely" to offend, can be extended readily to include successive categories representing declining marginality. When such extension is not limited by the countervailing principles embodied in legal defenses against the arbitrary use of the police power of the state, the "success" of crime control policy is seriously compromised.[13] It need hardly be argued that the goal of control policy is not reduction of crime at the cost of subverting the equally important community value of freedom from official repression.

Nonetheless, the limit within which crime may be reduced short of the use of police-state methods may well be open to determination. Ratios of arrests to arraignments may be examined to determine whether harassing enforcement pressure is systematically employed. Sentence severity on conviction for identical offenses may be compared across jurisdictions. Less directly, the data of public perception of and sentiment regarding the policies of justice agencies may be examined. Finally, evidence may be obtained in field studies regarding the use of crime control agencies in the service of chronic political conflict, particularly in communities characterized by sharply polarized, asymmetrical power groups.

DATA REQUIREMENTS FOR EVALUATION

The effort here has been to specify the goal of crime control policy in a manner that enhances the prospect of its definitive evaluation. It has been proposed that the goal of control policy be defined for each jurisdiction as reduction in the incidence of crimes below the average magnitude expected by virtue of its social composition, with the lower limit constrained by established libertarian considerations. In addition to providing specificity in goal definition for various types of jurisdictions, the inclusion of factors of social composition permits segregation of their effects on crime measures from those attributable to the action of control agencies.

However, the implementation of this evaluation design encounters problems of data availability, reliability, and validity. Some of these problems are common to any evaluation design, others are unique to the one here proposed. Three types of information are required, each of which may be currently unavailable, or available but seriously flawed. These include data on the incidence of crimes, on the response of the justice system, and on the social and demographic characteristics of populations.

DATA FOR THE CONSTRUCTION OF CRIME MEASURES

The first of these is information-yielding measures of the incidence of crimes. The deficiencies of record data are too well known to require detailed description here. They may be briefly summarized by pointing out that of all criminal acts that occur, reliable information is lacking respecting the proportion that are detected, reported, recorded, and responded to by arrests of suspects.[14] Only recently has a major survey been conducted to ascertain the ratio of criminal victimizations to reported crimes, although the variation in this ratio across different types of jurisdictions remains unknown.[15] No systematic information is available respecting variation in the ratio of reported to recorded crimes, a matter subject to both police discretion and political pressure. In addition, despite improvement over the past several decades, there remain problems of uniformity in the classification of offenses for purposes of reporting to state and national agencies which compile and publish crime statistics. Finally, the record data that are available are presented in unweighted form for the purposes of estimating crude crime rates. Little systematically derived information is available for the estimation of the seriousness of the crime problem in various jurisdictions, based on the variable distribution of reported crimes among the several categories of offense.

These limitations in the information available for the measurement of crime are currently all but intractable. Police agencies maintain crime records primarily for administrative purposes. Their use for evaluation purposes is typically confined to internal control functions such as estimating crime clearance rates and the like. The pressing task of police agencies is to respond with reasonable competence to the community demand for public order and for the safety of persons and property. Their immediate and ongoing concern, strictly speaking, is not with the crimes that occur, but of this number only with those that come or are brought to their attention. The records maintained of the traffic so generated are oriented to serving such legally mandated functions of enforcement as identifying suspects and moving them to the stage of adjudication. Deficiencies in the recording of reported crimes thus tend to occur in cases of reduced prospect of successful prosecution, whether caused by an overwhelming of police or court manpower availability, simple police incompetence, or judicial disinclination to convict for certain types of offenses. In brief, the functional constraints that shape the record data of police agencies render such data inappropriate as a direct measure of crime. Their improvement for this purpose is likely to occur only as the evaluation of policy becomes a matter of increasing concern to crime control agencies.

In the meantime, however, the record data as it currently exists may be used with caution as an indirect measure of crime. Very simply, the use of record data may be justified on the grounds that it furnishes some information where the alternative is no information.[16] Those who regard policy evaluation in this field as urgent face the hard choice of abandoning the effort or committing themselves to findings based on incomplete information biased in unknown ways. Two considerations argue for choice of the latter alternative. First, although information regarding the magnitude of the crime problem is crude and incomplete, it is not useless in the sense that it would be revealed by fuller data to be completely erroneous. Any given policy decision in the condition of no information may be construed as dichotomous with reference to its predicted effect on the crime rate when that rate is assumed to be unmeasurable, yielding equal probability that it will be predicted to increase or decrease that rate. The addition of any increment of quantitative information about crime, provided it is not completely erroneous, will raise the probability of a correct policy choice in direct proportion to the accuracy of the information content of that increment.

Second, although the existing record data on the magnitude of the crime problem is incomplete rather than false, it is biased in the sense that selective factors operate somewhat systematically to produce in the record data a distorted representation of the actual incidence and prevalence of types of offenses. Some information is currently available on two sources of distortion. Certain offenses are significantly underreported for fear of revealing victimization, as in cases of rape and assaults involving persons known to one another.[17] A second important source of bias is the patterned under-recording of certain offenses on the part of the police. There have been notorious instances of deliberately falsified recording by police agencies affected by a climate of local political corruption. But such practices in the past have been episodic, and with the general decline of the big city political machines they are likely to diminish as a problem of serious concern (Institute of Public Administration, 1952). A more significant determinant of chronic under-recording, in all likelihood, is community pressure on the police to attend to those types of offenses regarded as serious. Since the manpower resources of police agencies are limited, this has the effect of relative inattention to the less intolerable offenses reported, with consequent reduction in the completeness of their recording. Thus, under circumstances of average police honesty and over the long run, the offenses that tend to get recorded most punctiliously are those that most offend against community sentiment. Recorded crimes tend, operationally, to represent those acts against which the punitive sanctions of the law are mobilized. Few homicides, willful or negligent, go un-recorded.[18]

DATA FOR THE MEASUREMENT OF AGENCY RESPONSE

In contrast to reasonably standard and periodically published data for estimating crime rates, the data needed to assess the response to crime by the control agencies are neither routinely available nor centrally compiled and published. A notable exception is the state of California, where certain standard items on crime reports, arrests, charges, and court dispositions are tabulated by types of offenses and offenders for each of the state's criminal court jurisdictions. However, even there tabulations in full detail are not consistently available in published form, nor are data readily accessible on length of sentence for those committed to jails and prisons.

Agencies of criminal justice may be conceived of as that component of the social control system which is empowered to impose coercive sanction on those suspected of violating the law. Each of these agencies is located at a different point in a process through which suspects are transformed into convicted offenders. The form of sanction available to each agency differs according to its special function, ranging from the police power to detain and charge, through that of the prosecutor's office to seek conviction, and of the court to convict and sentence. The extent to which the sanction available at each of these points is in fact imposed constitutes a potentially measurable variable. How the level of sanction actually imposed at each of these points may be measured is dealt with below. The data requirements for the measurement of sanction level at each stage of the criminal justice process will here be briefly indicated.

Currently available in most police jurisdictions are statistics on arrests and charges. These permit an initial crude estimate of the level of sanction at the police stage by determining the ratio of arrests to crime reports. But such estimates can be only a crude measure of the certainty of arrest, since the denominator unit in the calculation of the ratio, reported criminal events, and the numerator unit, persons, are not identical. Moreover, data are commonly unavailable to ascertain the average number of crimes represented by each arrested person. The additional data required for a more adequate measure of the level of police sanction concern the disposition of cases of arrest. It is necessary to know, in cases of felony arrests, the proportion of those released without being charged, those in which the charge was reduced to a lesser offense, and those on whom the felony charge was filed for consideration at the pre-trial stage.

Similarly, at the pre-trial stage complete data are required covering each of the three main forms of possible action: dismissal, charge reduction, and acceptance of the police-initiated charge. However, this information should be supplemented if sanction at this stage is to be adequately measured. As is true of the police agencies, arraignment proceedings at the lower court level perform a crucial "gatekeeping" function. The acceptance, rejection, or modification of the police charge is a function of a subtle and complex interplay of diverse pressures. Judgments made at this point take into account not only the substantive weight of the evidence in support of the police charge, but reflect as well the prevailing state of antagonism or cooperation between and among the police, the judiciary, and the prosecutor's office. While pre-trial case dispositions provide the needed data for the measurement of net sanction imposition at this stage, the climate generated by the interaction among the agencies concerned contributes a qualitative component needed for the assessment of system response at this stage. For example, an equivalently high rate of charge reduction in two jurisdictions may reflect in one a prevailing tendency to negotiate both the charge and the plea, and in the other a practice of assessing the police charge solely on its merits. But the level of sanction experienced by the suspect in the two cases is likely to differ substantially. In the former he may anticipate an outcome based on the operation of factors extrinsic to the evidence of his culpability, while in the latter he may not. It is hence essential to have available detailed data on the considerations that have entered into the decisions of the various participants in the pre-trial process. As may be expected, this type of data is rarely systematically compiled in any jurisdiction, and is nowhere centrally available in conveniently tabulated form.

Indeed, the same problem of data deficiency respecting the

qualitative aspects of sanction exists with reference to both the "gatekeeper" points in the criminal justice system. Standard statistics compiled by police agencies are similarly incapable of reflecting crucial features of policy. The weight of police sanction is only broadly and imprecisely indicated by ratios of those arrested for felony crimes against whom such charges are not filed. For example, what may be defined as an "arrest" is subject to a good deal of variation as to the exact procedures entailed. Data on detention practices, such as street and station interrogation, are typically unavailable, representing a standard and on the whole a legitimate feature of police operations which may vary widely among jurisdictions in intensity and aggressiveness. The inclusion of data on these uses of the power of police sanction is essential for the measurement of system response at this stage. Such data are generally now unavailable, and where they are available they are not compiled in a form that is comparable across jurisdictions.

Data required to assess system response at the trial or conviction stage are perhaps the least problematic with respect to format. The legally prescribed categories of outcome, permitting direct measurement of sanction severity, include charge dismissal, acquittal, and conviction on either the original charge or on one that has been reduced or substituted. The single problem at this point is that these data are infrequently centrally compiled and tabulated, creating a serious obstacle to the efficient and economical conduct of policy evaluation studies in a comparative context.

The same problem limits the feasibility of measuring sanction at the sentencing stage. In addition, there exist at least two other problems of data access posing serious difficulty. First, sentence severity may be assessed from two quite disparate perspectives, that of some putative "general public," and that of the population of currently active offenders. So far as special deterrence constitutes a principal aim of crime control policy, that is, the deterrence of those whose likelihood of future offense has been established by the fact of past offense, the measurement of sentence severity requires information regarding its perception by members of this population. Legislatures commonly respond to increases in the incidence of crimes by increasing the severity of penalties. However, estimates of the increment of penalty increase sufficient to its deterrent aim are likely to be based on little more than the degree of indignation or anxiety which the offenses arouse. In brief, the weight of punishment experienced by the person accorded a particular sentence on conviction, or experienced by a particular class of offenders accorded particular types of sentences, can be ascertained by information which only they can provide. It is hardly necessary to add that such information does not exist. In its absence, the response of the criminal justice system at the point of sentence imposition can be only crudely approximated.

A related second problem of data availability for the assessment of the weight of formal punishment concerns information with respect to sentence implementation. Widespread contemporary use of indeterminate sentencing laws, and the broad latitude of discretion accorded prison officials and parole boards, renders uncertain the weight of sanction attached to imprisonment as a sentence. Needed, and neither readily nor easily available, are data on length of sentence served by persons from comparable jurisdictions committed for similar offenses.[19] Attribution of differential sanction severity weights to sentences ranging from fines through jail and probation to commitment to prison, however reasonably these weights may be derived, ignores the variation in severity that may attach to each. Fines may be light or onerous, probation may have stringent or relaxed conditions, and confinement in jails and prisons may be brief or prolonged. Moreover, the same sentence may be perceived and experienced as differentially severe by different categories of persons.

DATA FOR THE MEASUREMENT OF CRIMOGENIC FACTORS

Little problem is encountered in getting access to demographic data predictive of variation in crime measures. The U.S. Census reports provide detailed tabulations of age and sex structure, as well as ethnic and racial composition and socioeconomic status. With respect to the latter in particular, current census information furnishes a variety of useful indicators. Moreover, information that is not published in standard census volumes may be obtained on request from the Census Bureau's data repositories.

As may be expected, however, the efficiency of a number of such factors in predicting crime measures varies substantially in association with the population size of jurisdictions. For example, there are cogent theoretical grounds for questioning the constancy of the relationship between the socioeconomic status of a population and its crime rate. Indeed, the California study found that its index of SES, while highly predictive for crime rates in all counties, was substantially less so in counties with populations below 100,000.[20] Similar variation was found in the predictive efficiency of other demographic and social factors for jurisdictions which differed in social composition. Needed, consequently, are empirically derived refinements of prediction models designed to assess the crimogenic potential of various types of jurisdictions. Such refinements entail ascertaining the differential predictive weights to be assigned to standard factors for each kind of population, to be based on their observed relationship to their long-time average crime measures.

PROBLEMS OF METHOD AND MEASUREMENT

It would appear to be a simple matter to specify as the aim of crime control policy the deterrence of criminal acts by posing a threat of punitive reprisal. Punishment, both imposed and threatened, is widely accepted as the effective principle of deterrence, despite the controversies concerning the pragmatic or ethical justification of punishment. However, the designation of deterrence as the goal of crime control policy introduces problems of the greatest difficulty for the task of policy evaluation. Since evaluation entails measurement at some level if it is to be definitive, the problem arises of measuring deterrence effects.

What is meant by deterrence is the foregoing of an act which is assumed to have had the realistic potential of actualization. The difficulty here is that "not committing an act" is not a tangible event. It is neither an "entity" nor an "attribute" of an entity. Accordingly, the practice of treating non-acts as if they were things for the purpose of analysis creates complex problems of meaning.

For example, does the fact that an airline passenger does not skyjack his conveyence mean that he is being effectively deterred from so doing? The answer to this question depends, of course, upon whether the passenger is in fact inclined to commit the act, and whether, given the inclination, deterrence mechanisms (e.g., the airport passenger check, fear of life imprisonment) have worked. But even if it could be ascertained that such mechanisms were present, the passenger's exemplary behavior need not necessarily indicate effective deterrence. That he has not skyjacked in the past does not also mean that, given sufficient motivation, he will not attempt to do so in the future. In brief, the intangibility of the individual "non-act" embodies a very large set of possible meanings having their source in unascertainable motivations or lack thereof.

The problem is also present in the analysis of social aggregates. We customarily assume that the repertory of threat behavior at the command of individuals or institutions produces deterrent effects, but we can rarely be certain of this. For example, if the incidence of skyjackings were to diminish shortly after a federally imposed threat of a death penalty, such diminution would not be a logically necessary consequence of the threat. It could mean that a natural decrease in the behavior would have occurred without any official intervention, or it could also mean that the threat is unnecessarily harsh. Along these lines, Zimring has characterized two fallacies of assuming gratuitously a causal link between threat and deterrence as "Aunt Jane's Cold Remedy" and "Tiger Prevention" (Zimring, 1971).

The first fallacy takes its name from the ad: "Take Aunt Jane's Cold Remedy and your cold will go away within two weeks!" The catch is that most colds go away in two weeks with or without intervention. The disappearance of the ailment does not necessarily indicate that Aunt Jane's remedy is effective. The second fallacy, "Tiger Prevention," takes its name from "the story of the gentleman who was running about the streets of mid-Manhattan, snapping his fingers and moaning loudly, when he was intercepted by a police officer. Their conversation follows: P.O.: What are you doing? Gtlm: Keeping tigers away. P.O.: Why, that's crazy. There isn't a wild tiger within five thousand miles of New York City! Gtlm: Well, then, I must have a pretty effective technique."

The problem posed by the evanescent character of the deterred act may be solved in part by shifting the analysis from the individual to the community. Reduction in the incidence of offenses in a jurisdiction suggests as one possibility that criminal acts which might have occurred have been deterred. For example, if at Time 1 a community has the crime rate (x), and if at Time 2 that crime rate decreases appreciably to (x′), then it may be the case that (x − x′) represents the volume of potential and foregone criminal acts attributable to some specifiable features of crime control policy. Of course, to make the attribution validly it would be necessary to ensure that (x − x′) was not a result of naturally occurring fluctuations in crime rates due to quantitative or qualitative changes in the population, or the removal of some percentage of persistent law violators from the community, or attributable to historical factors such as changing definitions of crime. Crime rates could increase or decrease as a function of any or all of these factors while crime control policy remained constant. Only through the statistical control of these factors in accordance with a quasi-experimental design might it be possible to ascertain whether (x − x′) is related to policy.

However, it is necessary here to raise the caution that even if such an analysis were totally feasible, which it currently is not, it would tell us little about the operation of deterrence mechanisms in the minds of individuals. We may learn, for example, that an increase in the certainty of apprehension and of conviction and an increase in the severity of sentence does or does not have the effect of decreasing the incidence of offenses in the aggregate. But we will learn nothing from this kind of analysis about why these effects were produced on some but not on other kinds of potential offenders, representing the kind of knowledge required for the effective administration of the criminal law. Such knowledge is in principle within reach, but it requires a quite different type of analytic approach from that provided by aggregate studies.

Given a focus upon crime control policy at the community (as distinct from the individual) level, and assuming the availability of an adequate data base for statistical analysis, the problem remains of constructing valid measures of the concepts central to policy evaluation. Three principal categories of measures are needed: measures of crime, measures of criminal justice agency response, and measures of natural, crimogenic potential. While a number of techniques could be employed to quantify each of these three categories, the following discussion will describe the approach to the measurement problem employed in the California study.

MEASURES OF CRIME

Crime constitutes the dependent variable of deterrence research, for it is variation in its severity and frequency of occurrence that is posited to be a direct function of the action of criminal justice agencies. In the California study we chose to limit our analysis to felonies, and to develop three separate types of measures. First, we quantified the extent of crime in each California jurisdiction by measuring the number of felonies reported to the police per 100,000 population. This measure of the crime rate has been in general use for several decades and is published annually in the Uniform Crime Reports of the Federal Bureau of Investigation.

While the measure of the crime rate is satisfactory for many purposes, its major shortcoming is that all of the felonies that comprise it (i.e., homicide, assault, burglary, robbery, rape, grand larceny, and auto theft) are given equal weights. Since a major assumption of the study was that a jurisdiction with a low rate of serious felonies may have a problem equal in magnitude to that of a jurisdiction with a high rate of relatively nonserious felonies, we decided to construct a second measure of crime seriousness. To accomplish this, each of the felonies comprising the crime rate measure was assigned a weight reflecting its relative seriousness. For a given jurisdiction, the total number of felonies in given categories was multiplied by their respective weights, then summed, and divided by the total number of felonies reported.[21]

A third measure, that of crime, level, was developed to reflect simultaneously both the rate and the seriousness of crime. It was constructed by multiplying the crime rate of a given jurisdiction by its crime seriousness. Accordingly, a jurisdiction with a relatively high crime level would be one with a high frequency of very serious felonies. A jurisdiction with a relatively moderate crime level would be one with either a low frequency of serious offenses or a high frequency of nonserious offenses. Finally, a jurisdiction with a low crime level would be one with a low frequency and seriousness of felonious crime.

Ideally, all three measures of rate, seriousness, and level should be measured over time for each jurisdiction. By subtracting figures of later years from earlier years, it would then be possible to ascertain both quantitative and qualitative shifts in the magnitude of each jurisdiction's respective crime problem (i.e., $x - x'$). Such shifts could then be related to variations in the crimogenic potential of the communities that were studied.

MEASURES OF CRIMINAL JUSTICE AGENCY ACTIONS

The concept of criminal justice agency action entailed an expansion of the conception of criminal sanction of the single event of sentencing by the Superior Court. Agency response was viewed as a concatenated sequence of events involving the several agencies. It was assumed that each of the three major agencies—the police, the lower courts and the superior courts—possesses a unique sanction potential and that the interdependent patterning of this potential should have a marked effect upon fluctuations in crime.

As defendants are processed through the system, their appearance at each stage is contingent upon decisions made at each earlier stage, and each new decision will determine eligibility for any further action. Four key stages of proceedings against suspected and adjudicated felony offenders were defined. These include the police arrest stage, the pre-trial or lower court stage, the superior court or trial stage, and the sentencing stage. The assumption here was that, to offenders, each successive stage represents further risk or jeopardy of receiving the full weight of legal sanction. These stages were measured separately and then compared jointly to derive the *Sanction Pattern* of a jurisdiction.

For each of the jurisdictions under study, four indexes were constructed to measure the utilization of sanction resources at each of the above four key stages. These included measures of *Police*

Sanction Level, Pre-Trial Sanction Level, Superior Court Conviction Level, and *Sentencing Level.* [22] These measures were based on the notion that sanctioning gradients are employed not only by judges at the sentencing stage, but also at earlier stages involving the actions of police, lower court officials, grand juries and district attorneys. The validity of these measures is admittedly impaired by failure to take account of such factors as plea bargaining, bureaucratic data manipulations, and errors of record-keeping.[23] The measures nevertheless provided a general picture of the sanction practices of the California agencies and a basis for cross-jurisdictional comparisons.

MEASURES OF CRIMOGENIC POTENTIAL

A central thesis of this paper, it will be recalled, is that the crime problems of jurisdictions are, to varying degrees, directly attributable to the crimogenic potential of their populations. Accordingly, an assessment of the crime control policy of a jurisdiction requires that the impact of its population characteristics be measured and statistically controlled. In the California study, U.S. Census information was utilized to provide indicators of demographic factors traditionally found to be associated with crime. The census indicators used were socioeconomic level, percentage black, percentage 14 to 25 years of age, percentage male, percentage rural (i.e., percentage of persons living in towns with populations of 2,500 or less), and change in population size since 1960.

A METHOD FOR ASSESSING CRIME CONTROL POLICY

With the development of these three broad groups of measures the major task of the study was to develop a method by which the effectiveness of agency action of a community could be assessed relative to its natural crimogenic potential. Ideally such a method would proceed in three steps. As a first step, crime indicators for a sample of jurisdictions would be computed for at least two adjacent time periods. By a process of subtraction, the degree to which a jurisdiction experienced a notable increase or decrease in its crime problem would then be ascertained. In the second step, it would be asce̶   ̶ ̶ ̶d whether or not such changes in the incidence of crimes v̶   ̶nction of changing population characteristics. As a third   ̶eme cases would be identified. The extremes would include,   ̶ ̶one hand, jurisdictions with serious crime problems *not   ̶d for by changes in population characteristics* and, on the   ̶ ̶nd, jurisdictions with similarly unexplained extremely low v̶.̶ ̶ ̶ ̶ ̶ ̶evels. In the case of either set of extremes, the Sanction Pattern associated with either increased or decreased effectiveness could then be identified.

Despite their relatively comprehensive character, the data in the California study were not adequate to permit the implementation of this method. Data over time were not sufficiently complete to allow for a longitudinal assessment of changing patterns in crime and in agency action. However, it was possible to approximate crudely the ideal method through a *static* analysis of averaged crime statistics for the years 1968, 1969, and 1970.[24] Within this averaged time period, jurisdictions with extremely high or low crime measures whose values were not explained by crimogenic factors were isolated as follows. First, the 58 county jurisdictions of California were classified by four categories based upon population size: those with more than 500,000 population; those with populations between 100,000 and 500,000; between 25,000 and 100,000; and those with populations below 25,000. This classification was developed on the assumption that the effects of the crimogenic factors and the nature of sanctioning patterns would differ by size of county populations. Second, those counties with extremely high or low crime measures were identified. Third, a series of bivariate regressions were calculated within each population grouping to determine the degree to which extreme measures on crime were attributable to naturally occurring population characteristics. Thus, it was possible to identify those jurisdictions whose extreme crime scores were not "explained away" by their crimogenic factors.

No attempt is made here to describe the study in its entirety.[25] However, some of the findings are presented by way of illustrating a crucial feature of its methodology. Table 1 presents the findings

Table 1. SANCTION PATTERN, CRIME LEVEL, AND CRIMOGENIC POTENTIAL FOR COUNTIES OVER 500,000 POPULATION

County	Crime Level	Crimogenic Factors x_1 x_2 x_3 x_4 x_5 x_6 x_7							Sanction Pattern Police	Pre-Trial	Con-viction	Sen-tencing
Alameda	.394								0	−1	0	+1
Contra Costa	.298								−2	+1	0	0
Los Angeles	.412			+		+			+1	+2	−2	−2
Orange	.240								+2	−2	+1	+2
Sacramento	.232								−1	−2	+2	+2
San Bernardino	.254								+1	+2	+2	+1
San Diego	.207								+2	+1	−2	−2
San Francisco	.526	+	+	+		+	+		−1	0	+1	−1
San Mateo	.191	−	−	−		−	−	−	−2	−1	−1	−1
Santa Clara	.202								0	0	−1	0

Key: x_1 = % 14-25 years old; x_2 = % male; x_3 = % Black; x_4 = % more than 1.51 persons per room; x_5 = % lacking plumbing facility; x_6 = % growth 1960-1970; x_7 = % rural.

respecting the class of county jurisdictions with populations exceeding 500,000. Each of these counties is listed with its respective "Crime Level." Under the heading "Crimogenic Factors," a plus or minus sign indicates whether, on the basis of a given bivariate regression model, a jurisdiction's error of prediction (that is, "residual") was either greater than one positive standard deviation from the mean of the prediction errors, or less than one negative standard deviation away from the same mean. A minus sign under this heading indicates that a given jurisdiction's crime level was considerably lower than would be predicted on the basis of its crimogenic potential, while a plus sign indicates that it was substantially higher than would be predicted on the same basis. Under the heading of "Sanction Pattern," the table summarizes agency operation in the four main stages of the criminal justice process. In order to arrive at the figures reported, each of the four measures was standardized by assigning each jurisdiction a quintile rank relative to its position in the distribution of values for its population category.

San Francisco and San Mateo Counties emerged as the extreme cases. In both, their extreme crime measures are not for the most part accounted for by the crimogenic characteristics of their populations. For example, although the crime level of San Francisco County is adequately predicted by the two socioeconomic indicators, the remaining five factors do not account for its crime problem. Thus, it could be argued that it manifests a crime level that is far above what could be expected solely on the basis of natural community factors. The reverse tends to be true for San Mateo County. Its extremely low crime level does not appear to be accounted for by the absence of a natural crimogenic potential.

Examination of the sanction patterns of these two counties does not reveal a dramatic difference. San Mateo County, however, does exhibit a slight tendency toward the escalation of sanction between the arrest and pre-trial stages, maintaining a consistent level of sanction across the stages of conviction and sentencing. While San Francisco County exhibits a similar pattern of escalation between the arrest and pre-trial stages, it also exhibits a sharp drop in sanction level from the conviction to the sentencing stage. It might be suggested that a high sanction level at the conviction stage coupled with a relatively reduced level at the sentencing stage may impede the deterrent effect of criminal justice. But in view of the fact that the data are synchronic rather than diachronic, this inference must remain highly tentative.

Moreover, in the light of the serious data limitation problems discussed earlier, question may be raised whether the true determinant of a relatively successful crime control policy in populous jurisdictions is the pattern formed in San Mateo County. The pattern may itself be a random effect of unknown qualitative variables descriptive of police-community relations, relationships between the prosecutor's office and the lower court judiciary, of the availability and dedication of public defense counsel in felony cases, and the like. Needed to resolve this question is the refinement of the method employed by incorporating variables of this type into the agency sanction measures. Thus, while the California study was unable to arrive at definitive findings, it succeeded in defining the elements of a methodological paradigm that, with the addition of the appropriate more sensitive data, offers promise for advancing the evaluation of crime control policy.

SUMMARY

This paper has presented a discussion of some major conceptual and methodological problems in the evaluation of crime control policy. Crime control was defined as a specialized institutional response to the need for social control, and as limited programmatically to the use of coercive punitive sanction. The methodological problems of policy evaluation as well as some possible solutions were illustrated by drawing on the experience and findings of a study based on California data.

Principal next steps in research on the evaluation of crime control policy include improvement of data resources, as indicated in earlier sections of this report, and the development of more refined measurement methods. The assumption here made is that improved evaluation will identify those elements of policy which may account for crime levels that are by some criterion, excessively high. The criterion here proposed is that level of crime which has been "determined" by the social and demographic composition of the population of any given jurisdiction. The hallmark of effective policy, on this reckoning, is a crime level reduced below this point.

The determination of what that point may be in any jurisdiction becomes, then, of signal importance in the evaluation of crime control policy. In the California study it was found that the crime levels of most jurisdictions at the county level were within the range predicted by their gross social and demographic composition. But it is reasonable to assume that with the development of more adequate indicators of crimogenic potential and their application to the smaller units of police jurisdictions, it will be possible to identify a large number in which the crime rate exceeds expectation. Given such improved identification of smaller "deviant" jurisdictions, the question must then be addressed as to the features of their social and political organization which, reflected in enforcement and adjudication policies, may account for such deviance. On the assumption that crime control policy is a responsive expression of the political life of a community, the improvement of policy requires identification of the elements of the community's political pattern that obstruct more effective crime control, and an assessment of what may be required to remove such obstructions.

NOTES

1. For an early statement of this view, see Durkheim (1960: ch. 2), and Mead (1918: 577-602). More recent expositions are found in Erikson (1966), Dentler and Erikson (1957: 98-107), and Coser (1962: 72-181).

2. An exposition of this effect of the criminal law may be found in Andenaes (1966: 949-983).

3. See Claster (1967: 80-86) and Jensen (1968: 189-201).

4. Common textbook coverage of these correlations may be sampled in Reckless (1961: ch. 3-4).

5. Studies of the social ecology of crime reaching essentially similar conclusions date from the mid-nineteenth century in England and France. See Levin and Lindesmith (1971). An additional relevant early analysis may be found in Mayhew (1861).

6. Zimring and Hawkins (1968) suggest as a practical matter calibrating increases in punitive sanction to the precise point at which those most likely to commit offenses may be deterred.

7. For example, the difficult task of enforcing the essentially unenforceable sumptuary laws respecting such offenses as gambling and prostitution tends to reduce public confidence in crime control agencies. See Packer (1968).

8. The fact of such disjuncture forms the basis of an influential modern theory of deviant behavior. See Merton (1957: ch. 4).

9. For a general discussion of the uses of exculpation among delinquent boys, see Sykes and Matza (1957).

10. How private interests may condition the attribution of legitimacy to the authority of the law is analyzed in Weber (1947).

11. These are extensively dealt with in the body of commentary and analysis constituting the leading edge of development in contemporary criminology. A sampling of the "new" criminology may be found in Turk (1969) and Quinney (1970).

12. Notable in the findings of the California study was the very high proportion of county jurisdictions (80%) whose crime measures fell within the range predicted by their crimogenic potential. So far as this finding suggests the prevailing state of competence in the control of crime, we may characterize current control policy as largely successful in conducting a "holding operation." Whether the criminal justice system should be given high marks for this accomplishment will depend on the aspirations one may hold for the civic culture of the society.

13. When totally unchecked, the tendency to increase the number of categories construed as "marginal" can come to include virtually the entire population. An example of such mass paranoia in recent history is provided by the Stalin era in the Soviet Union. See Connor (1972).

14. For a discussion of the deficiencies of criminal statistics, see Sutherland and Cressey (1970: ch. 2).

15. The first large-scale systematic effort to ascertain the ratio of unreported to reported crimes was undertaken only within the last decade (President's Commission on Law Enforcement and the Administration of Justice: 1967). Continuous victimization survey work is currently under development through collaborative arrangements between

the U.S. Census Bureau and the Law Enforcement Assistance Administration (Dodge and Turner: 1971).

16. A reasonable case may be made for the use of the criminal statistics currently available. Cressey (1966: 146) has noted that

> Despite all their limitations, statistics on crime give information important to our understanding of crime and to hypotheses and theories about it. Similarities and differences in crime rates for certain categories of persons are so consistent that a gross relationship between the category and crime can reasonably be concluded to exist. In these cases, it is practical to assume that if a part of an observed relationship which is due merely to the methods of collecting statistics were eliminated, a real relationship would still remain. After specifying this assumption, we can go ahead and use the statistics. Even if they are gross, relationships which consistently appear and which cannot be readily 'explained away' by citing the inadequacies of crime statistics must be taken into account in any theory of crime and criminality.

17. Nonreporting because of distrust of the police remains a marginal case, largely confined to ghetto populations and to periods of exacerbated police-community relations. Growing police professionalization and the slow but rising recognition of the legal rights of minority racial and ethnic groups are likely to minimize this source of bias in the future.

18. This interpretation of the social basis of recorded crime is cognate with the contention that the relevant concern of legal scholars should be "law in action" rather than the content of legal statutes (Pound, 1923; Geis, 1959). Encoded criminal law is in large part a cumulative record of the success of multifarious groups at various points in time in enlisting the state's powers of coercive sanction in the protection and defense of their interests. But the balance of political power that obtained when particular laws were enacted undergoes change. These changes are registered in the nonenforcement, capped by periodic repeal or reduction of penalty for violation, of laws whose obsolescence marks the destruction of the powers of groups once dominant, or their disappearance from the political stage (Gusfield, 1963). Problems created by the progressive extension of the criminal law to the regulation of commerce are illustrative of the relationships among the factors of political power, enforcement, and the recording of offenses. Given the political power of commercial and financial interest groups, enforcement takes the form typically of regulation rather than the invocation of the penal sanction available in the applicable statutory law. Although the sanction response is thus moderated, a meticulously complete record of offenses is maintained (Sutherland, 1949). The fullness of recording in conjunction with the reluctance to impose severe sanction would appear to express sensitively the approximate equality of power between commercial interest groups and amorphously organized public opinion.

19. Recent studies of the deterrent effect of punishment, using only length of imprisonment as the measure of sanction, have been restricted to summary state data assembled by the U.S. Bureau of Prisons. The utility of such data is severely limited, among other reasons because the state as a jurisdictional unit is too heterogeneous with respect to the range of crime control policy across the local systems of which it is consituted. See Gibbs (1968); Tittle (1969); and Chirocos and Waldo (1970).

20. Because Fourth Count census data on occupation, income, and education were not yet available at the time the study was conducted, use was made of two housing indicators, proportion of dwellings lacking plumbing facilities and with more than 1.5 persons per room. These SES indicators predicted county crime levels (a measure combining rate and

seriousness) in 87.4% of counties with populations above 100,000, and in 78.3% of those with populations below this number.

21. The following weights were assigned to felony offenses: homicide, 26; forcible rape, 11; robbery, 5; assault, 4; burglary, 3; theft, 2; auto theft, 2. The weights were extrapolated from an earlier study by Sellin and Wolfgang (1964). While it would have been desirable to base the weights on a representative sampling of current opinion in California, such an undertaking was beyond the financing of the study.

22. Measures were constructed by the following formulas (N = number):

Police Sanction Level $=$ $\dfrac{(1 \times \text{N Felonies Released}) + (2 \times \text{N Felonies Filed as Misdemeanors}) + (3 \times \text{N Felonies Filed})}{3 \times (\text{Total N of UCR Felonies Reported to the Police})}$

Pre-Trial Sanction Level $=$ $\dfrac{(0 \times \text{N Released in Lower Court}) + (1 \times \text{N Refiled as Misdemeanors}) + (2 \times \text{N Superior Court Dispositions})}{2 \times (\text{Total N Felony Suspects Disposed in Lower Court}) + (\text{N Superior Court Dispositions})}$

Conviction Level $=$ $\dfrac{(0 \times \text{N Acquitted and Released}) + (1 \times \text{N Convicted of Misdemeanor}) + (2 \times \text{N Convicted of Lesser Felony}) + (3 \times \text{Convicted on Original Felony})}{3 \times (\text{Total Felony Suspects Disposed of in Superior Court})}$

Sentencing Level $=$ $\dfrac{(0 \times \text{N Fine Only}) + (1 \times \text{N Probation Only}) + (2 \times \text{N Jail and Probation}) + (3 \times \text{N Jail Only}) + (4 \times \text{N State Prison}) = (5 \times \text{N Death Penalty}}{5 \times (\text{Total Superior Court Convictions})}$

23. For example, police clearance rates may be manipulated to enhance the public image of enforcement efficiency (Skolnick, 1966).

24. Data on both crime and agency action for these three years were averaged for each county jurisdiction in an attempt to control for errors and annual fluctuations.

25. Also investigated in the study were the relationship of crime measures to the severity of punitive sanction; the extent to which the magnitude of the crime problem was differentially associated with factors of social composition and those of punitive sanction; the relative contribution of enforcement and adjudication to variation in crime measures; and the bearing of several aspects of police work on crime. The findings, briefly, were: (1) the more severe the punitive sanction, the lower the crime measure; (2) slightly more than half the variance in crime measures was "explained" by social and demographic factors, and another third by the sanction severity of criminal justice agencies; (3) of the justice system's contribution to variation in crime, most occurred at the stages of police sanction and sentencing; and (4) police sanction exhibited greater deterrent effect under conditions of high acceptance at the pre-trial stage of felony charge filings. For a complete report of the study, see Kobrin et al. (1972).

REFERENCES

ANDENAES, J. (1966) "The general preventive effects of punishment." University of Pennsylvania Law Review 14, 7: 949-983.

CHIRICOS, T. G. and G. P. WALDO (1970) "Punishment and crime: an examination of some empirical evidence." Social Problems 18 (Fall): 200-217.

CLASTER, D. S. (1968) "Comparisons of risk perceptions between delinquents and nondelinquents." Journal of Criminal Law, Criminology, & Police Science 58, 1: 80-86.

CONNOR, W. D. (1972) "The manufacture of deviance: the case of the Soviet purge, 1936-1938." American Sociological Review 37 (August): 403-413.

COSER, L. A. (1962) "Some functions of deviant behavior and normative flexibility." American Journal of Sociology 68 (September): 172-181.

CRESSEY, D. R. (1966) "Crime," in R. K. Merton and R. A. Nisbet (eds.) Contemporary Social Problems. New York: Harcourt, Brace, & World.

DENTLER, R. A. and K. T. ERIKSON (1957) "The function of deviance in groups." Social Problems 7 (Fall): 98-107.

DODGE, R. W. and A. C. TURNER (1971) "Methodological foundations for establishing a national survey of victimization." Presented at the meeting of the American Statistical Association, Fort Collins, Colorado.

DURKHEIM, E. (1960) The Division of Labor in Society. G. Simpson, trans. Glencoe, Ill.: Free Press.

ERIKSON, K. T. (1966) Wayward Puritans. New York: John Wiley.

GEIS, G. (1959) "Sociology, criminology, and criminal law." Social Problems 7 (Summer): 40-47.

GIBBS, J. P. (1968) "Crime, punishment, and deterrence." Southwestern Social Science Quarterly 48 (March): 515-530.

GUSFIELD, J. R. (1963) Symbolic Crusade: Status Politics and the American Temperance Movement. Urbana: University of Illinois Press.

Institute of Public Administration (1952) "Crime records in police management," pp. 114-116 in M. E. Wolfgang, L. Savitz, and N. Johnston (eds.) The Sociology of Crime and Delinquency. New York: John Wiley.

JENSEN, G. F. (1968) "Crime doesn't pay: correlates of a shared misunderstanding." Social Problems 17 (Fall): 189-201.

KOBRIN, S., S. G. LUBECK, E. W. HANSEN, and R. K. YEAMAN (1972) The Deterrent Effectiveness of Criminal Justice Sanction Strategies. Los Angeles: Social Science Research Institute, University of Southern California.

LEVIN, Y. and A. R. LINDESMITH (1971) "English ecology and criminology of the past century," in J. H. Voss and D. M. Petersen (eds.) Ecology, Crime, and Delinquency. New York: Appleton-Century-Crofts.

MAYHEW, H. (1861) London Labour and the London Poor. London: Charles Griffin.

MEAD, G. H. (1918) "The psychology of punitive justice." American Journal of Sociology 23 (March): 577-602.

MERTON, R. K. (1957) Social Theory and Social Structure. Glencoe, Ill.: Free Press.

PACKER, H. (1968) The Limits of the Criminal Sanction. Stanford: Stanford University Press.

POUND, R. (1923) Interpretations of Legal History. New York: Macmillan.

President's Commission on Law Enforcement and the Administration of Justice (1967) The Challenge of Crime in a Free Society. Washington, D.C.: Government Printing Office.

QUINNEY, R. (1970) The Social Reality of Crime. Boston: Little, Brown.

RECKLESS, W. C. (1961) The Crime Problem, 3rd ed. New York: Appleton-Century-Crofts.

SELLIN, T. and M. E. WOLFGANG (1964) The Measurement of Delinquency. New York: John Wiley.

SKOLNICK, J. (1966) Justice Without Trial. New York: John Wiley.

SMITH, R. A. (1970) "The incredible electrical conspiracy," in M. E. Wolfgang, L. Savitz, and N. Johnston (eds.) The Sociology of Crime and Delinquency. New York: John Wiley.

SUTHERLAND, E. H. (1949) White Collar Crime. New York: Dryden.

——— and D. R. CRESSEY (1970) Criminology. Philadelphia: Lippincott.

SYKES, G. M. and D. MATZA (1957) "Techniques of neutralization: a theory of delinquency." American Sociological Review 22 (December): 664-670.

TITTLE, C. R. (1969) "Crime rates and legal sanctions." Social Problems 16 (Spring): 409-423.

TURK, A. (1969) Criminality and Legal Order. Chicago: Rand McNally.

WEBER, M. (1947) The Theory of Social and Economic Organization. A. M. Henderson and T. Parsons, trans. Glencoe, Ill.: Free Press.

ZIMRING, F. E. (1971) Perspectives on Deterrence. Washington, D.C.: Goverment Printing Office. Public Health Service Publication No. 2056.

——— and G. HAWKINS (1968) "Deterrence and marginal groups." Journal of Research in Crime and Delinquency 5: 99-114.

10

SOCIAL SCIENCE EVALUATION AND CRIMINAL JUSTICE POLICY-MAKING: THE CASE OF PRE-TRIAL RELEASE

M I C H A E L   K E L L Y

University of Maryland School of Law

Pre-trial release is a critical stage in the criminal process in which a decision is made how a court is to be assured of the presence of a defendant at trial following apprehension by the police. In probably the majority of criminal cases in most American jurisdictions, no release issue arises either because the police arrest is in the form of a summons to trial (for example, in the case of a traffic or parking ticket), or because the entire procedure is so summary that there is little or no time between arrest and trial of the case. But for large categories of misdemeanor and felony charges involving crimes of most concern to the public and political officials, the release process and the mechanisms designed to assure a defendant's presence at the

AUTHOR'S NOTE: *I would like to thank Douglas Rosenthal, Roy Fleming, Herbert Kaufman, Tony Partridge, and Michael Millemann, whose aid and ideas, through discussions with me, may appear here in a form for which they have no responsibility.*

trial of the charges against him are an important stage of criminal proceedings (Amsterdam et al., 1967).

GENERAL BACKGROUND

The release process in this country is dominated by the use of money bail, that is, the posting of a form of performance bond, usually by a surety company, on behalf of a defendant. The dollar amount of the bond is forfeited to the court if the defendant fails to appear for trial. Typically, those who can afford the professional bondsmen's fees, and who are acceptable risks to the bondsmen, can obtain release from jail prior to trial, while the indigent generally spend their pre-trial time in jail. A wide variety of criticisms have been leveled at the money bail system. These include the effects on the court (and prejudice to the trial outcome) of a defendant who arrives in court directly from jail, the severe negative constraints of incarceration on effective case preparation by lawyers, the economic disruption that incarceration imposes on the families of defendants, the public costs of detention centers and jails, the less tangible public costs of educating young detainees in criminal activity through the socialization process in prison, as well as undermining respect for the deliberative fairness of courts (Harvard Civil Liberties Law Review, 1971). Further evidence (see below on the Bellamy Memorandum) suggests that detention has a marked, indeed integral, relationship with the disposition of criminal charges.

Over the last dozen years, an extraordinary outgrowth of controversy, legal exploration, administrative reform, and legislation have seriously cut back the monopoly of money bail as the method of assuring defendants' presence at trial. The bail reform movement is a classic mixture of American idealism, political inventiveness, and intellectual fashion that has, with some important exceptions, left intact the traditional money bail system.

Although there had been significant critiques and analyses of the bail system in the United States prior to the 1960s (Beeley, 1927; Foote et al., 1954; University of Pennsylvania, 1958), the generating event for bail reform appears to have been the development of a project in New York City by the Vera Foundation in 1961 in which judges were presented with verified information about such matters as defendants' home ties and employment status, in order to encourage them to release defendants "on their own recognizance" (i.e., formal promise to return). The results of the Vera Manhattan Bail Project showed that judges were more inclined to release defendants without bail where such information was at their disposal, and that defendants so released were remarkably inclined to return to court for trial—more so than defendants on money bail (Ares et al., 1963; National Conference on Bail, 1965; Botein, 1965). The Vera Project's success was rather skillfully broadcast and politicized through a series of national conferences (Freed and Wald, 1964; National Conference on Bail, 1965; Institute on Pre-Trial Release, 1965; Friedman, 1973), publications (Tompkins, 1964), sponsorship by the Department of Justice (Friedman, 1973), and the general enthusiasm of a new cause to which lawyers were particularly susceptible in the early 1960s. Replications of the Vera Project spread like "wildfire" (Botein, 1965: 331). By 1968 there were about 100 such release on recognizance (or R.O.R.) programs under development throughout the country (Friedman, 1973).

The interest in bail reform also generated programs of legislative change such as the Federal Bail Reform Act of 1966, and the model bail reform law prepared by the American Bar Association on which some states like Maryland, for example, have patterned their bail rules (U.S. Code, 1968: § 3041, 3141-43, 4146-52, 3568; American Bar Association, 1968). This legislation essentially attempts to change the criteria of committing magistrates (the court officials who make the release determination) from reliance on money bail as the standard of control over defendants to a presumption that R.O.R. is the standard rule. A variety of other methods short of money bail (such as releasing a defendant to the custody of reliable parties or agencies, imposing conditions on travel and living or associational arrangements) are also prescribed in most reform bail rules.

The political climate which kindled bail reform changed rather markedly by the end of the decade, when the new national administration sought to enact a measure which would articulate and legitimatize an underlying theme in the use of money bail, preventive detention.[1] After extensive debate, a preventive detention measure permitting a court to hold a defendant in jail on grounds of "dangerousness" was passed for the District of Columbia in 1970, but the new law was so laden with procedural safeguards that it has proven to be a hopelessly time-consuming and inefficient detention mechanism by comparison with money bail, and it has apparently fallen into disuse (Bases and McDonald, 1972).

The legal literature spawned from these developments is an extensive one ranging from pitched battles over preventive detention, to constitutional attacks on the money bail system, to largely laudatory reviews and advocacy of the Vera projects and bail statutes such as the Federal Act.

Despite the significant progress and change in pre-trial detention since the early 1960s, detention before trial still remains an extraordinarily widespread phenomenon. The number of detainees in jails and lock-ups at any one time roughly approximates the number of sentenced prisoners.[2] Although one must discount heavily for the effects of recidivism, it seems probable that on an annual basis, owing to the higher turnover in detention facilities, pre-trial detention affects perhaps as many as a million people a year, many times the number of sentenced individuals. There are some indications that the number of pre-trial detainees has actually risen during the period of bail reform agitation (OEO, 1972: 7).

EVALUATION AND BAIL REFORM

Social science evaluation, at it is characterized in this paper, comprises a wide range of fundamentally quantitative techniques of measuring and interpreting social phenomena: simple counting, the calculation of percentages and rates, cross tabulations, correlations and regression analyses, based among others upon random samples and comparisons between experimental and control groups, as well as the inferences and insights drawn from the use of such techniques: generalizations, outcome evaluations, projections, or policy analyses (Rossi and Williams, 1972; Wholey et al., 1971).[3] Such evaluative techniques and models are enormously useful in the legal analysis and administration of criminal justice programs, and they are increasingly being imposed and funded by the Law Enforcement Assistance Administration of the Justice Department. My concerns are with certain uses of these quantitative evaluation tools and the failure to understand some dangers as well as utilities of social science evaluation in criminal justice. I should also say that the area I intend to examine may be somewhat rare in the field of evaluation of governmental social programs, namely, it exists. Even more remarkable, much of the ongoing work in bail reform cannot be dismissed as either pathetic failures to account for ideological disagreements over program objectives or outright falsification to satisfy political needs. While significant problems of poor record-keeping and inadequate evaluation in the bail reform area exist (OEO, 1973a), there are many excellent examples of quantitative research.

Bail reform has always been dominated by numbers. From the early bail reform literature (Foote et al., 1954; University of Pennsylvania Law Review, 1958) to the recent arguments over preventive detention (Mitchell, 1969; Dershowitz, 1968; Tribe, 1970), statistics of release, recidivism, bail forfeitures, and failures-to-show have been the grist for the mills of constitutional debate. The entire discussion of bail has been a mixed empirical-legal argument.

The discussion-by-statistics in the bail debates is no novelty to a legal literature in which the "Brandeis" brief (empirically based legal arguments) has been a feature for well over half a century, and in which class-action litigation has enjoyed enormous popularity. Pre-trial release seems, however, particularly susceptible to quantitative evaluation: the process itself involves management of large volumes of defendants through a relatively speedy labeling process with a limited range of alternatives. The set of possible decisions appear to have little of the strategic and other complexities of, say, the trial process. We have, therefore, in bail, a social process or program with relatively useful statistical indicators—a readily available "data" base that most social scientists would welcome.

I want now to examine some issues regarding the use of quantitative evaluation in pre-trial release from three perspectives: social scientist, lawyer, and system manipulator or "reformer."

SOCIAL SCIENCE AND PRE-TRIAL RELEASE

Two recent studies of pre-trial release illustrate some of the fundamental problems faced by social scientists in evaluation of pre-trial release. A study by the National Bureau of Standards (Locke et al., 1970) (hereafter the NBS study) and a study by students at the Harvard Law School funded by the American Bar Foundation (Harvard Civil Liberties Law Review, 1971—hereafter, the Harvard study) examined, in the context of the preventive detention debate, the problems of "interim" crime, i.e., crime committed by released defendants prior to disposition of their case at trial. This recidivism issue touches on the underlying problem of all bail systems, namely, the extent to which pre-trial incarceration is used and is effective to prevent anticipated crime by apprehended suspects prior to disposition of the case at trial. The reform bail project initiators began to keep records on arrests of releasees prior to trial to prove that not only were released-on-recognizance defendants more likely to appear at trial than those released on bail, but also they were less likely to engage in criminal activity (Molleur, 1966: 33). The issue became politicized in 1969 when the Nixon Administration claimed that some form of explicit pre-trial detention (other than the form universally in use in this country, namely, high money bail) might have a significant effect on preventing crime (Mitchell, 1969).

The NBS study found, on the basis of an examination of 426 released defendants in the District of Columbia in the first half of 1968, that about 17% of defendants charged with felonies and 8% of defendants charged with misdemeanors (11% overall) were rearrested prior to trial. Only 7% of charged felons were rearrested for a felony (1970: 134). While persons arrested for "dangerous" crimes (defined as Robbery, Burglary, Arson, Rape, and Sale of Illegal Drugs under § 23-1331 of the D.C. Code—the criteria of the Preventive Detention Statute examined by both the NBS and Harvard studies) tended to be rearrested at a somewhat higher rate (25%) than felons in general, the NBS study found no significant correlations with (or "predictors" of) rearrest in such factors as initial charge, previous record, age, education, or community ties. Unemployment, however, appeared to be a prominent characteristic of rearrested defendants (1970: 134-151).

The most significant finding of the NBS study, however, was the development of an "exposure index" by which the researchers showed that generally the longer the period of release prior to trial, the greater the likelihood of rearrests. The NBS study also indicated the greater likelihood of rearrest during release pending sentencing and appeal than during release before trial (1970: 152-165).

The Harvard study is a full-scale, empirically based attack on the constitutionality of the preventive detention provisions of the District of Columbia Court Reform and Criminal Procedure Act (D.C. Cod Ann. § § 23-1321-1332). From a study of 657 defendants arrested for "violent" and "dangerous" crimes (generally speaking, Homicide, Kidnapping, Aggravated Assault, Rape, Arson, Burglary, Robbery, Extortion or Blackmail by threat of violence) in Boston during the first six months of 1968, the researchers found that 12.3% of the sample were rearrested prior to trial, and 9.6% were convicted for crimes while on bail or release; 4.1% of the sample were rearrested and convicted for dangerous and violent crimes (1971: 308-309). The Harvard study found no correlation with (or predictability of) subsequent criminal activity in such factors as the initial charges (including drug offenses), family ties, length of residence in the community, and (unlike the NBS study) employment or unemployment. Defendants with records of juvenile arrests, prior incarcerations, prior convictions, and two or more prior failures to appear at trial had substantially higher recidivism rates than those without such records (1971: 313). The main thrust of the Harvard study was to show that the combination of criteria listed in the D.C. Preventive Detention Bill for holding a defendant in preventive detention were so far from predictive accuracy (namely, more often wrong than right by a considerable margin) that constitutional problems of equal protection (unreasonable classification) and due process (failure to meet the test of rational relation) may result (1971: 333-347). The Harvard study tended to confirm the NBS study findings of the importance of time in bail crime: 29 of the 41 detected crimes and 15 of the 19 most serious crimes in Boston occurred after the sixtieth pre-trial day (1971: 360).

How accurate are these figures? The answer must be full of skepticism. The parameters of the studies, the framework of significant events, are keyed to the due process formalities of criminal procedure, an appropriate choice in light of the legal evaluation purposes of the studies. It is not clear, however, that events in the formal criminal process affect either the decision-makers or the defendants. Judges, or magistrates, or police officials who subscribe to forms of preventive detention or "crime control" views may not consider the timing of the threat of crime (that is, in the period prior to trial) to be of more relevance than the ostensibly criminal characteristics of the defendant in general. Nor is it obvious how, if at all, individuals engaging in antisocial behavior control or "time" their activity in anticipation of forthcoming trial, or, for that matter, whether they distinguish at all between pre-trial and post-trial time, in jail or on probation. There is therefore a strangely artificial quality to the entire analysis. Recidivism is a given: the only variable is the stage at which it occurs: pre-trial, post-trial, probation, or parole. The measure of interim crime is largely a measure of the speed of processing.

There are more obvious difficulties as well. The Harvard study researchers put it in this way:

> As long as some crimes go unreported, reported crimes go unsolved, false and mistaken arrests occur, pleas are bargained, innocent men convicted, and guilty criminals released erroneously or because of violation of their procedural rights, there can never be a completely accurate measure of recidivism [1971: 317].

While the Harvard analysts argue that serious felonies are less unreported, and less undetected and less unsolved, than other crimes, the relationship between arrest, conviction, and crime remains, at best, a highly tenuous one (President's Commission, 1967: 20-22). Moreover, the records in a given jurisdiction and the lack of care of the researchers may lead to inaccuracies, and out-of-state or out-of-jurisdiction crimes are generally not included (Locke et al., 1970: 131-133).

The two analyses differ markedly in the confidence placed in the data. The NBS study is replete with apologies, caveats, and a general sense of what an arduous and uncertain task it is to work with court records. One has the sense from the document (and I say this not having questioned any participants or close observers) of the sensitivity of the researchers toward charges that their work was too slow and too tentative to have been useful or particularly clarifying in the preventive detention debate. The Harvard study, on the other hand, bristles with confidence and contains not a breath of qualification of the accuracy or comprehensiveness of either their research or the primary records on which it is based. My own work in Baltimore puts me strongly in the NBS camp.

Any quantitative analysis which works off of records as bad as court records requires much in the way of judgment to interpret difficult, incomplete, and contradictory entries. What is more worrisome is the use of court records at all. There must be serious question, on several grounds, whether record (i.e., outcome) analyses accurately reflect what goes on in those courts and police districts where large numbers of defendants are labeled and released on a mass production basis. The abstraction of the records is severe and distorting: the records can lend dignity and weight to a process routinized and superficial; they can homogenize the unique and idiosyncratic;[4] they simply do not reflect the character, the quality, and procedural justice of a court operation. Moreover, they can be profoundly misleading about court activity.

Perhaps a useful example of the inaccuracies which plague pre-trial release studies is the recording of forfeitures or failures-to-appear. Courts keep a variety of records about people who fail to show at trial or at some preliminary stage before trial; some are listed as postponements; others, failures to appear at trial; still others are bail forfeitures (i.e., formal action declaring money bail forfeited or given up to the court because of the nonappearance of the bailed defendant), or bench warrants issued for the arrest of recalcitrant defendants who fail to appear. The judgment about, and corresponding record entry on, who is a fugitive from justice is undoubtedly handled differently by each jurisdiction, if not by each individual judge. At least in Baltimore, formal charges of failure to appear are routinely dismissed at trial, presumably because the want of appearance was excusable or not willful in some way. Rarely, if ever, does the literature on R.O.R. explain local forfeiture policies, and even such an explanation may not be much help. Are there, for example, differences in judicial attitudes toward blacks and whites, indigents and nonindigents, bail and R.O.R. expressed in terms of a propensity to record a formal failure to appear for the record and to issue a warrant? Such a difference, for example, may rest upon an evaluation by the judge of the reliability of the commercial bondsmen to pursue and produce an individual who fails to show, compared to a Vera-type project, or it may simply be a function of a predilection favoring bondsmen and a reluctance to forfeit bail. These uncertainties are part of the reason that comparative failure-to-appear rates and interim arrest rates published by bail reform projects are so difficult to interpret or believe. [5]

The use of evaluative techniques in the pre-trial release area raises the extraordinary discrepancy between our rather primitive under-standing of what "the data" means—that is, what kind of action it stands for—and the sophistication of quantitative methodologies with which researchers seek to manipulate the data. There is remarkably little in the literature that is descriptive of how the lower-level criminal courts operate.[6] Without this kind of system-wise background, quantitative analysis resembles building an elaborate castle on quicksand—that is how I would characterize attempts to develop comparisons of such activities as appearance and forfeiture rates between cities without enormous research and statistical control investments.

It is obviously an indefensible posture to despair of any quantitative analysis until "the data" reach perfection, or, what is perhaps more characteristic, to project grandiose information systems well beyond the capability of the court institutions to manage or finance. This discrepancy between ideal research con-ditions and real world data, and ideal experimental subjects and real social programs, is a constant and theoretically unresolvable theme in the world of social program evaluation (Rossi and Williams, 1972). The mark of sophistication in evaluation today no doubt is the ability to create "second best" solutions to arrive at relatively valid analyses which are compromises between the textbook models and the crude order of institutional measures.[7] The recidivism analyses discussed earlier are clearly "second best" efforts that are legitimate evaluative efforts, no matter how shakey and tenuous a connection the indicators of arrest and conviction may bear to recidivism during the relatively short timespan of pre-trial release. Moreover, they illustrate the utility of quantitative evaluation when the primary question posed is narrowed to the analysis of the validity of measureable standards to achieve measureable goals. The two studies showed why preventive detention defined in statutory terms would not work if it pretended to be an effective bar to pre-trial crime. The negative value of such research makes sense. The "positive" use of such tools, i.e., information about what does work to achieve certain goals, is a rarity.

The shadowy and problematic nature of the data and the difficult task of evaluators to reconstruct data and undertake sensible, less-than-ideal analyses does not, I imagine, distinguish pre-trial release from any field of evaluation of social policy. What is disconcerting in the criminal justice field is what might be termed the social structure of the response to these issues. We have all heard the usual lamentations about the fragmentation of the criminal justice system—its federal structure wedding it to a myriad of local jurisdictions around the nation and a further Balkanization of the structure that divides it between unstable and often warlike functional agencies. The consequences for evaluation are that very few organizations have the capacity or will to engage in systematic evaluation, let alone careful upgrading of the data reflecting the reality of their operations. All data are ammunition for the competitive games agencies feel compelled to play of justifying their effectiveness in the war on crime, or the Sisyphean struggle against the caseload.

What has resulted, as the pressures by LEAA have mounted for evaluation that extends beyond project monitoring, is that evaluation institutions and programs funded by the federal government have begun to assume a pathological cast. On the one hand, research organizations, consultant and university suppliers of social science analysis, commit themselves to growth in the form of the development of large-scale operations and capacity precisely because of their perceptions that methodological purity and the wretched quality of court data require extremely expensive reconstructions of data in parallel with existing data systems. Their interest is the development of organizational capacity large enough to carry on the quality and scale of research necessary to develop "responsible" (in their terms) evaluation (Rossi, 1971; Williams, 1970). On the other hand, LEAA, conscious perhaps of the danger of the increasing concentration of evaluation sophistication in organizational structures outside of court systems, is willing to fund the appetite of the courts for computer-based data systems, most of which only exacerbate data problems by ignoring the fundamental management aspects of data reliability and focus on compilation or scheduling problems. The direction of financing and activity tends to be either parochial or cosmic: either the self-serving statistics-mongering of agencies trying either to maintain their equilibrium in the budget process with the data from their new electronic box, or to jump through LEAA-imposed hoops for their grants' continuation; or large-scale "sophisticated stuff" that (assuming it is methodologically sound) is extremely expensive and largely ineffective in terms of policy-making because of the inevitable time lag and institutional distance involved in the relationship. What we are in desperate need of, and what cannot easily be programmed by LEAA methods, is careful handpicking of promising court environments and the development of evaluation *within* court management systems.

LAWYERS AND PRE-TRIAL RELEASE

Recently, a sociologist, Donald J. Black, characterized much of the legal literature on contemporary criminal justice issues, especially police, as legal effectiveness analysis, that is, a comparison of different forms of due process ideals with reality (Black, 1972). To no one's surprise, serious shortcomings or gaps between theory and practice are invariably uncovered. Black was critical of this approach because it leads nowhere in terms of development of a more comprehensive theory of law. He did, however, acknowledge that matching empirical findings to legal ideals could be justifiable in terms of providing evidence to legal reformers. In fact, some of the early legal effectiveness analyses on bail, the studies at the University of Pennsylvania Law School in the 1950s (Foote et al., 1954;

University of Pennsylvania Law Review, 1958), were powerful and superbly documented indictments of the traditional money bail system. The legal literature on bail since the initiation of the Vera Foundation project is a variant of legal effectiveness analysis: the predominant mode of analysis adds to the empirical accounts of "reality" (in the form of citing some quantitative accounts of bail practices), and to the discussion of the proper legal framework of bail, the citation of the Federal Bail Reform Act, or the Vera Project model as an encouraging and hopeful effort to reduce the enormity of the gap between the real and the ideal.[8] The underlying analysis, conducted with varying degrees of passion and scholarship, is generated from the perceived "gap," and the bail reform act or the Vera projects are convenient, consistently reported solutions. This kind of legal effectiveness analysis with prescribed antidotes is an example of what one scholar (in the different context of a critique of systems, not legal, analysis) calls "reducing wholes and blending parts," that is, the reduction of complex structures to separate parts and then making features of those parts comparable—a "profoundly limiting and distorting mode of analysis" (Tribe, 1972). The reason it is so limited is not simply that it derives much of the force of its argument from the value of proving yet again the staggering differences between due process procedural requirements and the criminal procedural reality, but also that it fails to probe the characteristics of the crime control institutional environment that are relevant and amenable to change.

The important issue is not the gap, but the advantages and limitations of alternate strategies of narrowing the gap. Here is where a purely legal or constitutional analysis is a form of reductionism, for quantitative analysis keyed to due process standards is not very helpful in examining who really contributes to setting policy in the system (e.g., police, judges, bondsmen), what are the origins of their policies, and what are the possibilities of change. The legal analysis of the bail problem has proven to be of rather short-term interest. I allude to what appears to be a prevailing sense in the scholarly legal world of having "solved" the bail problem with the enactment of the Federal Bail Reform Act of 1966.[9] Nothing, of course, could be farther from the truth. In Maryland, for example, there are extraordinary discrepancies between urbanized jurisdictions applying the same rule—discrepancies that are not simply attributable to the obviously contrasting crime patterns or appearance habits in the two jurisdictions. Baltimore in 1972 released about 20% to 25% of defendants on R.O.R.; Montgomery County, a suburban jurisdiction, released about 75% on either R.O.R. or a variant of it, personal bond (Kelly and Morlock, 1973: 11-12, 31-32). One would expect similar discrepancies to prevail in federal courts and in other jurisdictions which have "solved" the problem of bail through legislation. The only "solution" is, in my opinion, that bail has dropped out of scholarly fashion because there is so little fashion in the complexities of administration.

One factor that perhaps contributes to the sense of "solution" among lawyers is an assumption underlying the Bail Reform Act that lawyers and some form of quasi-adversarial proceedings (embodied in provisions mandating a judicial review of release decision of the magistrate within 24 hours) would become part of the release determination process (Wald and Freed, 1966; but see Bogomolny and Sonnenreich, 1969). The notion that the addition of the opportunity for lawyers to participate in trial-like proceedings at this early stage of the criminal process would significantly change the operations of pre-trial release systems is a profound misunderstanding of the role of professional criminal defense attorneys in courts. The extent of lawyers' willingness to participate (we found in Baltimore that less than 2% of the cases sampled involved lawyers at a bail review hearing) and the nature of the systematic accommodations defense lawyers make with courts raises serious questions of how beneficial the effect of professionalism and advocacy is in the criminal process (see Blumberg, 1967).

The other typical "solution" proposed in the legal literature, the Vera-type bail projects, are experiencing chronic and severe difficulties maintaining a stable existence (OEO, 1973a: 7-10), and are probably providing R.O.R. services to less than one in thirty persons in this country charged with minor crimes (OEO, 1973: 7-10).

One of the findings of our Baltimore work illustrates the complexity of legal solutions to release problems. Unlike the results of virtually all previous studies, we found that failure to be released on bail did not correspond to increased bail amount, nor with higher conviction rates and more adverse treatment by the courts compared with those released. An apparent abnormality of the Baltimore system was the extent to which defendants on low money bail (below $250) had significantly lower release rates (40%) than release rates of defendants placed on higher bail ($250 to $1,000—60% released; and $1,000 to $5,000—58% released). Moreover, these incarcerated low-bail defendants, again defying the findings of all previous studies, did far better in court: 39% of those incarcerated on low bail had their cases "nol prossed" (i.e., dismissed by the prosecutor) and over 64% of the low bails were not convicted, while only 15% of the freed low bails were nol prossed and 46% not convicted. Completely opposite results (that is, an apparent correlation between release on bail and "better" disposition results) obtained with defendants given high money bail (Kelly and Morlock, 1973: 15-18, 22-23).

The factors that led to these results were two due process reforms in Maryland law: the elimination of the crime of drunkenness in 1968, and the advent of the reform bail rule in 1971. The old routine before 1971 of immediate summary disposition of drunks with a three-to-five-day sentence in City Jail had, I think, evolved into a system of pre-trial incarceration on low bail of drunks charged with assault or disorderly conduct terminating with a "nol pros" (in effect, dismissal) of the charges at trial three to five days later. The new system is, of course, hardly distinguishable from the old in the defendant's eyes. For judges, it involved adaptation of "due process model" rules to effect "crime control model" attitudes (see Packer, 1968).

The policy resiliency and administrative adaptability of lower courts illustrated by this example are simply not part of most legal dialogues. It is precisely such critical institutional characteristics that legal effectiveness analysis fails to engage. It is result-oriented, not process-oriented (see Tribe, 1972). It is touting solutions that superficially address the gap between theory and practice, when the most critical problems are how can we go about analyzing and developing the reform strategies which affect the complex organizational structures of courts.

SYSTEM REFORM AND PRE-TRIAL RELEASE

We have alluded earlier to the heavily data-oriented nature of debate over bail. The figures in pre-trial release arguments have a peculiar utility that bears exploration. During the early days of bail reform in the early sixties, figures were compiled to show, among other things, that few defendants of limited means were freed prior to trial, and secondly, that defendants who met certain criteria of reliability (cast in terms of acceptable living situations, employment, and previous criminal record) could be counted upon to appear at trial with less risk of nonappearance than even those released on money bail. The arguments from the numbers were meant to point up the inadequacies of the pre-trial release system typical of courts and police departments nationwide. The figures were essentially the reporting systems of the Manhattan Bail Project in New York City and other projects modeled after Vera in Washington, D.C., and elsewhere. The projects were essentially designed to show up and embarrass the existing system, to illustrate that policy change was feasible and practical. These projects were pilot programs in the sense of showing the way to change in the systems in which they operated. Heavy reliance on the figures was critical to their efficacy and purpose. The projects deliberately and self-consciously set themselves to compete with, to outperform, the traditional methods of release, and their statistics were the proof of their argument.

The Vera-type programs were successful to the extent they "piloted" a system to change release attitudes and policies by legislation or by rules. While it seems obvious that the impact of the operations of reform pre-trial mechanisms lag far behind the intentions of legislative draftsmen (Bogomolny and Sonnenreich, 1969), it is fair, I think, to note that significant progress has probably been made in many jurisdictions in terms of extending use by courts of R.O.R. and other less onerous means of pre-trial release such as the 10% rule (by which defendants are released upon payment to the court of 10% of the bond set).[10] What is not clear is whether continuation of projects modeled on the Manhattan Bail Project is at all critical to the continuation or extension of the use of R.O.R. or other release methods.

The proliferation of the "pilot" programs during the 1960s was meant to prove the point of change, that is, to undertake advocacy by illustration. Their worth as institutions had to be measured by the extent to which they compelled the adoption of their perspective. Instead, the main strategy of the bail reformers was to advocate the adoption of the program itself. Replicating the Manhattan project was more the theme than achieving the Manhattan results. The "administrative strategy" (Dill, 1972) and justice-increasing "technology" (Friedman, 1973) were apparently never clearly distinguished from the mechanics of the technology and the administration of the strategy. The idea behind the Manhattan project became lost in the technique used to prove the idea. And the figures and quantitative studies used by programs served to mask this problem. The Manhattan replicas began to assess their worth in terms of the very measures (such as forfeiture rates and R.O.R. rates) they used to articulate the call for change. The same types of analyses were used, but the evaluation shifted from an effectiveness analysis of the entire pre-trial processing system to quantitative monitoring of the bail project itself. As the pilot programs either triggered superficial legislative change without significant administrative follow-through or failed to induce significant alteration in the release policies of the system, the figures were transformed into self-serving rationalia of an institution looking for measures of its survival, not for measures of the system's failures. Indeed, the most conspicuous failure of the Vera program may have been its breeding capacity: projects of indefinite duration and doubtful efficacy have sprung up all over the country on the doubtful premise that institutionalizing change within the court system was tantamount to changing the courts as institutions.

There are many reasons for the speedy transformation or premature institutional "aging" of Vera-type bail reform projects. Many of the programs were, from the start, exceedingly poor reproductions of the original model. For example, they mistakenly focused on the initial interview, rather than the more crucial verification and follow-up functions relating to defendants (Friedman, 1973). Some bail programs developed as administrative agencies identical to probation departments serving a crime control phi-

losophy of their judicial masters and appear in some cases to have
been designed to limit and forestall efforts to expand R.O.R.[11]
The personnel and internal organizational structure of the bail
projects have undergone critical changes. For example, in New York
City the Vera Project used eager law students for interviewing
personnel, a fact undoubtedly contributing in a major way to their
success and assuring the near impossibility of replication of success in
more bureaucratic organizational environments.[12] The transfer of
the Vera program to the New York City Probation Department
effected significant changes in the spirit and purposes of the program
and marked a decline in its efficiency (Friedman, 1973). Probation
officers, court clerks, judge-appointed bail investigators, and former
policemen have replaced the perhaps more energetic original Vista
volunteers and students (Wice, 1973a). Independently funded and
operated "pilot" programs have been shifted to the budgetary and
policy constraints of the courthouse. Increasing dependence on the
court agencies has major effects on release agency policies. Forest
Dill, in his superb study of the Oakland, California, Pre-Trial Release
Project spells out how an undesigned accommodation to the lower
court "organizational imperatives" occurs as a release project
becomes a servicing agency to judges, prosecutors, and defense
attorneys largely concerned with moving the caseload. Indeed, Dill
argues that for Oakland the prediction of case outcome was an
integral part of the initial release recommendation decision (Dill,
1972: 132-191). The apparently widespread use of "subjective"
decision techniques in release projects (Wice, 1973a) has moved far
from the Manhattan project's formula, which was at least an attempt
to develop systematic criteria for release. The small pilot programs
could effectively "cream" the best prospects for R.O.R. without
having to address themselves to the realities of extension of R.O.R.
to a substantial part of the defendant population.

It is not my purpose to review systematically the factors which
have led to extensive changes in the character of pre-trial release
programs. But it seems likely that the presence of quantitative
measures uncritically accepted as valid indices of success enormously
enhanced the process of change. To the project leaders, the statistics
had always seemed to justify the project, when in fact the uses of the

quantitative materials were being radically transformed from advocacy to self-justification. The figures were deceptive. The aura of objective value lent itself to change in the values of pre-trial release programs. For those programs—perhaps the majority—that never were reforming events, the figures lent not a continuity with an earlier stage but a deceptive solidarity with other programs or published materials. The figures in this case appear to have had a strongly supportive effect on the peculiar institutional ambiguities of bail reform programs, by which reformers and lower court managers with profoundly different purposes in mind could welcome the spread of Vera-type projects. The figures served as an effective disguise for very different organizational realities.

There are other instances of the diverting effect of the predilection for quantitative reporting. An elaborate, carefully designed OEO questionnaire sent to known pre-trial release programs in 1972 asked for extensive statistical and evaluative data, but there was no indication of their exploring the fundamental purposes of bail reform of reducing massive and unjust pre-trial incarceration: not a word about local jails, historical detention policies, or jail populations that ought to be critical to evaluation of project impacts (OEO, 1972b).

Another such example, I believe, is the Bellamy Memorandum, a study sponsored by the New York Legal Aid Society and published in March 1972, the main thrust of which was an analysis of the correlation (or explanatory relationship) between pre-trial incarceration (for inability to raise money bail) and disposition by prison sentence. The Memorandum is an elaborate, methodologically sophisticated analysis in support of the New York Legal Aid Society's suit, *Bellamy v. Judges of New York City,* to declare the New York City bail system unconstitutional as a violation of the Equal Protection and Due Process clauses of both the state and federal constitutions. The plaintiffs sought to obtain a remedy similar to the American Bar Association's *Standards Relating to Pre-Trial Release,* the Federal Bail Reform provisions, and Maryland District Court Rule 777, namely a presumption of release on recognizance, the preferential use of nonfinancial alternatives to bail, the use of money bail only as a last resort, a hearing, a statement of reasons for refusal to release on recognizance, and prompt automatic de novo review (Criminal Law Bulletin, 1972).

Using a sample of 857 cases of criminal defendants represented by the New York Legal Aid Society prior to December 15, 1971, who were charged generally with more serious crimes, the study examined the "ins" (that is, those who were detained) in comparison with the "outs" (that is, those released prior to trial through R.O.R. or ability to "make" bail). The study found enormous disparities between the "ins" and "outs" in terms of dismissals, probation, and prison sentences of varying length—all in favor of the "outs":

> those released have one chance in six of going to prison; by contrast, three out of five of those jailed receive prison sentences, and much longer ones at that. Furthermore, 33% of the released who were found guilty got a prison term as contrasted with more than 75% of the detained (Criminal Law Bulletin, 1972: 468).

The study then examined "legally relevant" explanations for the disparity in result by continuing to correlate results with "in" or "out" status while controlling for other explanations of differing results: seriousness of charge (felony or misdemeanor), type of crime, weight of the evidence (confession or "evidence found on the accused"), aggravated circumstances (injury, use of weapon, and resisting arrest), prior criminal record or lack thereof, and personal characteristics such as family ties and employment. The same, markedly different outcomes for releasees and detainees obtained, regardless of the other potential explanations of the outcome.

The Appellate Division of the New York Supreme Court, rejecting the Legal Aid position, reacted to the documentation in this way:

> Both experience and logic show us that, all other imperfections and discrepancies aside, the plaintiffs' figures and statistics are but a shadow of reality, misconstruing cause and effect and putting the cart before the horse. A judge in his expertise and in applying the bail rules heretofore set forth, . . . may decide to hold the defendant. It is not because bail is required that the defendant is later convicted. It is because he is likely to be convicted that bail may be required. To put it another way, "figures don't lie, but liars figure." . . . The factors for allowing bail, when properly applied, generally lead to a conclusion that those denied bail are more likely to be convicted, and if the statistics prove this out, as they do, it shows the system is working rather than, as plaintiffs contend, that it is, instead, detrimental to a defense against accusation [New York Supplement, 1973].

The nonresponse of the court to the issues raised by *Bellamy* must give serious pause to those who hope to confront directly, through constitutional litigation, the problems of pre-trial release. On the other hand, I would like to suggest that perhaps the "scientific" evidence of the Memorandum detracted from the case against bail. While there are some substantial methodological criticisms that can be leveled at the Memorandum,[13] the important issue is the way in which the litigants, perhaps for understandable strategic or political reasons, attempted to keep their argument abstract: "The inescapable conclusion," the Memorandum argues, "is that the fact of detention itself causes those detained to be convicted far more often and sentenced much more severely than those who are released" (Criminal Law Bulletin, 1972: 481). The "fact of detention itself" is, of course, not independent of the way the New York court system organizes itself to deal with its caseload. New York City is almost exclusively a plea-bargaining disposition system (unlike Baltimore, for example); and pre-trial release is, like the initial charge, one of the labels through which the bargainers assess the value of the offense "commodity." To speak of a separate, self-contained "bail system" is to miss the critical idea that bail is an integral part of the mass processing by which police, courts, prosecutors, and defense attorneys cope with their caseload. The Memorandum explained a correlation, not the system that creates the correlation. The Bellamy Memorandum is, above all, an indictment of the systematic way in which Legal Aid attorneys participate in that mass processing. Or, stated in more hygienic and simplistic terms, a fundamental defect of the statistics is that there was no control for the impact of counsel, to distinguish private counsel, the absence of counsel, or the experience and ability of counsel.[14]

SOME CONCLUSIONS

The cautions that the pre-trial release experience raise with respect to quantitative evaluation are not simply those of worrying about poor work, or misunderstanding about the proper role of scientific analysis. There are, I submit, built-in or systematic problems with quantitative evaluation. The financial and organizational costs of developing effective and accurate quantitative analyses in independent scholarly organizations with "credibility" seriously distract attention and resources from the more important job of developing within entry-level court systems the administrative and information capacities to make system improvements. The task of educating a class of people critically involved in the process of change—lawyers (who by training, incentive, or the social divisions within their own ranks are naive about the institutional arrangements of lower courts)—about the dangers and distractions of quantitative reporting and scientific analysis is a formidable one, particularly when the task is, I would venture to guess, so far from complete within the ranks of social scientists. The figures and quantitative analyses unleashed by automated data processing are tools of measurement that can be structured and used in a variety of ways. They certainly do not compel us toward what should be our fundamental concerns to make our courts more fair, humane, and effective. In fact, I think the record is to the contrary. The abstractions of measurement in this field of criminal justice policy seems to be inherently more distracting than enhancing to the process of analysis.

The history of the bail reform movement ought to be told, not by a lawyer, but by a political scientist or sociologist who can examine the strategies and direction of the reform from a perspective of the social structure and background of its leadership. The replication of the Vera pilot bail program in scores of cities throughout the country and the enactment of Federal Bail Reform were works of orthodoxy and institutional naiveté, at least for those who viewed the program as significant system reform.

There are lessons of the experience to date for lawyers, reform-oriented court administrators and LEAA officials, and social scientists, in addition to the obvious need for there to be much greater communication of their disciplinary insights and sharing of strengths. The fundamental lesson must be a greater appreciation of the institutional complexities and organizational "rules" of the courts with which they are dealing. For institutional reformers in the courts area, the experience with Vera-type projects suggests how crucial it is to think through the appropriateness of establishing a new administrative function that must depend for its support on the existing court case-processing system. The efforts underway in some jurisdictions to institutionalize a separate pre-trial services agency to combine various pre-trial diversion efforts with R.O.R. programs still raise questions whether separate agency status, even with independent funding, leadership, and personnel policies would be a significant strategic intervention in the lower court criminal process.

For lawyers, the lessons may be hard ones. The standard reaction of lawyers seeking to reform abusive criminal processes is to harken back to the trial model, on the assumption that the opportunity to individualize decisions respecting defendants through more extensive deliberation by an "impartial" tribunal (including advocacy settings and double-checking) is the only feasible as well as morally acceptable corrective. The fundamental theme seems to be to emphasize the importance of individualizing the release decision. By that I mean a concept of making a thorough investigation of an individual's background to assess factors that are likely to be associated with return to trial. To the extent that there is argument between those favoring individualization and general classification (Tribe, 1970: 390-392), it is a misleading distinction in the area of pre-trial release. The release decision is not a factual inquiry relating an action to general standards: it is a sociological inquiry, a prediction or guesswork based on certain assumptions about the ways people are likely to react. And regardless of whether there are applicable written standards, the decision-maker (desk sergeant, magistrate, bail bondsman, or judge) will make his decisions on some standards he feels are reliable. Even if not articulated, standards are still employed: "hunches"—subjective standards—are probably not random guesses but fairly regularized reactions of individuals related to their attitudes formed through background and training. The nature, then, of the factual inquiry in bail-setting is an elaboration of facts that facilitate assessment of the socialization of the defendant. The labeling inherent in release procedure, no matter how much deliberation is sought to be imposed on it, is invariably the result of quick decisions under a prevailing orthodoxy of release—liberal, conservative, or otherwise. It may be, then, that lawyers should acknowledge that a reason the current due process model is not working is that there are inherent in it reasons it will not work. It takes too much to make it work, and it must eventually accommodate itself to the local court leadership.

The need of proving the efficacy of pre-trial release mechanisms like R.O.R. and 10% bail (Rice and Gallagher, 1972) has long since passed. The idea that Vera-model programs as separate institutions would lead to a due process advance in pre-trial release ignores the critical determinant of pre-trial release policies, namely, the local court leadership. Where the local courts favor release, no separate institutional arrangements are necessary to support the humane "technologies" of pre-trial release. Where courts are doubtful, lawyers can join with government leaders responsible for funding and managing detention facilities to convince the local court leadership of the value of pre-trial release. Where the politics of local court leadership is antithetical to extension of pre-trial release measures (Wice, 1973b), it might be strategically and substantively better to explore alternatives other than the Vera model.

One model might be to press for more nondiscretionary mechanisms. The traditional bail schedule (which posts certain dollar amounts of bail applicable for different charges) at least has the virtue of being openly published, although it is a method benefiting bondsmen and leaving to police generally the discretion to refuse release. Nevertheless, charges are referenced in an open consumer price list and there is perhaps less by way of arbitrariness in the crude pricing of charges than the less open and often "subjective" decisions of Vera-type agency personnel. If combined with a 10% bail rule and used in tandem with a summons program (by which police issue "tickets" for minor violations) and summary trials of minor matters, a reasonably high percentage of defendants could be released from the system immediately.[15] Such a model would put highest priority on reduction, by open, nondiscretionary methods, of the number of detainees for which it would be necessary to entertain individualized information in the release decision. Of course, even a predominantly nondiscretionary system would face serious counterpressures. Policy decisions involving pre-trial release are not easy ones to prescribe in the face of organizational pressures from other crime control agencies. Lawyers, however, must begin to look closely at the realities of due process model release procedures and their effect on maintaining untoward detention practices in hostile lower court environments, and begin experimenting with new reforms.

Social scientists have a significant contribution to make if new forms of release reforms are instituted. They can analyze, validate, and, yes, perhaps even measure reform as field experiments (Campbell, 1969). I would add only two conditions to the involvement of social scientists: there should be a protocol requiring, first, that the introduction of every quantitative study include a list of all the known weaknesses in the data used and in the analysis and administration of the study; and second, the researchers should have spent enough time in the courts to have some real familiarity with the institutions whose life they are measuring.

NOTES

1. It is common practice for a court to detain a man through use of money bail (to prevent public outcry or anticipated future crime) simply by requiring such a high bond that a defendant cannot afford the bondsman's fee. The procedure is summary, and although challengeable by way of habeas corpus on constitutional grounds, there is little by way of standards to predict a successful challenge with any degree of reliability.

2. On March 15, 1970, the Census Bureau recorded 77,921 adults in municipal or county jails awaiting trial, not including state-operated detention centers, or police lock-ups (OEO, 1972). The Law Enforcement Assistance Administration reported, in a national census of juvenile criminal justice facilities, 11,189 juveniles awaiting trial on June 30, 1971 (Crime Control Digest, 1973: 5-6). Thus a one-day profile of jail facilities accounts for roughly 90,000 detainees. Data on the number of incarcerated adults in U.S. prisons in 1970 indicate a total of 71,671 in state correctional institutions (Federal Bureau of Prisons, 1970. The precise coverage of the data in this publication is far from clear. The figures do not include Alaska or Rhode Island totals). About an average of 20,000 prisoners were incarcerated in federal prisons in 1970 (Federal Bureau of Prisons, Weekly Statistical Reports).

3. I am thus referring to "scientific" analysis, not to such efforts as monitoring, cost analysis, and the like, however important these may be or however closely related, in certain instances, to effectiveness studies. My definition, by including projections and policy analyses, is somewhat broader than Wholey's.

4. In the Baltimore study it was obvious, for example, that a typical form of dismissal, the nolle prosequi or "nol pros," was used to terminate cases and also to initiate what were in effect 60-day commitments to state mental health hospitals for alcoholism treatment.

5. For an example of the wide disparities and difficulties in this area, see Wice (1973a). Different bases (total releasees, R.O.R. releasees, defendants supervised by bail projects,

defendants interviewed for release and recommended for release) complicate the calculations enormously. A major study of bail projects by the Center on the Administration of
Criminal Justice at the University of California School of Law at Davis has apparently
analyzed numerous data-comparison problems (telephone conversation with Wayne
Thompson, School of Law, University of California, Davis).

6. We could use the kind of ethnography for lower courts that Jonathan Rubenstein
(1973) has explored for police.

7. I am indebted to Lynn Curtis for this "second best" reduction of his more
sophisticated analysis of present-day social program evaluation.

8. While in an important sense, I will be caricaturing and stereotyping a wide variety of
legal work, the risks of such an approach will hopefully be outweighed by its usefulness. I
except from my generalizations Caleb Foote's superb series on the constitutional arguments
surrounding bail (1963). My models for the stereotype are Paulsen (1966) and the
Vanderbilt Law Review (1967) articles.

9. No one that I am aware of has the naiveté to state that bail problems have been
solved. What I refer to is the extraordinary popularity or fashionability of writing about bail
in the 1960s that has diminished to a trickle of articles in legal journals in the 1970s, fed
only by the interest and controversy generated by the Nixon Administration's preventive
detention proposals and enactment of the D.C. Crime Act in 1970 (Tompkins, 1964; Smith,
1969; Reader's Guide to Legal Periodicals, 1960-1974).

10. Wayne Thompson, a researcher at the Center on the Administration of Criminal
Justice at the University of California at Davis, in his forthcoming volume on Vera-type bail
projects indicates that a considerable advance in the use of R.O.R. and other methods of
avoiding incarceration has occurred in the United States since the advent of the Manhattan
Bail Project.

11. The OEO (1973a) reported that 28% of the 88 projects reporting recommend 30%
or less of the defendants they interview. See also the extensive, extraordinarily charitable,
and carefully worded evaluation of Bogomolny and Gaus (1972).

12. There were probably special "Hawthorne" effects since the staff could not help but
be apprised of the important, pioneering, and carefully watched experiment they were
conducting.

13. See Hindlang (1972). The decision in the Memorandum to count sentences of "time
served" (namely, a finding of guilty, a sentence equal to the length of pre-trial incarceration,
and counting of pre-trial time to satisfy the sentence) as a form of disposition seems to
undermine the analysis that pre-trial incarceration is outcome determinative of trial
disposition. It requires no analysis to show that a "time served" sentence is outcome
determinative. It is a perfect fit. Under the Bellamy Memorandum standards, an incarcerated
defendant who is put on probation is *less* badly treated than the defendant who gets "time
served" and is freed. At the very least, the Memorandum should have explained the extent
of "time served" sentences and their impact on their analysis. Another factor (other than
the indigency of Legal Aid clients) which seems to enhance the perfection of the
correlations is the fact that the profile of crimes charged involves far more serious crimes
than ordinary arrest activity would generate. As we have suggested from the Baltimore
experience, minor crimes and misdemeanors probably generate quite different bail and
release patterns than felonies.

14. This failure may be particularly important in light of the results found in Boston
showing significant disparities between the results of court-appointed counsel and private
attorneys (Bing and Rosenfeld, 1970).

15. Speedier trials and better enforcement of release violations and the development of conditional release mechanisms are obviously desirable (Harvard Study, 1971: 359-368). There is evidence that misdemeanor defendants are more likely to fail to appear than felony defendants (Foote et al., 1954: 1062; Molleur, 1966: 33), which would seem to call for more use of summary trials or better reminding methods for releasees charged with misdemeanors.

REFERENCES

American Bar Association Project on Minimum Standards for Criminal Justice (1968) Standards Relating to Pre-Trial Release, Approved Draft, September, 1968. New York: Institute of Judicial Administration.

AMSTERDAM, A. G., B. L. SEGAL, and M. K. MILLER (1967) Trial Manual for the Defense of Criminal Cases, Vol. I. Philadelphia: American College of Trial Lawyers, Joint Committee on Continuing Legal Education of the American Law Institute and the American Bar Association, and National Defender Project of the National Legal Aid and Defender Association.

ARES, C. E., A. RANKIN, and H. STURZ (1963) "The Manhattan Bail Project: an interim report on the use of pre-trial parole." New York University Law Review 38 (January): 67-95.

BASES, N. C. and W. F. McDONALD (1972) Preventive Detention in the District of Columbia: The First Ten Months. Washington, D.C.: Vera Institute of Justice and Georgetown Institute of Criminal Law and Procedure.

BEELEY, A. L. (1927) The Bail System in Chicago. Chicago: University of Chicago Press.

BING, S. R. and S. S. ROSENFELD (1970) The Quality of Justice in the Lower Criminal Courts of Metropolitan Boston. Boston: Lawyer's Committee for Civil Rights Under the Law.

BLACK, D. J. (1972) "The boundaries of legal sociology." Yale Law Journal 81 (May): 1086-1100.

BLUMBERG, A. S. (1967) Criminal Justice. Chicago: Quadrangle.

BOGOMOLNY, R. L. and W. GAUS (1972) "An evaluation of the Dallas Pre-Trial Release Project." Southwestern Law Journal 27 (August): 510-537.

BOGOMOLNY, R. L. and M. R. SONNENREICH (1969) "The Bail Reform Act of 1966." Arizona Law Review 11 (Summer): 201-227.

BOTEIN, B. (1965) "The Manhattan Bail Project: its impact on criminology and the criminal law processes." Taxes Law Review 43 (February): 319-331.

CAMPBELL, D. D. (1969) "Reforms as experiments." American Psychologist 24 (April): 409-429.

Crime Control Digest (1973) Volume 7 (June 29): 5-6.

Criminal Law Bulletin (1972) "The Bellamy Memorandum." Volume 8 (July): 459-566.

DERSHOWITZ, M. (1969) "Preventing preventive detention." New York Review of Books. (March 13): 22.

DILL, F. (1972) "Bail and bail reform: a sociological study." Ph.D. dissertation. University of California, Berkeley.

Federal Bureau of Prisons (1970) National Prisoner Statistics, State Prisoners: Admissions and Release, 1970. Washington, D.C.: Government Printing Office.

——— (various dates) Weekly Statistical Reports.

FOOTE, C. (1965) "The coming constitutional crisis in bail." University of Pennsylvania Law Review 113 (May and June): 959-999, 1125-1185.

——— J. P. MARKLE, and E. A. WOOLLEY (1954) "Compelling appearance in court: administration of bail in Philadelphia." University of Pennsylvania Law Review 102 (June): 1031-1079.

FREED, D. J. and P. WALD (1964) "Bail in the United States: 1964." Working paper for the National Conference on Bail and Criminal Justice.

FRIEDMAN, L. S. (1973) "The evaluation of a bail reform." New Haven: Institute for Social and Policy Studies, Yale University, Working paper W4-7.

Harvard Civil Rights-Civil Liberties Law Review (1971) "Preventive detention: an empirical analysis." Volume 6 (March): 300-396.

HINDLANG, M. J. (1972) "On the methodological rigor of the Bellamy Memorandum." Criminal Law Bulletin 8 (July): 507-513.

HRUSKA, R. L. (1969) "Preventive detention: the Constitution and the Congress." Creighton Law Review 3 (Fall): 36-87.

Institute on the Operation of Pre-Trial Release Projects and the Justice Conference on Bail and Remands in Custody (1965) Bail and Summons: 1965. New York: National Conference on Bail and Criminal Justice.

KELLY, M. J. and L. MORLOCK (1973) "Pre-trial release in Baltimore: a report to Judge Robert Sweeney on the operation of Rule 777 in District Court One of the District Court of Maryland." (unpublished)

LOCKE, J. W., R. PENN, J. RICK, E. BUNTEN, and G. HARE (1970) Compilation and Use of Criminal Court Data in Relation to Pre-Trial Release of Defendants–Pilot Study. National Bureau of Standards Technical Note 536. Washington, D.C.: Government Printing Office.

MITCHELL, J. M. (1969) "Bail reform and the constitutionality of preventive detention." Virginia Law Review 55 (November): 1223-1242.

MOLLEUR, R. R. (1966) Bail Reform in the Nation's Capital, Final Report of the D.C. Bail Project. Washington, D.C.: Georgetown University Law Center.

National Conference on Bail and Criminal Justice (1965) Proceedings and Interim Report of the National Conference on Bail and Criminal Justice. Washington, D.C.: Office of Juvenile Delinquency, Department of Health, Education and Welfare.

New York Supplement (1973) "Bellamy v. The Judges and Justices Authorized to Sit In the New York City Criminal Court." 342 N.Y.S. 2d 137. St. Paul, Minn.: West Publishing.

Office of Economic Opportunity Pre-Trial Release Program (1973a) "Survey of pre-trial release programs." Unpublished staff paper dated March 8.

——— (1973b) "Name and location of pre-trial release activities." Unpublished staff paper dated February 26.

——— (1972a) "The OEO pre-trial release program." Unpublished staff paper dated May 10.

——— (1972b) "Bail project questionnaire."

PACKER, H. L. (1968) The Limits of Criminal Sanction. Stanford: Stanford University Press.

PAULSON, M. (1966) "Pre-trial release in the United States." Columbia Law Review 66 (January): 109-125.

Reader's Guide to Legal Periodicals (1960-1974) New York: H. W. Wilson.

RICE, P. R. and M. C. GALLAGHER (1972) "An alternative to professional bail bonding: a 10% cash deposit for Connecticut." Connecticut Law Review 5 (Fall): 143-203.

ROSSI, P. H. (1971) "Observations on the organization of social research," in R. O'Toole (ed.) The Organization Management and Tactics of Social Research. Cambridge: Schenkman; reprinted in Rossi and Williams (1972).

——— and W. WILLIAMS [eds.] (1972) Evaluating Social Programs—Theory, Practice, and Politics. New York: Seminar Press.

RUBENSTEIN, J. (1973) City Police. New York: Farrar, Straus, & Giroux.

SMITH, S. C. (1969) "Selected writings on bail." (February). New Haven: Yale Law Library.

The President's Commission on Law Enforcement and Administration of Justice (1967) The Challenge of Crime in a Free Society. Washington, D.C.: Government Printing Office.

TOMPKINS, D. C. (1964) Bail in the United States: A Bibliography. Berkeley: Institute of Governmental Studies, University of California.

TRIBE, L. H. (1972) "Policy science: analysis or ideology?" Philosophy and Public Affairs 2 (Fall): 66-110.

——— (1970) "An ounce of detention: preventive justice in the world of John Mitchell." Virginia Law Review 56 (April): 371-407.

University of Pennsylvania Law Review (1958) "Comment, a study of the administration of bail in New York City." Vol. 106 (March): 693-730.

Vanderbilt Law Review (1967) "Note, bail reform in the state and federal system." Vol. 20 (May): 948-962.

WALD, P. M. and D. J. FREED (1966) "The Bail Reform Act of 1966: a practitioner's primer." American Bar Association Journal 52 (October): 940-945.

WHOLEY, J. S., J. W. SCANLON, H. G. DUFFY, J. S. FUKUMOTO, and L. M. VOGT (1971) Federal Evaluation Policy. Washington, D.C.: Urban Institute.

WICE, P. B. (1973a) "Bail reform in American cities." Presented at the Midwest Political Science Association Annual Meeting.

——— (1973b) "Bail reform in American cities." Criminal Law Bulletin 9 (November): 770-797.

WILLIAMS, W. (1970) "The capacity of social science organizations to perform large-scale evaluative research." Seattle: Institute of Governmental Research, University of Washington, Public Policy Paper No. 2; reprinted in Rossi and Williams (1972).

ABOUT THE CONTRIBUTORS

MICHAEL H. BEST is Associate Professor of Economics at the University of Massachusetts. He has published articles on inflation and development economics and is a member of the Board of Editors of *Review of Radical Political Economics.* His forthcoming book (with William E. Connolly) is entitled *The Politicized Economy.*

DAVID A. CAPUTO is Associate Professor of Political Science at Purdue University, where he teaches urban politics, intergovernmental relations, and public policy analysis. He is the author of *American Politics and Public Policy: An Introduction; Organized Crime and American Politics;* and a co-author (with Richard L. Cole) of *Decentralization and Urban Politics: The Case of Revenue Sharing.* He has published articles in *Public Administration Review, Midwest Journal of Political Science, Urban Affairs Quarterly, Publuis,* and the 1974 *Municipal Year Book.* His research interests deal with the politics of federalism and intergovernmental relations, urban politics, policy analysis, and population policy. He is currently completing a policy-oriented urban politics manuscript.

RICHARD L. COLE is Assistant Professor of Political Science at George Washington University, where he teaches urban politics, state politics, and methodology. He is the author of *Citizen Participation and the Urban Policy Process;* co-author (with David A. Caputo) of *Decentralization and Urban Politics: The Case of Revenue Sharing;* and has published articles in *Public Administration Review, American Journal of Political Science,* the 1974 *Municipal Year Book,* and *Social Science Quarterly.* His research deals with the measurement of policy impact, political trust, urban politics, and political methodology.

JAMES S. COLEMAN is Professor of Sociology at the University of Chicago. He was senior author of the government publication,

Equality of Educational Opportunity (1966), popularly known as "The Coleman Report."

WILLIAM E. CONNOLLY is Professor of Political Science at the University of Massachusetts, Amherst. He is the author of *Political Science and Ideology* and *The Terms of Political Discourse,* and editor of *The Bias of Pluralism* and *Social Structure and Political Theory.* He and Michael Best are currently working on a text in political economy.

THOMAS J. COOK is Associate Professor of Political Science at the University of Illinois at Chicago Circle. He received his Ph.D. from Florida State University in 1969, and taught at Pennsylvania State University before coming to Chicago Circle. He was Principal Investigator on an NSF grant evaluating volunteer programs, and has served as a consultant on program evaluation to federal, state, and local governments. He currently serves on the editorial boards of *Experimental Study of Politics* and *Policy Studies Journal.*

KENNETH M. DOLBEARE is Professor of Political Science at the University of Massachusetts, Amherst. He is the author of several books on American public policy and political thought, and is currently working on developing new ways of understanding the effects of public policies from the perspective of consumers.

JOHN A. GARDINER is head of the Department of Political Science of the University of Illinois at Chicago Circle. He previously taught at the University of Wisconsin—Madison and the State University of New York at Stony Brook, and served as Assistant Director of the National Institute of Law Enforcement and Criminal Justice. He is the author of *Traffic and the Police* and *The Politics of Corruption,* and co-editor of *Theft of the City: Readings on Corruption in Urban America* and *Crime and Criminal Justice: Issues in Public Policy Analysis.*

RONALD W. JOHNSON, Assistant Professor of Political Science at Pennsylvania State University, received his Ph.D. in 1970 from the State University of New York at Buffalo. He is the co-author with Robert D. Lee, Jr., of a graduate-level textbook titled *Public Budgeting Systems* (1973). Other publications include articles in the *Policy Studies Journal* and *Methodology for Policy Impact Analysis*

(1975). He is currently the President of the Centre County Child Development Council, a nonprofit corporation providing day care services in several centers in Centre County, Pennsylvania.

MICHAEL KELLY was appointed Dean of the University of Maryland School of Law in February 1975. He was a Fellow of the National Institute of Law Enforcement, 1974-1975, where his research focused on criminal justice policy problems. He has served in a variety of policy-making posts in local government—as an aide to the Mayors of Boston and Baltimore as well as Director of the Baltimore Mayor's Coordinating Council on Criminal Justice.

SOLOMON KOBRIN is Senior Associate, Social Science Research Institute, and Emeritus Professor of Sociology—both at the University of Southern California. Publications reflecting his current research interests include journal articles in areas of criminal justice planning, policy evaluation, the sociology of deterrence, and theories of crime and delinquency.

STEVEN G. LUBECK received his Ph.D. in Sociology (1969) from the University of Southern California and is currently working as a Research Analyst for Los Angeles County Mental Health Services. He has co-authored two research monographs, *Explaining Delinquency* and *The Silverlake Experiment,* and several articles in scientific journals. His current research interests include psychiatric emergencies, the politics of madness, and the social psychology of time.

STUART S. NAGEL is Professor of Political Science at the University of Illinois and a member of the Illinois bar. He is the author or editor of *Policy Studies and the Social Sciences, Policy Studies in America and Elsewhere, Improving the Legal Process: Effects of Alternatives, Environmental Politics, The Rights of the Accused: In Law and Action,* and *The Legal Process from a Behavioral Perspective.* He has been an attorney to the Office of Economic Opportunity, Lawyers Constitutional Defense Committee in Mississippi, National Labor Relations Board, and the U.S. Senate Subcommittee on Administrative Practice and Procedure.

ROGER B. PARKS is a Research Associate with the Workshop in Political Theory and Policy Analysis at Indiana University and is currently Co-Principal Investigator on a National Science Foundation

(RANN) funded study of the organization of police services in 200 metropolitan areas in the United States. Previous research includes studies of police services in Indianapolis and in the St. Louis area, as well as methodological studies of multi-mode measurement approaches applied to a variety of public services.

FRANK P. SCIOLI, Jr., is Associate Professor of Political Science at Florida State University, where he teaches courses in policy evaluation, public administration, and organizational behavior. His co-authored publications include *Methodologies for Analyzing Public Policy* (1975; with T. Cook) and "Communications and Candidate Selection" (with J. Dyson). He is co-founder and co-editor of the journal *Experimental Study of Politics,* and co-editor of the *Policy Studies Journal.*